DUNE AND PHILOSOPHY

T0246762

The Blackwell Philosophy and Pop Culture Series
Series editor: William Irwin

A spoonful of sugar helps the medicine go down, and a healthy helping of popular culture clears the cobwebs from Kant. Philosophy has had a public relations problem for a few centuries now. This series aims to change that, showing that philosophy is relevant to your life – and not just for answering the big questions like "To be or not to be?" but for answering the little questions: "To watch or not to watch *South Park*?" Thinking deeply about TV, movies, and music doesn't make you a "complete idiot." In fact it might make you a philosopher, someone who believes the unexamined life is not worth living and the unexamined cartoon is not worth watching.

Already published in the series:

DUNE AND PHILOSOPHY

MINDS, MONADS, AND MUAD'DIB

Edited by

Kevin S. Decker

WILEY Blackwell

Registered Office
John Wiley & Sons, Inc., 111 River Street, Hoboken, NJ 07030, USA

Editorial Office
9600 Garsington Road, Oxford, OX4 2DQ, UK

For details of our global editorial offices, customer services, and more information about Wiley products visit us at www.wiley.com.

Wiley also publishes its books in a variety of electronic formats and by print-on-demand. Some content that appears in standard print versions of this book may not be available in other formats.

Library of Congress Cataloging-in-Publication Data applied for
Paperback ISBN: 9781119841395

Cover Design: Wiley
Cover Image: © Nataniil/Shutterstock

Set in 10/12.5pt Photina by Straive, Pondicherry, India

SKY10075170_051424

Contents

Contributors
Navigators, Mentats, Fremen, and Bene Gesserit

Galipcan Altinkaya decided to pursue an academic career after trying his luck and failing miserably at being a professional baliset player. He is currently an assistant researcher in the Ege University Department of Philosophy, writing his dissertation on Avicenna's psychology. His ulterior motive is to learn from the philosophers how to predict the future purely for personal gain. He insists that Avicenna gave him his blessings in person in a dream after a night of heavy melange use.

Steve Bein is Associate Professor of Philosophy at the University of Dayton, where he is a specialist in Asian thought. He has written chapters for 11 different volumes on philosophy and popular culture, on topics ranging from *Blade Runner* to Wonder Woman. He's also a science fiction and fantasy novelist, and his sci-fi short stories make the occasional appearance in Philosophy and Science Fiction courses across the US. Steve knows fear is the mind-killer, and he can recite the Litany Against Fear by heart. However, these days he thinks the Litany Against Wasting Your Whole Night Watching Netflix is just as important.

Matthew Crippen has wormed his way across the world, touching down for visits in about 60 nations and holding academic positions in five, as well as doing other jobs ranging from teaching and performing music to coaching gymnastics to machete work on farms. The intercultural waters of his life – which range from living in Egypt and Korea to excavating indigenous ruins to tramping through African bush on anti-poaching patrols – has spiced his *Dune* chapter. It has also flavored his research, which burrows through the sands of history, cognitive science, and cross-cultural value theory informed by one another and orbiting ecological concerns.

Kevin S. Decker is Professor of Philosophy at Eastern Washington University. He has edited or co-edited more than a dozen anthology books in philosophy and popular culture and is the author of *Who Is Who? The*

Philosophy of Doctor Who. He failed the gom jabbar test on his first try, so his saga is over.

Alexandru Dragomir is an Assistant Professor in the Department of Philosophy at the University of Bucharest. He actually took up saber fencing after reading *Dune*, but had to quit to pursue his dream of becoming a Mentat-philosopher. Currently, he's doing research on the ethics of human enhancement and the problem of post-personhood. This involves mostly "armchair" conceptual analysis, so he won't get to travel the galaxy with a pain box in one hand and a gom jabbar in the other in search of superbeings.

Sam Forsythe studied philosophy and war studies at King's College London, and now works as a researcher at the Peace Research Institute Frankfurt while finishing up his doctorate at Goethe University, Frankfurt. He has recently contributed chapters to the *Springer Handbook of Abductive Cognition* (2022), the *Routledge Handbook of Disinformation and National Security* (2022), and his first book, *Every Day Catastrophes*, will be published by Urbanomic/MIT Press in 2022. His current research interests led him into the wilderness between scientific inquiry, strategic rationality, and international politics, where he navigates using the concepts of C.S. Peirce as a philosophical para-compass. Otherwise, Sam spends his time as a good Fedaykin ought to: studying the secret Chakobsa hunting language and practicing prana-bindu grappling arts.

Luke Hillman did his graduate studies at the University of Arkansas and the University of Oklahoma, despite no formal Bene Gesserit instruction. His contribution in this volume is his first Wiley Blackwell publication, but hopefully not his last. His philosophical interests include philosophy of religion, philosophy of language, and Wittgenstein. Ever since Luke bought his first copy of *Dune* at a garage sale in high school, he's remained awestruck by Herbert's expansive universe, captivated by the history of House Atreides, and lost in the smell and taste of spice melange.

Ilmari Hirvonen is a doctoral student working on the philosophy of pseudoscience at the University of Helsinki. The Orange Catholic Bible has become quite familiar to him since, in his spare time, Hirvonen has been dabbling in the philosophy of religion. His other work and interests lie within metaphilosophy, epistemic justification, the epistemology of modality, philosophy of language, history of empiricism, and the Bene Gesserit venture of creating the Kwisatz Haderach. Hirvonen also makes Filmbooks on philosophy and worldview studies for high school students.

A.M. Houot completed his master's degree in Philosophy of Science, Technology, & Society at the University of Twente in The Netherlands. He podcasts, blogs, writes articles, and will pursue further graduate work. He is currently working on his first book, about psychedelics. *Dune* has been his favorite science fiction story since childhood, before he even knew what mind-altering drugs were. A friend of Frank Herbert once sent him peyote as a cure for writer's block; fortunately, A.M. did not experience writer's block at any point during the writing of his chapter.

Aaron Irvin is Associate Professor of the Ancient World at Murray State University. His research examines human organization, government, empire, and religion in the Roman world. Completely lacking any sense of rhythm, he can proudly boast that he has never attracted a sandworm.

Kara Kennedy is a researcher, writer, and educator in the areas of science fiction, writing, and digital literacy. She completed her doctoral dissertation on the Bene Gesserit in the *Dune* series and is the author of *Women's Agency in the "Dune" Universe: Tracing Women's Liberation Through Science Fiction*. She has also published articles on world-building in *Dune* and runs the blog DuneScholar.com. She put off taking the gom jabbar test for too long and is now on the run from the Sisterhood as a suspected thinking machine.

Tomi Kokkonen is a philosopher of science, mind, and technology, with both personal and professional interest in science fiction. He has a PhD in theoretical philosophy and a MSocSc in practical philosophy, both from the University of Helsinki. This doubling down in philosophy is but one reason his colleagues consider him a genuine thinking machine. His dissertation discussed human evolution, a vision of which revealed itself to him after a feast of spicy food and Irish water of life. He currently works on how to introduce AI applications in society in ethically responsible ways. This is going to lead to a disaster, but someone has to take the first steps on the Golden Path.

Mehmet Kuyurtar has completed both his undergraduate and graduate degrees from the Ege University Department of Philosophy, Turkey. His main research interests and publication areas include moral and political philosophies of Alfârâbî and Ibn Khaldun. Also, out of contempt against the Missionaria Protectiva, he studies religious pluralism and liberation theologies. In 2016 he participated in the organization of the International Borkluce Mustafa Symposium. Since the Harkonnen raids of January 6, 2017, he and his co-workers have been defending the Ege University Department of Philosophy against the evil empire.

R.S. Leiby is a PhD candidate in philosophy at Boston University. She has recently contributed a chapter to Wiley Blackwell's *The Expanse and Philosophy*. When she's not thinking about political philosophy or science fiction, she's eagerly awaiting the Butlerian Jihad (since only the absolute destruction of thinking machines will get her off of the internet and back to work on her dissertation).

"Greg Littmann," intoned Korba of Muad'Dib's Quizarate, "you are accused of being a philosopher, of conducting a personal hunt for truth rather than accepting the truth of Muad'Dib or submitting to any orthodoxy." Numb with terror, Littmann only shook his head. Korba glanced at the charge sheet. "You're Associate Professor in the Philosophy Department at SIUE," he pointed out. Littmann tried to speak but no words came. "The charges state that you willfully and with malice aforethought did publish on paradoxes of self-reference, evolutionary epistemology, and the philosophy of professional philosophy, among other topics. And not content to keep your heresies to academia, you wrote chapters for the public, tying philosophical issues to popular culture. You have contributed to numerous such volumes, including books dedicated to *Black Mirror*, *Doctor Who*, *Game of Thrones*, Neil Gaiman, Stephen King, *Star Trek*, and *Star Wars*." Littmann looked desperately to his lawyer, who avoided his eyes and studied the courtroom floor. Korba put down the charge sheet and smiled. "Dr. Littmann, we Fremen have a saying. *Polish comes from the cities, wisdom from the desert.* Perhaps if you are quick, you will find some wisdom before Shai-Hulud takes you. Take him away."

Matti Mäkikangas is a teacher and an author of philosophy and worldview studies. His philosophical interests lean toward ethics and political philosophy and his worldview toward the needs of the invisible nobodies. On some mornings, Matti wakes up from dreams where he finds himself leading a great revolt against venture capitalists and fossil-fuel-driven conglomerates.

Ethan Mills is an Associate Professor of Philosophy at the University of Tennessee at Chattanooga, where he trains student-Mentats in the weirding ways of Greek and Asian philosophy as well as philosophy and popular culture, including a course during which students make their own horror films. When he's not writing articles and books about classical Indian philosophy, he follows a Golden Path of engaging philosophically with popular culture in a mélange of locations from *Philip K. Dick and Philosophy* (2011) and the *Journal of Science Fiction and Philosophy* to his personal blog: *Examined Worlds: Philosophy and Science Fiction*. He became a *Dune* fan at age 15, but his attempts to usurp the Imperium were thwarted by his lack of water discipline and love of walking in rhythm.

Jennifer Mundale is an Associate Professor of Philosophy and Cognitive Science at the University of Central Florida. She finds gholas intriguing and sometimes wonders if she is one. Her chapter would have been done sooner but the Mentat she hired to do the research ran off with a Bene Gesserit to market skincare products on Arrakis.

William Peden researches the philosophy of economics at Erasmus University Rotterdam, The Netherlands. He wrote his PhD thesis at Durham University (UK) after studies in Cambridge (UK) and Edinburgh. Before all that, he was a high school student in Scotland, where *Dune* was one of his first experiences of philosophy. Unfortunately, his school banned Frank Herbert's books as senior English literature dissertation topics, due to "insufficient literary merit" (the list of forbidden subjects also included anything by Tolkien, Bram Stoker, Isaac Asimov, and Ian Fleming!). After waiting so many years to write about the Duniverse, he is glad that this volume will prove just how much there is to say about it.

Edwardo Pérez spent years as a Spice Driver, learning the Fremen ways and the cries of the water-sellers (Soo-Soo Sook!), before giving it all up for the contemplative life of an English professor. While the skill set Edwardo acquired comes in handy during faculty meetings and "office hours," it's the eyes – the blue within blue within blue – that keep his students mesmerized through lessons on critical and rhetorical theory. And it's the secret stash of melange, hidden in a compartment carved into the pages of Aristotle's *Rhetoric*, that allows Edwardo to endure semester after semester of endless grading. Kull Wahad!

Kenneth R. Pike teaches philosophy and law at the Florida Institute of Technology, where from his office window he watches spaceships leave the planet. He writes at the intersection of moral theory and technology, and is especially interested in the challenges posed by values inculcation – both in his own four children, who are probably not gholas, and in the mechanical minds he hopes will one day constitute humanity's collective offspring. As an aspiring transhumanist and techno-optimist, he will be first against the wall when the Butlerian Jihad comes.

Zachary Pirtle, PhD, is an engineer and policy practitioner working on lunar exploration. He also teaches systems engineering and publishes research in philosophy of engineering, including the co-edited book *Engineering and Philosophy: Reimagining Technology and Social Progress*. He wanted to help Leto II with the Golden Path, until one day he sparked the fury of the Worm.

James R.M. Wakefield teaches political theory and government at Cardiff University, Wales. For reasons that made sense back in graduate school, he writes mainly about Italian philosophy, and sometimes translates it into English. He also has interests in ethics, the philosophy of education, and neglected thinkers of the past. When not worrying about these things, he's usually pretty good value in a pub quiz. After spice melange, his favorite spice is probably smoked paprika. It's so versatile!

Zach Vereb teaches philosophy, critical thinking, and environmental ethics at the University of Mississippi. There, he goes off on tangents about the mental lives of zombies and the virtues of coffee (the true spice of earth). Zach also thinks anime is cool, and so recently published a chapter in *Neon Genesis Evangelion and Philosophy* with Open Universe. Since he began practicing kung fu, Zach often lets his hands do too much talking. One day he even hopes to master the crysknife.

Introduction

"He Who Controls the Spice Controls the Universe"

Kevin S. Decker

A beginning is the time for taking the most delicate care that the balances are correct. This every sister of the Bene Gesserit knows.

Dune

Frank Herbert's *Dune* is a space-opera treasure trove, and its sequels show it to also be a Pandora's Box of latent surprises and long games. In the Duniverse we explore *so many* things – survival, honor, deep ecology, strategy, weird psychic and physical capabilities, psychology, gender, prophecy, religion, and cultural mutation over millennia. But one omnipresent theme in the *Dune* tales – a theme that also characterizes the popularity of the book series and film and television adaptations – is *endurance*. Paul Atreides finds a way to endure his tests for taking over the Ducal seat from Leto. Jessica and Paul endure the Arrakeen desert's daily hostility – sand getting everywhere, winds whipping at hundreds of miles per hour, every drop of water needing to be saved, and, of course, the sandworms. And the *Dune* saga endures – over the six books that Frank Herbert published between 1965 and 1985, to the many prequel and sequel books written by Herbert's son Brian and Kevin J. Anderson, loads of fanfic, Sci-Fi Channel television miniseries, and two-and-a-half feature films and counting (Alexander Jodorowsky's *Dune* was never filmed, but Jodorowsky's mid-1970s script adaptation would have resulted in a 14-hour film; and that deserves a little credit). Director Denis Villeneuve's latest adaptation, released in 2021, garnered enough critical praise and audience fervor to justify at least one sequel. The brief timeline of the *Dune* series included in this book shows that even without dipping into the *XD* Duniverse – mostly constituted by the quasi-canonical writings of Herbert *fils* and Anderson – the stories of the great houses of the Landsraad, the Emperors, and the God Emperor unfurl over a jaw-dropping 16,000 years' span of time. *That's* endurance.

The Duniverse began in two novellas, *Dune World* and *The Prophet of Dune*, serialized in *Analog* between 1963 and 1965. Herbert developed the sands and sieves of what would become *Dune* the novel with the editorship of the great John W. Campbell. For the magazine *Analog* (formerly *Astounding Science Fiction*), Campbell "demanded that his writers try to think out how science and technology might really develop in the future – and, most importantly, how those changes would affect the lives of human beings."[1] This new level of sophistication raised *Analog* above its peers in the dust chasm of SF pulps, and many of the chapters in this book stress the importance of Herbert's careful research in historical, cultural, and ecological themes – among others – to meet the demands of Campbell's stricter approach.[2] Knit together and published in 1965 by Chilton (yes, the publisher of those incredibly detailed car manuals), the *Analog* novellas became *Dune*, winner of the prestigious Hugo and Nebula Awards.

Dune was part of the New Wave of science fiction of the 1960s and 1970s, which was characterized by literary experimentation with shifting styles, differing narrative points of view, and unreliable narrators, and with the integration of elements of the "psychedelic" culture of the period. Authors like Herbert, Joanna Russ, Harlan Ellison, Philip K. Dick, and Ursula K. Le Guin represent this movement. In the *Dune* books, plots are often driven by futuristic developments of psychedelic culture like mind-expanding drugs (Arrakis's spice melange), psychic powers (the weirding ways of the Bene Gesserit), dystopian themes (the culture of House Harkonnen, the genetic manipulations of the Tleilaxu), race memories, and martial arts that allow control of the mind and the body. All are explored in their philosophical richness in the pages of this book.

Many of the chapters you're about to read rightly emphasize the ecological themes of Herbert's book series. The immersive experience Herbert wished for readers of *Dune* was based on his own immersive experiences in the Pacific Northwest. John Notarianni of Oregon Public Broadcasting wrote:

> In the early 20th century, the coastal Oregon city of Florence was under threat of being consumed by the nearby dunes that were being whipped across human structures by the coastal winds. Roads, railroad tracks, even homes were being swallowed up by blowing sand. Starting in the 1920s, the US Department of Agriculture ran a program to try and stabilize the dunes by planting European Beach Grass . . . Herbert came to Florence in 1957, planning to write an article documenting this battle between man and nature. He was awestruck by the power of the blowing desert sand. As he wrote in a letter, "These waves can be every bit as devastating as a tidal wave in property damage."[3]

In turn, the scenarios of Herbert's Duniverse frequently depict not only the uncontrollable power of nature's majesty, but also the sublimity of its vast expanses of space and time. Fans frequently recommend reading Herbert to initiates based on the scale of *Dune*'s worldbuilding. Whether the treachery of twisted Mentat Piter De Vries or the Golden Path plotted out meticulously by the God Emperor Leto II, strategic and military brinksmanship often takes years or centuries to play out.

The great achievement of the 24 philosophers represented in this book is how they deploy their synthetic imagination. Without even needing to convert the poisonous Water of Life, the philosopher has the ability to see the big picture – how things are and how they could have been. She can also tease out the implications of the smallest threads of relevance, whether from Herbert's books or from the Denis Villeneuve film adaptation. This kind of guidance, reminiscent of the teaching of Socrates or Hypatia, isn't a luxury when exploring the vastness of the Duniverse – it's a necessity.

So it's entirely appropriate to acknowledge the influence on this volume of the first, groundbreaking book about the philosophical themes of *Dune*, editor Jeffrey Nicholas's 2011 *Dune and Philosophy: Weirding Way of the Mentat*. When I met Jeffrey at a Spokane-area Ethics Bowl shortly before his book was to be published, I was both excited for its release and disappointed that I hadn't thought to submit a chapter proposal myself. It's satisfying to finally be able to offer up one's own contribution to the enduring *Dune* phenomenon.

A note on the many editions of *Dune*: as a worldwide publishing phenomenon, there are numerous publishers of the book series, volumes of which have been translated into at least 14 languages. Each chapter author has been asked to identify their preferred edition, and page references in their chapter will follow that edition.

My family – Suzanne, Kennedy, Ethan, Jack, my brother Keith and his family, and my mother, Carolyn, provided support in many ways while I edited and wrote, and I appreciate them beyond words. Partners in philosophy and pop culture Jason T. Eberl, Rob Arp, and Bill Irwin also deserve a big "thanks!" The existence of this book also acknowledges the daily inspiration, challenge, and joy that my colleagues in Philosophy and the Humanities at Eastern Washington University provide, which it turns out is absolutely necessary while trying to produce a book like this in the middle of climate change catastrophes and the COVID-19 pandemic. So I cannot offer thanks enough to Kerri Boyd, Garry Kenney, Scott Kinder-Pyle, Chris Kirby, Kathryn Julyan, Terry MacMullan, Mimi Marinucci, and David Weise. This book is dedicated to them, and in memoriam to a colleague lost too soon, Henry-York "Hank" Steiner, who loved stories.

Notes

1. Trevor Quachri, "History of Analog Science Fiction and Fact," *Analog Science Fiction and Fact*, at https://www.analogsf.com/about-analog/history.
2. A captivating tale of the early days of Campbell's editorship and the way in which he cultivated SF Golden Age authors can be read in Alec Nevala-Lee's *Astounding: John W. Campbell, Isaac Asimov, Robert A. Heinlein, L. Ron*

Hubbard, and the Golden Age of Science Fiction (New York: Dey Street Books, 2018).

3. John Notarianni, "How an Oregon Battle Between Human and Nature Inspired Frank Herbert's 'Dune,'" *Oregon Public Broadcasting*, October 23, 2021, at https://www.opb.org/article/2021/10/23/florence-oregon-movies-dune-frank-herbert-science-fiction-novels.

A Brief *Dune* Series Timeline

1000 BG	Beginnings of space travel.
201 BG	The Butlerian Jihad begins.
108 BG	End of the Butlerian Jihad.
88 BG	Battle of Corrin; House Corrino establishes the Imperium.
80 BG	Founding of the order of Mentats.
0 AG	Founding of the Spacing Guild; Royal Houses of the Landsraad established; CHOAM (*Combine Honnete Ober Advancer Mercantiles*) founded.
2000 AG	The Great Convention is signed, saying that the combined power of the Great Houses may destroy anyone who uses atomic power against human beings; the Commission of Ecumenical Translators compiles the Orange Catholic Bible on Old Earth; Great Convention rule observed throughout the galaxy for the next 8000 years.
10111 AG	House Harkonnen gains stewardship of Arrakis, holding the planet in quasi-fief under a CHOAM company contract to mine the spice melange.
10156 AG	Elrood IX dies; Shaddam Corrino IV becomes Padishah Emperor.
10176 AG	Paul Atreides is born.
10189 AG	Leto Atreides I master trains a small, Sardaukar-level force, threatening the Emperor.
10191–95 AG	Events of *Dune* (published 1965).
10203 AG	Events of *Dune Messiah* (published 1969) begin.
10212 AG	Events of *Children of Dune* (published 1976) begin.
13712 AG	Events of *God Emperor of Dune* (published 1981) begin.
15212 AG	Events of *Heretics of Dune* (published 1984) begin.
15214 AG	Events of *Chapterhouse Dune* (published 1985) begin.

SONGS OF MUAD'DIB: CULTURE AND RELIGION IN *DUNE*

Liberating Women's Bodies
Feminist Philosophy and the Bene Gesserit of *Dune*

Kara Kennedy

Maybe Frank Herbert was too subtle in crafting the powerful and influential female characters in *Dune*, since some readers seem to overlook them. Women are everywhere in *Dune*, especially the members of the Bene Gesserit Sisterhood. From Princess Irulan and Reverend Mother Gaius Helen Mohiam, to Lady Margot and Lady Jessica, Bene Gesserit women's voices and choices play crucial roles in the book.

But *Dune* doesn't seem to be a work of science fiction that promises a future of gender equality. Although set in the far future, it resembles a past of feudal dukes, barons, and counts owing loyalty to an emperor, who bequeaths planetary fiefs and favors as he sees fit. In this medieval setting, the women of the Bene Gesserit don't hold the same roles or have the same responsibilities as men. Instead, they still hold traditional female roles: concubines, wives, advisors, and religious figures.

Jessica is Duke Leto Atreides's bound concubine who bears an heir, Paul, and uses her business training to serve as Leto's secretary. While Leto's busy engaging in strategic military planning on Arrakis, she is instructing their new servants how to set up their household. At a formal dinner banquet, she plays the gracious hostess, calling for more dishes and making small talk with their guests. Leto sits at the head of the table and is the person called away when a potential emergency arises. Among the Fremen, Jessica is not allowed to be her own champion when Jamis calls for a ritual fight. These and many other examples show that Jessica isn't given the same opportunities or made part of the same action as men.

Mohiam is the Padishah Emperor Shaddam IV's advisor and Truthsayer. She is trusted by him and provides crucial advice during his final confrontation with the Atreides family. But she is not a ruler; she must rely on her authority as a high-ranking Bene Gesserit and her ability to Truthsay. She may evoke fear, but she has to channel political influence through others, usually men.

Dune and Philosophy, First Edition. Edited by Kevin S. Decker.
© 2023 John Wiley & Sons, Inc. Published 2023 by John Wiley & Sons, Inc.

The characters Margot and Irulan have more limited appearances, but also appear bound to follow the lead of the men in their lives. Margot travels with her spouse, Count Hasimir Fenring, who is the Emperor's friend and confidant. Irulan accompanies her father, the Emperor, to Arrakis and agrees without resistance to a marriage alliance with the Atreides family.

This does not mean the Bene Gesserit are sitting around letting men run the show, though. They maintain a silent partnership in the CHOAM corporation and have an agreement with the Emperor to keep a Bene Gesserit on the throne. Meanwhile, they have a nearly covert operation involving a genetic master plan, missionary work, and highly specialized training.

Given these factors, *Dune* appears to create an environment with separate gendered spheres in which men and women often have different responsibilities, activities, and skills. Women have their own thing going on, but they do it behind the scenes and don't occupy roles with overt authority. This is not a universe in which women and men are equal.

The Female Body: Friend Not Foe

If we look at what's happening with the female body, though, *Dune* promises more freedom for its women. The Bene Gesserit do not see their bodies as obstacles to their active and purposeful existence in the world. They reject the idea that women are inferior or less capable of doing things than men simply because they're female and can get pregnant. Instead, they embrace the fact that they can choose to birth children and control their genetic lineage. They see vast potential in the body that members of the Guild or Mentats have overlooked or neglected. The Bene Gesserit view the body as a valuable vehicle through which to perceive the world and achieve their aims. In other words, the body is a way for them to be active agents of their own lives rather than something that holds them back or weakens them. By striving toward a balanced relationship between mind and body, they uncover a possible future in which women creatively utilize their potential to make their mark on the world.

Philosophers can help us understand how the depiction of the Bene Gesserit can be considered a science fiction vision of feminism despite *Dune*'s lack of gender equality. In her groundbreaking 1949 book *The Second Sex*, Simone de Beauvoir (1908–1986) takes a bold step by saying that girls don't just naturally take on the characteristics and stereotypes associated with femininity and womanhood. There is no inner "feminine essence" driving their behavior: "One is not born, but rather becomes, woman."[1] In Beauvoir's view, what happens is that girls are socialized early on to think of themselves as weaker and so gradually feminize themselves. They are told to be modest, charming, and graceful to be accepted by society. But though they are rewarded for restricting themselves and becoming "proper" women, they are also often treated as less valuable than their male counterparts in society. Over time, gendered restrictions and limitations become normalized, so it appears that women are destined by a "feminine essence" to always have certain attitudes and behaviors.

In the world of *Dune*, the Bene Gesserit have recognized the importance of socialization and flipped it on its head. Under the pretense of preparing girls to be concubines or wives placed in noble houses, they have developed a comprehensive education program that emboldens girls with a wealth of knowledge. In a presumably all-female schooling environment, girls are expected to study and master a broad range of subjects. Jessica tells the Fremen housekeeper, the Shadout Mapes, that "Tongues are the Bene Gesserit's first learning" and shows off her fluency in Chakobsa, an ancient hunting language.[2] At the dinner banquet, she recalls a Bene Gesserit teacher's lesson on espionage and counter-espionage while she uncovers a Harkonnen spy. Far from being merely a beautiful concubine and hostess, Jessica is a highly trained woman who actively uses her skills to analyze those around her and determine their level of threat to herself and her family on Arrakis.

Yet socialization also includes how girls learn to view themselves in relation to their body. Beauvoir says that in many cases, girls do not receive training in athletics, are forbidden from fighting or climbing or other "dangerous" activities, and are persuaded to avoid pushing their limits.[3] This can have severe, long-lasting effects on their beliefs and behaviors, for "To lose confidence in one's body is to lose confidence in one's self."[4] Beauvoir takes issue with these structures of sexism, suggesting that if girls were raised with the same expectations, freedom, studies, and activities as boys, they would grow up free from feelings of weakness, passivity, and inferiority. If girls and women did not experience their body as something to be ashamed of, or a handicap on their ability to do things, they could enjoy a more active and independent engagement with the world, just like men enjoy. They could see themselves as people who initiate, rather than people who passively sit on the sidelines. Beauvoir advocates for women to recognize themselves as fully capable human beings and explore the many possibilities that have historically been denied to them.

Understanding that an academic education is not comprehensive enough, the Bene Gesserit also focus attention on the body and its potential to empower girls and women. Rather than forbid intense physical activities, they encourage girls to perfect their skills in areas such as fighting. Jessica is more than capable of handling herself in sticky situations. We only get a couple sentences describing Jessica using her skill in a tussle with Stilgar, and it is over quickly: "A turn, a slash of her arm, a whirling of mingled robes, and she was against the rocks with the man helpless in front of her."[5] But Stilgar is in awe of her "weirding ability of battle" that requires no weapons, and this helps show us how amazing her skills are to "maste[r] an armed Fremen."[6] Her body is the only weapon she needs, having been trained in the art of combat at her Bene Gesserit school. In fact, the Bene Gesserit are actually the standard of measurement for combat. In the Appendix in *Dune*, the definition of the Sardaukar, the Emperor's feared soldier-fanatics, states that "their cunning abilities at in-fighting were reputed to approach those of a Bene Gesserit adept."[7] The Sardaukar only *approach* the skills of the Bene Gesserit! Although the Bene Gesserit certainly don't seek out a fight and aren't soldiers, their special combat skills give them the confidence and strength to move through a dangerous world as women.

Iris Marion Young (1949–2006) takes Beauvoir's rejection of a natural "feminine essence" a step further in "Throwing Like a Girl: A Phenomenology of Feminine Body Comportment Motility and Spatiality." Young looks closely at the female body and how its movements and limitations are conditioned by socialization. She's interested in how the female body orients itself toward its surroundings and why we might already find gender differences in body behavior and movement in children as young as five.

Why should there be such a thing as throwing like a girl, considered a derogatory accusation? If the human body is primarily used to accomplish tasks – whether those be throwing a ball, lifting a box, or walking to work – why do boys and men attempt these tasks with more ease and free motion than girls and women? Why are girls and women more likely to experience their bodies as a fragile impediment, instead of as a durable instrument that gets things done? For Young, responses might include lack of practice, lack of confidence, and a woman's perception of herself as being an object rather than an initiator. A woman sees things happening to her, instead of her making things happen. She worries about being treated as an object rather than as an equal human being. What is needed is for her to have complete trust in her body to do what she wishes, so she does not see her body as a burden that holds her back.

In the *Dune* universe, the Bene Gesserit give girls so much practice in honing their skills that it almost guarantees they will grow into supremely confident women who trust their bodies to follow through on any action they desire. When Jessica is confronted with potentially hostile Fremen – the Shadout Mapes and Stilgar – she secretly readies her body for battle through "the waiting whipsnap of her muscles."[8] There is no sense that she views her body as something fragile or burdensome. She has full faith in her body to initiate action, thanks to her Bene Gesserit training.

Young argues that if women were not "physically inhibited, confined, positioned, and objectified, they could see themselves as agents who could go out and master a world that belonged to them."[9] There is one example of Jessica being inhibited that stands out as a clear contrast to how she normally operates. After being drugged by the traitor in the Atreides household, Jessica awakes to find her mind and body are sluggish and she has been bound and gagged. With both her and Paul thrown into an ornithopter to be dropped in the desert by the Harkonnen, she must wait for her ungagged son to assist her in getting her gag removed before she can take control of the situation. In this case, she is restricted from immediately confronting the challenge ahead of her because the Harkonnen knew "what a deadly creature" she is and prepared accordingly.[10] But at other times, when her body is not confined, Jessica does appear to be a woman who rises up to meet what life throws at her.

Liberated Women

The Bene Gesserit in *Dune* represent a fulfillment of the ideal of the liberated women Beauvoir and Young describe. They are a pseudo-religious organization that encourages its members to perceive and use their bodies differently than we might expect of women in a medieval, feudal age, or indeed by the standard of today's societies. Sisters and Reverend Mothers measure themselves against Bene Gesserit standards, not male standards. In fact, looking at gender in *Dune* from this angle provides a richer and more comprehensive understanding of its women than examining gender roles in terms of equality.

If women were "given the opportunity to use their full bodily capacities in free and open engagement with the world" and encouraged "to develop specific bodily skills," they could overcome some of the challenges in a sexist society and make their goals a reality.[11] They could avoid the hesitancy and timidity that can get in women's way. The Bene Gesserit show this in action. The body is a core part of their toolkit, not an obstacle. And everything they do is geared toward a goal, whether small or large, immediate or far-reaching.

The Bene Gesserit have certainly developed specific bodily skills, and these extend beyond their more obvious fighting ability. They train in the art of minute perception, honing their eyes, ears, and other sensory organs to notice the smallest of details of their environment. Jessica frequently uses this ability to assess novel situations, the potential for danger, and the best course of action. During virtually every step of her and Paul's journey on Arrakis, they are processing sensory information in subtle ways, using their training to navigate and survive in an often hostile environment. At the banquet, she is "following the conversation with Bene Gesserit intensity" and reading the body language of key political figures on Arrakis to determine whose loyalties lie where.[12] For instance, she determines that the banker is terrified of Dr. Liet-Kynes after hearing the fear in his voice and seeing it in his face, his breathing, and the pulsing of a vein at his temple. In an encounter with the Shadout Mapes, Jessica reads the "petit betrayals" in Mapes's actions and appearance as Jessica reveals her knowledge of the Bene Gesserit-implanted legends while also preparing to defend herself against a possible attack.[13] Her keen perceptive abilities serve her well, as she gains valuable political insights that help her survive and establish a secure foothold on the planet.

Another useful skill the Bene Gesserit master is that of the Voice. This mysterious ability involves a Bene Gesserit pitching her voice in a targeted way to control another person. It is essentially a voice of command that cannot be resisted without special training. Mohiam commands Paul to draw closer to her when she prepares to administer the test of the gom jabbar. She also commands him to stop turning his head to look at the needle at his neck. Paul knows she is using the Voice, but he isn't trained well enough to resist it or use it himself. Jessica uses the Voice to put Thufir Hawat in his place, literally, and show him a glimpse of her powerful ability to control virtually anyone she wishes. The Voice combines skills in perception and vocal regulation to turn the mouth and vocal cords into a vehicle for women to bend others to their will. It is a special ability that only Bene Gesserit women have until Jessica trains Paul to use it, and so it's not something uniquely feminine, but instead a skill that requires practice to acquire. The Voice empowers women with confidence, because they know they can get things done quickly and efficiently and protect themselves in dangerous situations if need be. It's a kind of shortcut to power, to be used sparingly.

A larger-scale version of the Voice is the Missionaria Protectiva, a long-term project involving Bene Gesserit women traveling to the far reaches of the Imperium to sow religious myths to ensure a safe reception if later necessary.[14] Although we do not meet any missionaries, we can speculate that these women must be sufficiently trained in a number of skills to successfully establish themselves in remote places. They have to survive in body and spirit while also persuading the locals to believe the religious dogma they bring along. On Arrakis, they are so successful that the Fremen even adopt their terms, including Reverend Mother. Centuries later, all Jessica has to do is prove herself as a Bene Gesserit to begin to win the loyalty of a new people.

A Balance Between Mind and Body

One of the key ingredients of the Bene Gesserit's success is their emphasis on balance between the mind and the body. Unlike the Spacing Guild, which prioritizes mathematics, and Mentats, who prioritize logic, the Bene Gesserit embrace a more thorough understanding of their capabilities and talents. They escape the trap of *Cartesian mind–body dualism*, a philosophy that has filtered into culture to position women on the lesser side of artificial divisions: men/women, masculine/feminine, mind/body, logical/ emotional, rational/irrational, and active/passive.

Cartesian dualism is named after René Descartes (1596–1650), the French philosopher and mathematician considered to be the father of modern philosophy. Descartes popularized the theory that the mind and body are different kinds of "stuff," or metaphysical substances. This theory was supposed to answer old and lingering questions about the relationship of the mental and the physical in human life: How do they influence each other? What is consciousness and how is it related to the brain and body? Descartes' famous "I think therefore I am" reflected his belief that thinking alone could be proof of the existence of a person. Descartes thus put a high value on the mind and its ability to think, and believed the body was a complex machine that mostly worked autonomously unless the human mind commanded it, through the power of the will, to behave in desired ways.

Dualism has cast a long shadow in Western philosophy, making human bodies out to be burdens entrapping the minds within. In particular, the female body has been treated as a nuisance, even by feminists. It's often been considered a physical limitation that keeps women wrapped up in menstrual cycles, pregnancies, and inactivity, leaving them unable to develop their minds.

As we've seen, the Bene Gesserit take a different view in their philosophy. They don't affirm the body in its natural state, since they distrust instinctive behavior. After all, they administer the gom jabbar test to determine whether a person is human, and those who fail to keep their hand in the pain box are killed by the poison needle. But the Bene Gesserit do value the body once it has been trained to work in harmony with the mind. This gives them more flexibility in the use of human capabilities than the members of the Spacing Guild or the Mentats, who neglect the potential of the body.

In fact, Herbert must look to Eastern philosophies – and their view of the whole human and its interdependency with the world – in developing the Bene Gesserit's beliefs and activities. This not only bolsters the complexity of the characterization of their order; it also makes us look at avenues of strength and power beyond what we might expect from conventional gender roles.

Supernormal Powers Through Discipline

Principles from Indian philosophy make up a central part of the Bene Gesserit's operations. Their training focuses on prana-bindu, a form of total nerve and muscle programming. The terms *prana* and *bindu* come from Sanskrit. There, *prāṇa* refers to vital breath or animating force, and *bindu* means either a particle or the expression of highest consciousness.[15] As the breath of life, prana provides the "electricity" needed for the vitality of the body's organs.[16] In yogic meditation, *prana* is viewed as the link or bridge between mind and body.[17] It is also the feeling of harmony grasped when there is balance in internal and external influences on a person such as eating, exercise, and right thinking.[18]

Indian philosophy differs from Western thought in its view that the mind is part of the body instead of the two being separate kinds of "stuff," like in Cartesian dualism.[19] It is believed that through disciplining the mind and body through asceticism and yoga, a person can reach a deep state of meditation and attain a higher plane of consciousness and supernormal powers of action and knowledge.[20] Yoga represents "a set of disciplines of behavior, body, and mind, in which a practitioner gains progressive control and mastery over their psychophysical makeup."[21]

The Bene Gesserit's training in prana-bindu has many similarities to yogic practice. Prana-bindu allows its members virtually complete control over their bodily functions, including control of their breathing to the point of hibernation. Jessica shows her supreme control of her breath when she puts herself into such a state after getting caught in a sandslide. She "compose[s] herself in bindu suspension to reduce her oxygen needs" and her heartbeat slows down until Paul can dig her out.[22] Hers is completely normal behavior for those trained by the Bene Gesserit. It's Paul who makes a fuss after the sandslide, not her, and she chides him for his panic and tells him to get practicing his prana-bindu lessons again.

Prana-bindu can also be used to control other people's minds and bodies by implanting subconscious controls into them. Margot recognizes that the Sisterhood might want to control Feyd-Rautha Harkonnen at a future point, so she plans to "plant deep in his deepest self the necessary prana-bindu phrases to bend him."[23] This is future-proofing – like the method of the Missionaria Protectiva – that ensures women can control a dangerous person if the need arises. Sure enough, in a critical scene at the end of the novel, Jessica suspects Feyd-Rautha has been implanted by prana-bindu phrases, letting Paul know of this advantage in case he needs it in his duel with the Harkonnen. Paul refuses to say the trigger word, but stating his refusal to do so in the heat of combat causes a slight hesitation, enabling him to kill Feyd-Rautha, who had been gaining the upper hand in the fight.

The Bene Gesserit highly value the kind of self-control gained through focused attention to the body. This links with yoga and its focus on the breath and internal awareness of the body and its relationship with the mind. Appreciating the body for its capabilities and being able to control its natural processes are part of the Bene Gesserit way of being. But Indian philosophy is not the only Eastern philosophy that supports their order.

Indirect Action Through the Way

Taoism also appears in the workings of the Bene Gesserit order. One clue to its influence is the name of the Bene Gesserit Way, similar in name to the Tao ("Way") in Taoism. The Bene Gesserit also seek the Kwisatz Haderach ("Shortening of the Way"), referring to someone who can "bridge space and time" through special mental powers.[24] Women follow the Bene Gesserit Way through participating in the extensive training regimen we've already discussed.

As a philosophy, Taoism embraces balance, as shown through the symbolism of yin and yang. The Tao is a force flowing through the world that maintains balance in the cosmos. Following the Way means striving to live in harmony with nature, rather than fighting against the flow of life. Taoism urges us to simply accept things as they are instead of trying to control and dominate the natural order, a theme familiar in Western philosophy.

Taoism also contains the paradoxical idea of *wu-wei*, a strategy of non-action that actually allows the most effective action to happen. In other words, acting in harmony with one's surroundings and the natural flow of the universe leads to the right consequences. One example in the key text of Taoism, the *Tao-te-ching*, is a wheel. At a glance, the hub of the wheel appears as a passive center that does nothing. But actually, the hub is essential to the function of the rest of the wheel. There is also the example of water, which is "soft" and seems to have no effect on hard rocks or mountains as it finds paths of least resistance through valleys or down mountainsides. However, over time, water reshapes the hardest rocks and mountains by carving paths through them and shows itself to be a strong force.

Taoist-inspired philosophy emerges on two levels for the Bene Gesserit. First, the individual Bene Gesserit avoids challenging others outright. Sisters and Reverend Mothers prefer to work covertly to accomplish their goals. When Jessica and Paul stumble upon Stilgar's hunting party, she refrains from using the Voice on Stilgar though she senses danger. Instead, she gathers more information and appears to go along with Stilgar's reasoning. It's only when she realizes he's going to eliminate her that she engages in combat. Even then, she first tricks him by doing "a slumping, deceptive faint to the ground."[25] By going along with the flow of events, she places herself in a better position to demonstrate her skills and thus secures his admiration and promise of safety. Her initial appearance of passivity and naivete translates into a better outcome than direct confrontation.

Second, at a collective level, the Bene Gesserit have a long-term strategy to improve humanity without the need to occupy official ruling positions in the Imperium. In Mohiam's conversation with Paul after he survives the gom jabbar test, she explains that the Bene Gesserit want to prevent humans from falling into enslavement by thinking machines again, as happened before the Butlerian Jihad. One of their main ways of preventing this is their breeding program: they carefully select bloodlines with favorable genetic material and place women as concubines or wives within noble houses to bear children. Training the body in prana-bindu is key to running this type of breeding program since it gives them control of their pregnancies. The result is that the Bene Gesserit are set to produce the ultimate superhuman that they can take charge of.

All of this occurs under the noses of men. When Paul asks his mother if his father knew her plan to birth and train the long-awaited Kwisatz

Haderach, her response indicates Leto's ignorance. When Paul discloses
the Bene Gesserit's breeding plans in front of the Emperor, Mohiam screams
for him to be silenced, hissing, "You mustn't speak of these things!"[26] They
have been patiently waiting for many generations, working with the flow
of the universe rather than trying to abruptly alter it to their will. Although
they end up losing control of Paul, he stands as an incredible product of
their selective breeding and training in the Bene Gesserit Way.

What's interesting about the women of the Bene Gesserit in *Dune* is not
necessarily the political or social roles they hold, though some of them are
quite influential. It's their dedication to training and the incredible bodily
and mental feats they display, albeit subtly. *Dune* may not give us gender
equality, but it turns dualistic thinking on its head by uplifting the female
body as an essential tool for women to take control of their own destiny.
This science fiction story shows us women who are confident, goal-oriented,
and tough as nails while also being concubines, wives, and mothers.

Notes

1. Simone de Beauvoir, *The Second Sex*, trans. Constance Borde and Sheila
   Malovany-Chevallier (New York: Vintage, 2010), 330.
2. *Dune* (New York: Berkley, 1984), 53.
3. Beauvoir, *The Second Sex*, 397.
4. Beauvoir, *The Second Sex*, 399.
5. *Dune*, 281.
6. *Dune*, 282.
7. *Dune*, 528.
8. *Dune*, 277.
9. Iris Marion Young, "Throwing Like a Girl: A Phenomenology of Feminine
   Body Comportment Motility and Spatiality," *Human Studies* 3 (1980), 152.
10. *Dune*, 164.
11. Young, "Throwing Like a Girl," 152.
12. *Dune*, 136.
13. *Dune*, 53.
14. Timothy O'Reilly, *Frank Herbert* (New York: Frederick Ungar, 1981), 47.
15. W.J. Johnson, "prāṇa," in *A Dictionary of Hinduism* (Oxford University Press,
   2009); John Bowker, "bindu," in *The Concise Oxford Dictionary of World
   Religions* (Oxford University Press, 2003).
16. Ernest Wood, *Yoga* (Harmondsworth: Penguin, 1962), 177.
17. Sthaneshwar Timalsina, "Liberation and Immortality: Bhuśuṇḍa's Yoga of
   Prāṇa in the Yogavāsiṣṭha," in Knut A. Jacobsen ed., *Yoga Powers:
   Extraordinary Capacities Attained Through Meditation and Concentration*
   (Boston: Brill, 2012), 305.
18. Leonard M. Scigaj, "*Prana* and the Presbyterian Fixation: Ecology and
   Technology in Frank Herbert's *Dune* Tetralogy," *Extrapolation* 24 (1983), 345.
19. Chakravarthi Ram-Prasad, *Indian Philosophy and the Consequences of
   Knowledge: Themes in Ethics, Metaphysics and Soteriology* (Aldershot:
   Ashgate, 2007), 91.

20. Stuart Ray Sarbacker, "Power and Meaning in the Yogasūtra of Patañjali," in Knut A. Jacobsen ed., *Yoga Powers: Extraordinary Capacities Attained Through Meditation and Concentration* (Boston: Brill, 2012), 199.
21. Sarbacker, "Power and Meaning," 197.
22. *Dune*, 249.
23. *Dune*, 338–339.
24. *Dune*, 522.
25. *Dune*, 281.
26. *Dune*, 478.

2

What Do Zendaya's Blue Eyes Really Mean?

Edwardo Pérez

Blue is a significant color in science fiction: *Star Trek*, *Star Wars*, *Avatar*, Marvel, and DC all have aliens, mutants, and superheroes that come in shades from aqua to cerulean to cobalt. In *Dune*, however, blue isn't a skin tone, it's an eye color – not for aliens, but for humans. Specifically, it's meant to visualize and symbolize the Fremen, and anyone who is either addicted to spice or has been around it long enough for their eyes to change.

With an all-white cast in David Lynch's 1984 film[1] and in the *Dune* (2000) and *Children of Dune* (2003) Sci-Fi Channel miniseries, the blue eyes didn't really offer anything more than an easy visual shorthand – because an altered look for eyes is another sci-fi signifier. Yet in Denis Villeneuve's *Dune*, the use of blue eyes on multiracial and multiethnic actors suggests we consider ideas about race, culture, power, and privilege – considerations that not only speak to the contemporary moment, but also ones that illuminate and call for a reinterpretation of the cultural philosophy of Herbert's books.

"The unreadable total blue eyes of the spice diet"

Villeneuve's 2021 film casts Zendaya (African American) as Chani, Oscar Isaac (Guatemalan) as Duke Leto Atreides, Jason Momoa (Hawaiʻian/Native American) as Duncan Idaho, Javier Bardem (Spanish) as Stilgar, and Babs Olusanmokun (Nigerian/American) as Jamis, as well as many other diverse and multicultural actors in various roles. This offers a clear contrast to the previous casts – most notably, Villeneuve assigns Sharon Duncan-Brewster (a British woman of African descent) the role of Liet-Kynes, played by Max von Sydow in the 1984 film. Indeed, even Timothée Chalamet (Jewish American with French heritage/dual citizenship) as Paul Atreides and Rebecca Ferguson (Swedish) as Lady Jessica reinforce the diversity of ethnicity and color

Dune and Philosophy, First Edition. Edited by Kevin S. Decker.
© 2023 John Wiley & Sons, Inc. Published 2023 by John Wiley & Sons, Inc.

in Villeneuve's film. Put another way, this kind of racial representation doesn't just reflect our culturally blended contemporary society, it cinematically creates a spectrum of color rather than a monochromatic template. Accordingly, the blue eyes of Zendaya and Duncan-Brewster are not just visually striking, they're culturally striking, especially in light of contemporary philosophy of intersectionality and critical race theory. Thus, Villeneuve's *Dune* isn't just re-colored, it's re-contextualized to fit a twenty-first-century awareness regarding diversity and cultural pluralism.

What is the deeper meaning to audiences seeing a cinematic adaptation of *Dune* filmed with a group of actors of color? And does the use of blue eyes on actors like Zendaya add a layer of philosophical and cultural weight to the narrative that was effectively absent in previous adaptations? Is Villeneuve's *Dune* bringing an already-existing subtext to the foreground? Or is the use of cultural color in Villeneuve's version of *Dune* superficial, highlighting the cultural disparities between races rather than reconciling them?

"The blue of the Ibad"

In 1968, third-grade schoolteacher Jane Elliot's "blue eyes/brown eyes" experiment with Iowa school children helped reveal interesting behaviors bearing on racism and whites' treatment of people of color. Several decades later, in 2012, *Vibe* magazine recognized what they called "eye color privilege," leveling harsh criticism toward Black women who chose to change their eye color with fashion contact lenses. The color of your eyes can often be significant in our society, especially for people of color. Certainly, this is the case with blue eyes in *Dune*, which are clearly telling to the Fremen and for the narrative as a whole.

Blue eyes in *Dune* allow readers and characters to recognize those who live with spice either by proximity, diet, or addiction. In *Dune*'s mythology, this is called having the "Eyes of Ibad." Seeing a brown-eyed Sean Young in 1984 with blue eyes in the role of Chani might not seem strange (cheesy visual effect notwithstanding). Yet, seeing Zendaya and Sharon Duncan-Brewster with blue eyes is striking, isn't it? Even if we're used to seeing colored contacts and Rihanna's green orbs, seeing Black women like Zendaya and especially Duncan-Brewster (who is several shades darker than Zendaya) with blue eyes signals something different about the ways in which we've been conditioned to view culture in light of physical appearance – Zendaya might only have about seven minutes of screen time (and Duncan-Brewster about the same) in Villeneuve's "Part One," but her presence (mostly in Chalamet's Paul's dreams) haunts the film.

It's also interesting to consider that Zendaya's complexion (or Duncan-Brewster's or Bardem's) isn't too different from what Herbert likely envisioned for the "sand people called Fremen."[2] We easily equate the desert landscape and its spice with the Middle East and its oil – and Herbert employs words and names from various languages around the world, such as Hebrew, Navajo, Turkish, Finnish, Aztec, Greek, and even Russian and Old English. As Herbert explained in a 1969 interview, "in studying sand dunes, you immediately get into not just the Arabian mystique, but the Navajo mystique and the mystique of the Kalahari primitives."[3] Maybe Villeneuve's *Dune* casting better resembles Herbert's inspiration than Lynch's or the Sci-Fi Channel's miniseries. Certainly, if you're trying to evoke Arabian, Navajo, and the San people from the Kalahari Desert, Zendaya seems more appropriate than Sean Young or the Czech Barbora Kodetová (who played Chani on Sci-Fi).

But what about the name, Chani Kynes? "Chani" is Hebrew in origin while "Kynes" seems to be a variation of the English *Kyne*, which means "royal" (and owes its etymology to the Old English word *cyning*, which means king). From these cultural perspectives, Young and Kodetová seem a better fit. So, how are we supposed to understand this? Should Chani be played by a Hebrew-English (or Hebrew-English looking) actress because of her name? Or should she be played by a dark-skinned actress because of her geography? How far do we take our interpretation of the casting of a character like Chani?

In the novel, we first learn of Chani through a dream Paul describes to the Reverend Mother, but all we're told is that Paul sees "a girl there – very skinny with big eyes. Her eyes are all blue, no whites in them."[4] When Paul finally meets Chani (more than 300 pages later!) and she says, "I am Chani, daughter of Liet,"[5] Herbert writes:

> The voice was lilting, half filled with laughter . . . The figure in front of [Paul] turned into the moon's path and he saw an elfin face, black pits of eyes. The familiarity of that face, the features out of numberless visions in his earliest prescience, shocked Paul to stillness . . . And here was the face, but in no meeting he had ever dreamed . . . He scrambled out of the cleft, followed the swirling of her robe across a tumbled landscape. She moved like a gazelle, dancing over the rocks. Paul felt hot blood on his face, was thankful for the darkness. *That girl!* She was like a touch of destiny. He felt caught up on a wave, in tune with a motion that lifted all his spirits.[6]

So, maybe Villeneuve's casting of Zendaya has nothing to do with race, but more to do with finding an actress that physically fits Herbert's description.

Still, it's an interesting (and of-the-moment) casting choice. Zendaya is certainly popular – with a slew of television and film roles, including MJ in the Sony Spider-Man films and Rue in HBO's *Euphoria*. And she's a good actress, perfectly representing not just her ethnicity, but also her generation, with a wistful, otherworldly gaze (that seems to be perpetually sad and frustrated), portraying (with a sense of knowing gravitas) the angst Generation Z seems to feel about the future bequeathed to them by older generations.

Zendaya, like many in her generation, advocates for the equal rights and acceptance of others across racial, gender, and sexual spectrums. Her appearance suggests a possible fluidity of sexual identity, as she wears designer dresses as well as men's suits and neckties, like model Cara Delevingne. Zendaya's unique intersectionality is perhaps what most sets her apart from previous actresses to portray Chani. The reason why intersectionality matters in current feminist theory might help us better appreciate all of this.

"The shaded slits of blue within blue"

For all the progress feminism has achieved, its progress hasn't equally applied to all women, especially women of color. As Ruby Hamad notes, feminist history and tradition belong primarily to white women, and women of color "are always perceived as lesser women" because "every experience of marginalization is made more acute when race is thrown into the mix."[7] This is what makes Chani problematic, too. The casting in Lynch's *Dune* and in the Sci-Fi Channel miniseries could be interpreted as substituting a white woman's experience for a woman of color's experience, and, as Hamad notes, they are not interchangeable. This becomes problematic if Chani is meant to represent the Fremen, an oppressed desert-dwelling people.

Of course, we could suggest something similar with Zendaya, couldn't we? Is Zendaya's Chani substituting a woman of color's experience for the experience of a white (Hebrew-English) woman? Does Zendaya appropriate white culture? Or does Zendaya, with her own exotic-sounding name, better depict the *identity* of Chani, who isn't Hebrew-English so much as a dune dweller? Does Sean Young or Barbora Kodetová appropriate the culture of dune dwellers? And what about the gender-swapped role Duncan-Brewster embodies as Liet-Kynes?

Cultural appropriation occurs when a culture's practices, experiences, and knowledge are adopted by outsiders – and adoption can occur in both intentional and unintentional ways. Erich Hatala Matthes observes, "Cultural appropriation can often seem morally problematic," but, he says, it also "has received scant attention from philosophers."[8] Matthes borrows Loretta Todd's understanding of *cultural autonomy*, that members of a culture have a right to their "origins and histories as told from within the culture and not as mediated from without."[9] Matthes offers a strong argument for the claim that cultural appropriation is morally problematic because it's harmful to the culture being appropriated. Matthes doesn't think that all cultural appropriation is equal: "it is only objectionable when a member of a dominant cultural group appropriates from a member of a marginalized group" because "no reasonable person thinks that, for instance, an indigenous person does something wrong by employing some Western artistic style."[10]

Is this correct? If so, then Lynch's *Dune* film and the 2000 and 2003 miniseries could pose moral problems because they appropriate the marginalized dune-dwelling cultures I've suggested that Herbert had in mind, allowing white actors to represent them. Likewise, Villeneuve's 2021 *Dune*, by casting actors closer to what Herbert had in mind, offers a more culturally appropriate representation, at least in the sense that most of the actors of color hail from historically oppressed cultural groups. Indeed, to take Herbert at his word, the most accurate cultural representation would be to cast Fremen with actors of Arabian, Navajo, and Kalahari descent. For Villeneuve's version, then, darker skin tones are all that's needed to suggest the cultures Herbert envisioned. Is this still cultural appropriation? Does it remain morally problematic? Or is it close enough?

Perhaps these remaining questions are why, as Matthes notes, philosophers such as James O. Young remain skeptical about the harmfulness of cultural appropriation. Indeed, can we really say the representation by white actors in the earlier versions is *harmful* to Arabian, Navajo, and Kalahari cultures? And, does the use of Black, Hispanic, and Asian actors in Villeneuve's 2021 version also harm different cultures, those from which Herbert drew his inspiration? Harm (and certainly the intent to harm) is often hard to discern, isn't it? It's worth pointing out that Herbert drew inspiration from three very different groups of people, linked not by a shared culture or geography but by the *nature of their habitat*. So it's difficult to detect any specific cultural ownership of the Fremen. But it's also difficult to accept a future that negates non-whites and that essentially allows the history of oppressed non-whites to be told by a group of whites with non-white names and, of course, blue eyes.

"Without any white in them at all"

Alice Walker, in her essay "If the Present Looks Like the Past, What Does the Future Look Like?" connects color, oppression, and the future of Black people through her idea of *colorism*. This refers to the "prejudicial or preferential treatment of same-race people based solely on their color"; for Walker, colorism "like colonialism, sexism, and racism impedes us."[11] By "us," Walker means the Black community, where variations of skin tone sometimes cause strife. As Walker explains:

> What black women would be interested in, I think, is a consciously heightened awareness on the part of light black women that they are capable, often quite unconsciously, of inflicting pain upon them; and that unless the question of Colorism . . . is addressed in our communities and definitely in our black "sisterhoods" we cannot, as a people, progress.[12]

For Walker, darker-skinned Black women represent "our essential mother – the blacker she is the more us she is – and to see the hatred that is turned on her is enough to make me despair, almost entirely, of our future as a people."[13] Underlying Walker's fear is the fact that the past for Black people was rooted in the goal of escape:

> Escape the pain, the ridicule, escape the jokes, the lack of attention, respect, dates, even a job, any way you can. And if you can't escape, help your children to escape. Don't let them suffer as you have done. And yet, what have we been escaping to? Freedom used to be the only answer to that question. But for some of our parents it is as if freedom and whiteness were the same destination, and that presents a problem for any person of color who does not wish to disappear.[14]

As Kimberly Jade Norwood and Violeta Solonova Foreman observe, Walker's colorism extends beyond same-race concerns. Norwood and Foreman trace distinctions of skin color to antiquity – from Greeks and Romans who "used white lead as a cosmetic to lighten their skin" to Cleopatra using mercury and "asses' milk" to "keep her skin light," to agrarian societies who "placed value on white skin to distinguish the upper class from outdoor laborers" to Aztec women who "used to smear themselves with an ointment made of yellow earth . . . since golden skin was considered more attractive than brown."[15] As Norwood and Foreman note: "Western colonization, however, used colorism to dehumanize enslaved populations, thus making discrimination based on skin color more than a class imperative, turning it instead into a system of hatred and denigration."[16]

So, for Norwood and Foreman, colorism isn't just a same-race issue, it's a "global phenomenon" that applies not just "within racial communities but also between them."[17] This is what makes the absence of color in the filmed adaptations of *Dune* from 1984, 2000, and 2003 so striking and, frankly, implausible, and it's what makes Villeneuve's *Dune* seem more plausible – as much as a fantasy set so far in the future might plausibly represent humanity's descendants to our twenty-first-century minds. But this plausibility increases in the context of the murder of George Floyd, the Black Lives Matter movement, debates on immigration and refugees, the issue of voting rights being curtailed for people of color, and the myriad instances of colorism continuing to take place around the world. For Villeneuve's *Dune*, the plausibility centers on the depiction of the Fremen.

"Blue within blue within blue"

The culture of the Fremen is built around two things: spice and dunes (with gigantic worms!). Given the value of spice and the harsh conditions of the desert, the Fremen live a difficult, oppressed life. Their blue eyes could also be seen as "branding," if you will, a mark forced upon them by virtue of being Fremen. They don't choose to have blue eyes. Their eyes turn blue because of where and how they live, a reality they can't change – at least until Paul Atreides shows up.

These facts strengthen our interpretation of the earlier *Dune* adaptations as cultural appropriation. What makes Villeneuve's film seem more realistic is not just his vision of people of color as dune-dwellers, but – because *Dune* is set in the future (10191) – it seems wrong to portray the future as being only white. If anything, white skin color will likely be the minority, if not a rarity in future generations, as different groups of people continue to blend with one another.

So not only do the all-white versions of *Dune* appropriate culture, they also stake a white claim to the future, erasing the existence of any other ethnicities. In this whiteness, identity no longer has anything to do with skin color. Rather, identity is reduced to eye color, with blue equating to addiction and oppression. Thus, by casting Zendaya (and Javier Bardem and many other actors of color) as a Fremen, Villeneuve reclaims the culture of people of color and he reframes the future, showing that people of color not only continue to exist, they unfortunately continue to be oppressed.

This aligns with Herbert's vision. Lorenzo DiTommaso notes that Herbert believed that humans are unequal, explaining that "in *Dune* this fundamental imparity stems from [the Butlerian] Jihad's general and insidious effects upon every level of Imperial society."[18] As such, "some lives have a diminished value, others a greater value, and those of 'humans' (as opposed to less-aware 'people') exceptional worth."[19] Indeed, as Herbert wrote: "I now know . . . that all humans are not created equal. In fact, I believe attempts to create some abstract equalization create a morass of injustices that rebound on the equalizers."[20] DiTommaso argues that "the final historical effect of the Butlerian Jihad is the search for humanness" in which the Bene Gesserit "attempt to shatter the limits of the question 'What is it to be human?'"[21] He adds, "The sisterhood's plan is to lift Homo sapiens from animal awareness to people, to humans, and then to trained humans and perhaps beyond."[22] Crucially, Paul is working to this plan when he responds "to Liet-Kynes' question about the possible use of an Imperial Ecological Testing Station on Dune: 'To make this planet a fit place for humans.'"[23] What does Paul really mean by "humans" in his response to Liet-Kynes?

We've already said that Herbert seems to have modeled the Fremen on Arabian, Navajo, and Kalahari peoples – what Joel P. Christensen refers to as "a Bedouin-type culture."[24] Yet, given Herbert's thoughts on equality and the Bene Gesserit plan, it implicitly seems as if color is equated with *being less than human* in Herbert's framework, especially if we consider the fact that Paul isn't just a savior, he's a *white* savior.[25] This holds true in Villeneuve's version, too, perhaps even more so, given Villeneuve's choices in casting the Fremen as people of color, which further emphasizes Paul as a white savior.[26] No offense to Timothée Chalamet, but it would've been more culturally interesting if Villeneuve had cast someone like Dev Patel, Riz Ahmed, or even Elliot Page, who, though white, would have depicted a very different identity for Paul (and, if we're recasting, how about Zoe Saldana, Gemma Chan, or Gal Gadot as Lady Jessica?).

To be fair, Chalamet is one of the finest actors of his generation and his androgynous looks convincingly capture both the masculine and feminine sides of Paul's personality, something essential to his portrayal. Maybe color isn't as important to consider for Paul as it is for Chani and the Fremen; but what does it say that, even in the future, people of color continue to need to be saved by white men? Is this really what the future will be like? Does it matter that *Dune* is a fantasy future and not a possible future tied to our actual history? Given all this, what do Zendaya's blue eyes really mean?

"I am Chani, daughter of Liet"

Perhaps the awareness in Villeneuve's casting reflects views on representation of race and ethnicity that our society has embraced since Herbert's novel was first published in 1965 and Lynch's 1984 film was released – and even since the miniseries aired in 2000 and 2003. Yet, in casting actors of color as Fremen and Paul as a white savior, it seems Villeneuve (for all his gifts as a director) only reinforces the value of whiteness by failing to envision a better future for people of color. As such, it seems Zendaya's eyes only mean that people of color continue to be oppressed – which is exactly what she ponders in her voice-over that opens the film:

> At nightfall the spice harvesters land. The outsiders race against time to avoid the heat of the day. They ravage our lands in front of our eyes. Their cruelty to my people is all I've known. These outsiders, the Harkonnens, came long before I was born. By controlling spice production, they became obscenely rich. Richer than the Emperor himself. Our warriors couldn't free Arrakis from the Harkonnens, but one day, by Imperial decree, they were gone. Why did the Emperor choose this path? And who will our next oppressors be?

This might help illuminate Herbert's vision of inequality and emphasize the theme of oppression, but it doesn't change *Dune*'s message that people of color not only don't belong in the future, they don't have a future.[27] For what kind of future do people of color have to look forward to when they're depicted as oppressed addicts, unable to free themselves without the help of a white messiah?[28]

Notes

1. People of Italian and Spanish heritage have, at least in the era of mass media, been labeled "white" in terms of race, so the presence of José Ferrer, Leonardo Cimino, Silvana Mangano, and Honorato Magaloni in Lynch's film is not multiracial casting.
2. *Dune* (New York: Ace, 2005), 5.
3. From an interview with Willis E. McNelly, 1969. For an audio recording of the interview, see: ansionnachfionn.com/2017/10/23/willis-e-mcnelly-interviews-frank-herbert-author-of-dune-1969. For a transcription of the interview, see: sinanvural.com/seksek/inien/tvd/tvd2.htm.
   Also, the "primitives" of the Kalahari are known as the San people, hunter-gatherers who've lived in the Kalahari for 20,000 years.
4. *Dune*, 31.
5. *Dune*, 362.
6. *Dune*, 362–363.
7. Ruby Hamad, *White Tears/Brown Scars: How White Feminism Betrays Women of Color* (New York: Catapult, 2020), 13.
8. Erich Hatala Matthes, "Cultural Appropriation Without Cultural Essentialism?" *Social Theory and Practice* 42 (2016), 343, 344.
9. Matthes, "Cultural Appropriation," 347.
10. Matthes, "Cultural Appropriation," 347.
11. Alice Walker, "If the Present Looks Like the Past, What Does the Future Look Like?," in *In Search of Our Mother's Gardens: Womanist Prose* (New York: Harcourt, 1983), 290.
12. Walker, "If the Present Looks Like the Past," 290.
13. Walker, "If the Present Looks Like the Past," 291.
14. Walker, "If the Present Looks Like the Past," 291.
15. Kimberly Jade Norwood and Violeta Solonova Foreman, "The Ubiquitousness of Colorism: Then and Now," in Kimberly Jade Norwood ed., *Color Matters: Skin Tone Bias and the Myth of a Postracial America* (New York: Routledge, 2014), 9–10.
16. Norwood and Foreman, "The Ubiquitousness of Colorism," 10.
17. Norwood and Foreman, "The Ubiquitousness of Colorism," 9.
18. Lorenzo DiTommaso, "History and Historical Effect in Frank Herbert's 'Dune,'" *Science Fiction Studies* 19 (1992), 311.
19. DiTommaso, "History and Historical Effect in Frank Herbert's 'Dune,'" 311.
20. DiTommaso, "History and Historical Effect in Frank Herbert's 'Dune,'" 311.
21. DiTommaso, "History and Historical Effect in Frank Herbert's 'Dune,'" 317.
22. DiTommaso, "History and Historical Effect in Frank Herbert's 'Dune,'" 317, 318.
23. DiTommaso, "History and Historical Effect in Frank Herbert's 'Dune,'" 318.
24. Joel P. Christensen, "Time and Self-referentiality in the *Iliad* and Frank Herbert's *Dune*," in Brett M. Rogers and Benjamin Eldon eds., *Classical Traditions in Science Fiction* (Oxford: Oxford University Press, 2015), 166.
25. As David Ehrlich frames it in his review of Villeneuve's film: "Paul is Jesus Christ as a eugenics experiment designed by space witch Charlotte Rampling, who paired Duke Atreides (a bearded and winsome Oscar Isaac, who gets to yell 'Desert power!' several times) with a very special concubine (the ever-capable Rebecca Ferguson), and the Bedouin-coded Fremen of Arakis are happy to

accept this foreign twerp as their prophet." David Ehrlich, "'Dune' Review: Denis Villeneuve's Epic Spice Opera Is a Massive Disappointment," *IndieWire*, September 3, 2021, at Indiewire.com/2021/09/dune-review-denis-villeneuve-1234660459.

26. Indeed, he is a clear contrast to Zendaya's skin tone.
27. Several characters of color don't even make it to the end of Villeneuve's film – Villeneuve might adhere to Herbert's narrative, but it's noticeable that Isaac, Momoa, Duncan-Brewster, Chen, and Olusanmokun all get killed off.
28. Even Paul's defeat of Jamis, which ends Villeneuve's Part One, is depicted as a noble act, as if Paul killing his first man (a Black man painted with a stereotypical savage brush) somehow makes Paul heroic rather than blameful.

3

The Golden Path and Multicultural Meanings of Life

Ethan Mills

Leto II discusses not just the meaning of life for individuals as for ancient Earth philosophers from the Buddha and Socrates to Albert Camus and Susan Wolf, but the meaning of life for humanity itself. Furthermore, Leto II and Bene Gesserit Other Memory gave humanity a vast historical consciousness. The spice liberated us from cultural myopia, allowing us to learn from all teachers of the past. In changing what it means to be human, this historical consciousness enhanced our humanity.

From *The Golden Path to Meaning: A Philosophical Inquiry into the Thought of the Tyrant* by Falsafa Lukoru, Lecturer in Ancient Earth Philosophies, Chapterhouse Institute of Hermeneutics

If you're philosophically inclined enough to pick up a book on *Dune* and philosophy, you've probably occasionally stepped back from your busy life of making plans within plans and wondered: *what does it all mean?* In *God Emperor of Dune*, Leto II talks with the Duncans, Moneo, and Hwi Noree not just about the meaning of life for individuals, but for humanity as a whole, across vast reaches of time. We work and love and laugh and cry, which all feels imbued with meaning and purpose as we do it, but eventually, we die: "Leto spoke with infinite sadness: 'You, too, shall pass away. Will all your works be as dust forgotten?'" he says to his majordomo Moneo.[1]

Death is a Harkonnen traitor waiting to spring a trap in your sietch of meaning: if everything you do in life will someday be gone, what's the point? Leto II might provide a way out of this trap. He looks not at individual lives, but at humanity itself. He believes that ensuring the survival of humanity enhances its meaning for humans living now. At one point Leto II describes "the silent prayer for my intercession in all things – that humankind may never end."[2]

Dune and Philosophy, First Edition. Edited by Kevin S. Decker.
© 2023 John Wiley & Sons, Inc. Published 2023 by John Wiley & Sons, Inc.

But is he right? As Buddhists and Zensunnis say, everything is impermanent. Whether humans die out or evolve into Stage Four Guild Navigators, eventually there will be no humans – neither individuals nor the species. Does this fact make life as a human less meaningful today?

To answer, we'll need to direct our inner eyes toward Frank Herbert's use of non-European languages and ideas (especially from the Arabic language and the Islamic world). What can this teach us about the need to learn from *all* human cultures to gain a more complete answer to the question of the meaning of life for humanity?

But first let's take a planetological survey of the issue of meaning for individuals, going back tens of thousands of years before the reign of the God Emperor to see what four promising candidates (mentioned in the epigraph above) have had to say about the most famous philosophical question of all: What is the meaning of life?

Albert Camus: Meaning Messiah

French-Algerian philosopher, author, and journalist Albert Camus (1913–1960), in *The Myth of Sisyphus*, offers up "absurdity" in answering this question. He doesn't mean an everyday sense of absurdity, as in, "The hats the Bene Gesserit wear in the 2000 *Dune* miniseries are absurd." Instead, Camus points to the stark contrast between the way we humans feel the world should be (as a place that makes sense and is infused with meaning) and the way the world appears to us in light of scientific developments of the early twentieth century (a universe indifferent to human yearnings for meaning). As Camus says, "The absurd is born of this confrontation between the human need and the unreasonable silence of the world."[3]

Think of a Sardaukar warrior on Arrakis, far from friends and family. He might console himself that he's serving the Emperor of the Known Universe and making the folks back home proud. But, from a wider perspective, why do it? After all, the Emperor won't be around forever (at least not if Muad'Dib has anything to do with it!), and eventually everyone he knows will be lost in the sands of time. All the while the universe itself marches on – galaxies spinning, pulsars pulsing, and stars going supernova – without any care for the fate of our poor Sardaukar.

But what about the heroes of the *Dune* universe? Surely Duncan Idaho, Lady Jessica, Paul Muad'Dib, St. Alia of the Knife, and God Emperor Leto II make a bigger dent in the grand scheme of things than the Sardaukar! But even if you adjust your scope of reference to be a bit wider, even these don't measure up, cosmically speaking. To put it bluntly, the universe doesn't give a worm shit about humanity, much less millennia-long Atreides family drama. Even worse, the universe is not even the kind of thing that *can* care about us, having no personal qualities like desires, cares, and plans. Human efforts are completely insignificant in the grand scheme of things. No matter how hard we try to make a dent in the vast goings on of the universe, our fate is the same. We tried – and died. The end.

This might bum you out. You might even wonder if it's worth going on. Some people might contemplate suicide like Alia did in *Children of Dune*. But Camus differs: for him we should live on *despite* and *in defiance* of absurdity. Shake your fist at the universe! Camus points to the ancient Greek myth of Sisyphus, whom the gods condemned to roll a boulder up a hill over and over again, without end. Camus says that in the face of it all, "One must imagine Sisyphus happy."[4]

Can you really imagine Sisyphus happy? Camus is reacting to a world-view, shared by monotheistic religions (Christianity, Judaism, and Islam), that meaning and values ultimately rest with God, the creator of the universe. By the mid-twentieth century, though, new scientific advances, combined with the horrors of modern warfare and genocide, made this comforting monotheistic worldview about as shaky as a Duncan Idaho ghola when the God Emperor's in a bad mood. But could there be more satisfactory answers from outside these monotheistic religions? Let's give it the old Chapterhouse try, starting with the Buddha.

The Buddha: Children of Meaning

The Buddha (Siddhartha Gautama) lived in India and Nepal around the fourth century BCE. After out-meditating everyone in the Ganges Valley, the Buddha figured out that the fundamental problem of human existence is suffering, but not just suffering like stubbing your toe or having to wait another year to see Villeneuve's *Dune* because of the pandemic.

The Buddhist idea of suffering is one of great depth. Later Buddhist philosophers like Vasubandhu (around 400 CE) theorized that suffering comes in three types: explicit suffering, suffering produced by change, and suffering due to being conditioned. Stubbing your toe is explicit suffering, while a change in the release date of *Dune* is suffering produced by change. The last type, suffering due to conditioning, is complex. We suffer like this when we take ourselves to be something we're not, in particular when we believe we have permanent selves that serve as our "essence."

Selfish people like the Harkonnens develop plans within plans aiming to please themselves, when there is no self to please! The Buddha wouldn't be surprised they don't seem happy, despite their debauchery. But people who act out of an understanding that we're all in this together – as Paul and Leto claim to do, and Jessica might actually do – tend to do better. The Buddha has a lot of abstract arguments against the self I won't go into here, but the basic idea is that selfish desires are the cause of suffering, so we can have fewer selfish desires if we stop believing there's a self![5] The Buddha is often quoted as saying, "Both before and now, I declare only suffering and the cessation of suffering."[6] So for the Buddha, the meaning of life is to end suffering. Which is no small feat – your own Golden Path!

Camus wouldn't be impressed. You *could* end suffering, but so what? Eradicating suffering is no less absurd in an uncaring universe (still less absurd than those Bene Gesserit hats in the *Dune* miniseries, though). And, even worse, would a life without suffering even be meaningful? For Camus the struggle itself is meaningful.

Personally I'm not as much of a fan of struggle as Camus or the Bene Gesserit. I'm inclined to agree with Buddhists and think it would be nice if we could end suffering, but let's leave that one to the Mentats for now.

Socrates: Heretics of Meaning

Like the Preacher in *Children of Dune,* but with a better sense of humor, Socrates (470–399 BCE) spent his golden years hanging around annoying people, much to the delight of young Athenians like Plato (428–348/7 BCE). And like the Preacher, this eventually landed Socrates in trouble. He was charged with corrupting the youth, not believing in the city's gods, and practicing his own eccentric religious ideas. Plato's *Apology* details his response to these charges, and includes one of his most quotable lines: "the unexamined life is not worth living."[7]

Thankfully he doesn't mean examination like what Reverend Mother Gaius Helen Mohaim has in store for young Paul at the beginning of *Dune*. Socrates' examination involves fewer gom jabbar tests, weird boxes, and Litanies Against Fear, but it does involve asking difficult questions, not only of others but of yourself. You might critically examine one of your values, like justice or piety, and see whether you can adequately define that concept. It sounds easy, but try it! Whether Socrates thinks there are answers found at the end of all this examination has been debated for thousands of years. But for Socrates the meaning of life is to examine life.

However, an examined life can't escape absurdity. Sure, Socratic examination might be part of Camus' defiant creation of meaning, but so might a life of artistic and literary accomplishment. And, of course, examined lives are lost in the sands of Arrakis (or time) as much as unexamined ones.

Susan Wolf: Chapterhouse – Meaning

Susan Wolf is a philosopher who teaches at the University of North Carolina, Chapel Hill, Earth (Before Guild). On the meaning of life, Wolf says it's in your self-interest to have a meaningful life, and some pursuits and goals are meaningful for everyone – things from this list aren't just subjective likings. You don't need to pursue *everything* on this list, nor even know everything that's on it. Consider that Muad'Dib and Leto II have *some* idea what the Golden Path entails, but not even these prescient beings can see every step.

For Wolf, "Meaning arises when subjective attraction meets objective attractiveness."[8] Those words ("subjective" and "objective") are a philosophical Sardaukar ambush waiting to happen, so let's use an example for what Wolf means. Imagine you're a Mentat in training, learning to let your mind think on its own, waiting to stain your lips with the sapho juice. If you were bored with the whole Mentat training, it wouldn't be meaningful: this is the "subjective" part of meaningfulness. But then, becoming a Mentat is supposed to be a meaningful thing in itself (objectively speaking): it allows humanity to uphold the ban on thinking machines after the Butlerian Jihad and provides valuable services for important leaders.

To get a sense of Wolf's point, ask yourself: Why do people find things meaningful? You might say you think something's meaningful just because you prefer it. Emperor Shaddam IV would say power is meaningful since he prefers it over other things, like taking relaxing seaside vacations on Caladan. Or you might say that things are meaningful because they're pleasurable, and a life filled with more pleasure (hedonism) is a better life. You don't have to be as extreme as the Harkonnens and take as much pleasure as possible all the time, but maybe you think the point of life overall is to enjoy it or have fun.

But if you allow your Mentat reflexes to push deeper, you might ask: why should I prefer one thing over another? The Emperor prefers power *because* he thinks it's meaningful, and not the other way around. As for pleasure, not all pleasures are meaningful. An eccentric Fremen might get a lot of pleasure out of counting the grains of sand in the Habbanya Erg, but most wouldn't find that particularly meaningful. Besides, people do all sorts of unpleasurable things for the sake of meaningful things – Feyd and Rabban endure their uncle's tasteless jokes because they think family ties are meaningful!

So why not say that meaning is what drives a lot of our preferences and desires, rather than the other way around? Why not say that meaning is objective in some sense? This idea is strengthened by looking at specific things on the objective list: maintaining relationships, raising children, learning, ending suffering, philosophical examination, or reading *Dune*. If this way that most people actually think about meaning is right, then maybe Wolf has a point, and maybe other ideas from the Buddha or Socrates could even be included on the objective list.

You don't need spice-induced prescience to see Camus' response to this: these kinds of activities may be worth pursuing, but they don't last. You and everyone you know will meet Shai-Hulud in the desert of oblivion one day. Here Wolf has an interesting response. She claims Camus' view "expresses an irrational obsession with permanence."[9] *Of course* human activities don't last forever. But so what? Why should the meaning you and

I find in thinking philosophically about the *Dune* universe be lessened because it won't last forever? Aren't some things *more* meaningful precisely because they don't last forever?

We'll come back to those questions, but first let us go tens of thousands of years into the future. Make way for God Emperor Leto II!

The Golden Path and Humanity: God Emperor of Meaning

The Golden Path is kind of a big deal. It takes center stage with Leto II in *God Emperor of Dune*. There Leto says, "And what is the Golden Path? you ask. It is the survival of humankind, nothing more or less. We who have prescience, we who know the pitfalls in our human futures, this has always been our responsibility."[10]

Thirty-five hundred years after *Children of Dune*, Leto II has been fused with the body of a sandworm, a process giving him thousands of years of life and making him the God Emperor of humanity. Leto II is one of the most awesome characters in fiction: he can access Other Memories from all human history and has a prescient ability to see much of the future.

Frank Herbert uses this character to think deeply about politics, religion, violence, sex, gender, boredom, logic, and history, among other things. *God Emperor* is the most philosophical book of an already philosophical series. Its title character is actively *doing* philosophy by adding to the questions we can ask about the meaning of human life, including one that few, if any, philosophers have asked: *what is the meaning of life for humanity as a whole?*

Leto thinks species death is a tragedy threatening to erase whatever meaning our lives might have. But instead of following Camus' path of shaking his fist at the universe and finding meaning in spite of absurdity, Leto's answer is the millennia-long project of the Golden Path. "'As long as there is life, every ending is a beginning,' he said. 'And I would save humankind, even from itself . . . This is why no death in the perpetuation of humankind can be a complete failure,' he said."[11] In his secret journal, Leto writes,

> Nothing within these memories remains completely without meaning or influence, not as long as there is a humankind somewhere. We have that bright Infinity all around us, that Golden Path of forever to which we can continually pledge our puny but inspired allegiance.[12]

Leto explicitly denies that he became God Emperor to enjoy a long lifetime.[13] The point is the continuation of humanity. But as it turns out, nobody's a fan of Leto's methods, which include his millennia-long absolute dictatorship, brutal military rule by his army of Fish Speakers, and total economic control through possession of most of the spice in existence. No wonder everyone calls him the Tyrant.

But why does he do all that? Leto tells Siona, who is a descendant of the Atreides but also Leto's would-be assassin:

> "Without me there would have been by now no people anywhere, none whatsoever. And the path to that extinction was more hideous than your wildest imaginings." "Your *supposed* prescience," she sneered. "The Golden Path still stands open," he said.[14]

And in conversation with his betrothed, Hwi Noree, Leto says of his draconian "Golden Peace," "Here, there, everywhere. People will look back on my tyranny as *the good old days*. I will be the mirror of their future."[15] But is all this tyranny really necessary? Does Leto actually see the future, as Siona wonders? Why should we take his word for it? Let's set these issues aside for now.[16]

Leto assumes that for the life of humanity to have any meaning, it must survive into the far future, if not forever. This justifies his lonely yet brutal life. But is that assumption correct? Remember Susan Wolf's concern about Camus' obsession with permanence; Leto is similarly obsessed. It doesn't take a Reverend Mother to see that humanity won't last forever. The majority of other species that have existed have died out. Why should we be any different?

Even if we do survive, our descendants in the far future might become something different, wholly post-human. They might evolve into higher stages of Guild Navigators. The hybrid Leto wonders if he's really human, lamenting his "lost humanity."[17] Maybe Buddhists and Zensunnis are right: everything is impermanent. According to the Buddha, our refusal to accept impermanence is a major cause of suffering. We expect things to last forever. But they never do. And we suffer for it.[18]

I agree with Wolf: hanging your hopes for meaning on mere permanence is not the way to go. After all, something can be meaningful even if it doesn't last forever: a long but finite Golden Path could be a vitally important item on the objective list of meaningful things for human beings (and worm-human hybrids, stage three Guild Navigators, and so on). But what would a more complete, humane Golden Path look like? Looking at Frank Herbert's own use of concepts from a variety of real-life cultures can help us think through these issues.

Orientalism or a Multicultural Golden Path?

In US science fiction at the time of *Dune*'s publication in 1965, Herbert's non-Western influences – especially from the Islamic world and Buddhism – were nearly unique. Herbert uses Arabic words like *jihad* and *mahdi* as well as Persian *Padishah* and Sanskrit *prāṇa-bindu*.[19] The influence of Japanese Zen Buddhism is pervasive in some of his seemingly paradoxical statements modeled on *kōans*, not to mention the Zensunnis, who suggest a marriage of Zen Buddhism and Sunni Islam.[20]

It's no secret Herbert was interested in a wide variety of cultures; his son Brian reports that as part of the counter-culture of the San Francisco Bay area in the 1960s, Frank Herbert was interested in the Chinese *I Ching* and Japanese Zen Buddhism. While writing what would become *Dune* (originally serialized in *Analog* as two shorter works, *Dune World* and *The Prophet of Dune*), Frank Herbert read widely on these and other topics while studying Arab history.[21]

But does Herbert's use of these ideas become what Edward Said (1935–2003) called "Orientalism," the construction of a non-Western Other for Western purposes, a continuation of European colonialism by scholarly means?[22] Orientalism was originally an eighteenth- and nineteenth-century intellectual project that sought to understand non-Western nations colonized by European powers, usually by depicting the cultures of colonized nations as the mystical, irrational, feminine Other to the West's scientific, rational, masculine Self. The idea was to make Western political domination seem inevitable or justifiable. Despite the end of actual political colonization in the twentieth and twenty-first centuries, Orientalism has remained a pervasive cultural pattern: consider everything from Western news coverage of the Middle East and the language used to justify Western military interventions in the "War on Terror" to the fact that American actors of Middle Eastern or South Asian descent are more likely to be cast as terrorists in American TV shows than teachers or wacky neighbors.

Given this, Herbert might have been using "exotic" or "foreign" ideas to put his audience at a distance from their own presumably Western cultural homes and setting himself up as the authority on these cultures.[23] And in having Paul arrive as the savior of the Fremen, Herbert may be utilizing the troubling theme of the "white savior."[24]

But is this fair? After all, creative writing teachers tell you, "write what you know," and Frank Herbert just happened to know a lot. As his son Brian writes, he imagined a more multicultural future than most white American authors at the time: "He observed that bits and pieces of the diversified past were entrenched in our own language and culture, and he saw no reason why this pattern of creation would not continue to hold course."[25]

Concerning the second point, the issue of the white savior: why do the Fremen need Paul, anyway? Is this suggesting that marginalized groups need white people to save or rule them tens of thousands of years into the future? Maybe not. We could question whether twenty-first-century ideas about race even make sense in the *Dune* universe. After all, our concepts of race are only a few hundred years old. But this misunderstands the issue of Orientalism, which is after all a problem for the reception of the work by its audience, not necessarily within the world of that work (the world of *Dune* is about as far removed from our world as science fiction gets). Present-day audiences tend to assume Greek-named Atreides are white while Arabic-sounding Fremen are not, so this audience might read it as a white savior story.

On the other hand, Herbert also undermines the white savior theme. The mythology predicting Paul's coming to Arrakis was implanted in Fremen culture by the Missionaria Protectiva. Paul isn't really a "hero" – his ascension to power causes suffering and death for billions. And Jessica has deep and justified misgivings about Paul's journey.[26]

Dune is too complicated for easy answers, but we can't totally absolve the book series of Orientalism. I think there are elements of it there. The role of the white savior trope is troubling, even if it's subtly undermined. And however well-intentioned Herbert was in using Arabic and other languages, the global power dynamics in which we live influence how his work is received, and likely will for some time. For that matter, the *Dune* series is problematic in other ways, too, from the homophobic depictions of the Baron Harkonnen to the series' rather *blasé* attitude toward eugenics and the weird stuff about sex and gender in the later books.

But you can criticize something and still like it. And I still like *Dune a lot*. One reason is that Herbert was trying – in his own imperfect way – to imagine a multicultural future for humanity, one not dominated by Western cultures.[27] And this attempt might be just what we need in order to think about the meaning of life for humanity.

Multicultural Meanings of Life

To wander back onto the Golden Path, Herbert's imperfect efforts, as well as Leto's example in *God Emperor of Dune*, show that learning from *all* of humanity is a key to the meaning of life. It's only by learning from humanity's diverse cultural gifts that we can appreciate the meaning of life for our species, dramatized by the cultural syntheses in the *Dune* universe as well as diverse Other Memories like Leto's.[28] Finally, laying out my plans within plans: I think Wolf is on to something with the concept of objectively meaningful goals for life, and if we want to find out what sorts of meanings there might be on that list for humanity as a species, we need to set our gazes far beyond the horizons of a single culture. How can you figure out the human condition or understand basic truths about human life if you're only listening to small group of voices? If we learn anything from the *Dune* series (especially *God Emperor* and its sequels), it's that narrowmindedness is a danger to us all.

My academic specialization is in the philosophical traditions of classical India, including Buddhist philosophy, and Herbert is one reason for that. He introduced me to the idea that humanity is larger than the myopic idea of "the West." When I was young, I didn't understand Herbert's cultural references or how they might be echoes of Orientalism, but I've spent the time since learning more about some of those ideas and cultures. My own studies have both enhanced and complicated my appreciation for the *Dune* series, and I've found that another way to avoid the traps of Orientalism is to check out science fiction from various parts of the world; let writers from various cultures speak for themselves![29]

As in *Dune*, in life there are no easy answers. Yet I hope you'll embark upon your own Golden Path to contemplate what it means to be human in a vaster and more philosophically inclusive sense. And don't forget to ask your local Mentat for help!

Notes

1. God Emperor of Dune (New York: Berkley Books, 1981), 261.
2. *GED*, 174.
3. Albert Camus, *The Myth of Sisyphus and Other Essays,* trans. Justin O'Brien (New York: Vintage Books, 1955), 28.
4. Camus, *The Myth of Sisyphus,* 123.
5. A good place for Mentats to start gathering data about Buddhist arguments against the existence of the self is chapter 3 of Mark Siderits, *Buddhism as Philosophy* (Indianapolis: Hackett, 2007).
6. This quote is repeated many times in early Buddhist texts (not quite as many as the Litany Against Fear is repeated in the *Dune* saga). For one example, see the *Discourse on the Parable of the Water Snake* in *Early Buddhist Discourses,* trans. John J. Holder (Indianapolis: Hackett Publishing, 2006), 115.
7. Plato, *Apology* in *The Trial and Death of Socrates,* 3rd ed., trans. G.M.A. Grube, rev. John M. Cooper (Indianapolis: Hackett Publishing, 2000), 38a.
8. Susan Wolf, "Happiness and Meaning: Two Aspects of the Good Life," *Social Philosophy and Policy* 14 (1997), 211.
9. Wolf, "Happiness and Meaning," 215.
10. *GED*, 10.
11. *GED*, 221.
12. *GED*, 258.
13. *GED*, 247.
14. *GED*, 292–293.
15. *GED*, 203.
16. For a discussion of how the Golden Path plays out in *Heretics of Dune* and *Chapterhouse: Dune,* see Leo Wiggins and Abu Zafar, "The Golden Path," *Gom Jabbar: A Dune Podcast,* June 18, 2021, at: https://www.spreaker.com/user/14333325/gjep26-the-golden-path.
17. *GED*, 91.
18. Maybe Leto would disagree about impermanence. At one point he makes a casual remark about the nature of time: "The universe is timeless at its roots and contains therefore all times and all futures" (*GED*, 187). Does this provide a way for humanity to live forever? To even understand this, you have to become something more than human. On the other hand, take the school of Buddhist philosophy called *Sarvāstivāda* (literally, "all exists-ism") that believed that the fundamental units of reality (what they called *dharmas*) must exist simultaneously in the past, present, and future.

19. For an extensive study of Arabic words in *Dune*, see Khalid Baheyeldin, "Arabic and Islamic Themes in Frank Herbert's *Dune*," *The Baheyeldin Dynasty,* January 22, 2004, at https://baheyeldin.com/literature/arabic-and-islamic-themes-in-frank-herberts-dune.html. For a fascinating and nuanced discussion focusing on the word *jihad* and its replacement with "crusade" in early trailers for Villeneuve's *Dune,* see Ali Karjoo-Ravary, "In *Dune,* Paul Atreides Led a *Jihad* Not a Crusade," *Al Jazeera,* October 11, 2020, at https://www.aljazeera.com/opinions/2020/10/11/paul-atreides-led-a-jihad-not-a-crusade-heres-why-that-matters.

20. While Herbert's influences are mostly from Asia and the Islamic world, there are other influences. For example, *Tleilaxu* and *axlotl* are based on Nahuatl (Aztec) language.

21. Brian Herbert, *Dreamer of Dune: The Biography of Frank Herbert* (New York: Tor Books, 2003), 160–170.

22. Edward W. Said, *Orientalism: 25th Anniversary Edition* (New York: Vintage Books, 1994).

23. For a recent discussion of Orientalism with regard to the Villeneuve film, see Siddhant Adlakha, "*Dune* Is a Sprawling Orientalist Fever Dream," *Observer,* October 8, 2021, at https://observer.com/2021/10/dune-review-timothee-chalamet-zendaya-oscar-isaac.

24. Another version of this concern can be found in the issue of casting in film adaptions of *Dune*, as discussed by Edwardo Pérez in his chapter in this book as well as N. Jamiyla Chisholm, "'Dune' Adaptation Accused of Erasing Middle Eastern Actors," *Colorlines,* September 10, 2020, at https://www.colorlines.com/articles/dune-adaptation-accused-erasing-middle-eastern-actors.

25. Brian Herbert, *Dreamer of Dune: The Biography of Frank Herbert* (New York: Tor Books, 2003), 189.

26. For a nuanced treatment of this issue, see Emmet Asher-Perrin, "Why It's Important to Consider Whether *Dune* Is a White Savior Narrative," *Tor.com,* March 6, 2019, at https://www.tor.com/2019/03/06/why-its-important-to-consider-whether-dune-is-a-white-savior-narrative. For some interesting perspectives on *Dune* from Muslim readers including Khalid Baheyeldin, Salman Sayyid, and Sami Shah, see "The Book of *Dune*," *Imaginary Worlds Podcast,* Episode 72, July 12, 2017, at https://www.imaginaryworldspodcast.org/episodes/the-book-of-dune.

27. I discuss similar issues with regard to Ursula K. Le Guin's use of philosophical Daoism in Ethan Mills, "Ursula K. Le Guin's Science Fictional Feminist Daoism," *Journal of Science Fiction and Philosophy* 3 (2020), 1–21, at https://jsfphil.org/vol-3/le-guins-science-fictional-feminist-daoism.

28. Another excellent example is Octavia E. Butler's Earthseed duology. Earthseed is an *ethos* for an envisioned community that accepts human diversity and has the long-term goal of human interstellar travel. Octavia E. Butler, *Parable of the Sower* (New York: Aspect Books, 1993); Octavia E. Butler, *Parable of the Talents* (New York: Aspect Books, 1998).

29. Just a few places to start (your local Mentat can help you find more): Emad El-Din Aysha, "Science Fiction By, About, and For Arabs: Case Studies in De-Orientalizing the Western Imagination," *ReOrient* 6 (2020), 5–19; Nisi Shawl ed., *New Suns: Original Speculative Fiction by People of Color* (Oxford: Solaris, 2019); Tarun K. Saint ed., *Gollancz Book of South Asian Science Fiction* (New Delhi: Hachette India, 2019).

4

Messiahs, Jihads, and God Emperors
Should Humanity Just Give Up Religion?

Greg Littmann

"Statistics: at a conservative estimate, I've killed sixty-one billion, sterilized ninety planets, completely demoralized five hundred others. I've wiped out the followers of forty religions which had existed since–"

"Unbelievers!" Korba protested. "Unbelievers all!"

"No," Paul said. "Believers."

"My liege makes a joke," Korba said, voice trembling. "The Jihad has brought ten thousand worlds into the shining light of–"

"Into the darkness," Paul said. "We'll be a hundred generations recovering from Muad'Dib's Jihad. I find it hard to imagine that anyone will ever surpass this." A barking laugh erupted from his throat.

"What amuses Muad'Dib?" Stilgar asked.

"I am not amused. I merely had a sudden vision of the Emperor Hitler saying something similar. No doubt he did."

Dune Messiah

Should humanity just give up religion? You might believe so if you think the depiction of religion in the *Dune* saga is anywhere near realistic. What tragedy flows from the coming of the Fremen Messiah! Sixty-one billion dead! Ninety planets sterilized! Paul was supposed to bring the universe to paradise, but as his son, Leto II, notes, "Muad'Dib's religion had another name now; it was Shien-san-Shao, an Ixian label which designated the intensity and insanity of those who thought they could bring the universe to paradise at the point of a crysknife."[1]

And Paul's Jihad (or "holy war"), is only the start of the suffering. Having conquered humanity, Paul becomes dictator of an oppressive theocratic empire that brutally crushes dissent. Muad'Dib's government becomes a "bureaucratic monster" under which a "smell of blasphemy"

Dune and Philosophy, First Edition. Edited by Kevin S. Decker.
© 2023 John Wiley & Sons, Inc. Published 2023 by John Wiley & Sons, Inc.

arises from questioning government edicts.[2] After Paul abdicates, things get worse as his deranged sister Alia takes the throne and has control of the state religion. The religion grows more corrupt to suit the needs of the religious bureaucracy. The Preacher (Paul in disguise) counsels: "The religion of Muad'Dib is not Muad'Dib."[3] He accuses the priests of Muad'Dib of having abandoned him, and warns: "Holiness has replaced love in your religion."[4] Leto II observes: "Muad'Dib's high aims had fallen into wizardry which was enforced by the military arm of Auqaf."[5] Leto succeeds Alia as ruler and is worshipped as a living God. With his life unnaturally extended by transforming into a human–sandworm hybrid, Leto will rule humanity as "God Emperor" for three and a half millennia. He's deliberately tyrannical, so that humanity never again puts up with being subject to such absolute control.

Neither Paul, nor Alia, nor Leto II believes their own religion. Yet they use religion as a tool of political control, manipulating the Fremen to do their bidding. Fremen culture makes them particularly vulnerable to political exploitation because "law and religion were identical, making disobedience a sin."[6]

Of course, the cynical use of religion to manipulate politics was routine long before Paul came along. For millennia, the Bene Gesserit manipulated religious opinion throughout the empire to support their political agenda, despite lacking religious faith themselves. As Alia states, "Bene Gesserits have always been short on faith and long on pragmatism."[7] Leto II claims that in all history, the Bene Gesserit are the best at religious "rhetorical despotism."[8] Fremen religion had been carefully cultivated by the Bene Gesserit Missionaria Protectiva, their "black arm of superstition" responsible for manipulating primitive cultures.[9] It's the seeds planted by the Missionaria Protectiva that allow Paul and Jessica to survive among the Fremen, and which enables Paul to become the Fremen Messiah. After the death of Leto II, the Bene Gesserit use their religious influence to assemble armies of their own, and when the Honored Matres, degenerate Bene Gesserit offshoots, invade the old empire, they too control armies with the same religious power.

Prior to Paul's Jihad, humanity was ruled by House Corrino. Despite the agnosticism of the ruling class, the Corrino Padishah Emperor retained power with the support of his feared Sardaukar terror troops, who are motivated by their own "warrior religion."[10] Even the Guild (again explicitly agnostic) has been known to manipulate humanity through religion, as when it facilitated the creation of the Orange Catholic Bible, intended to provide a common holy book uniting all human religions and so increasing political stability.

Religion in the *Dune* universe represents the future of the religions we have today, especially the monotheistic religions. The religious views of the entire Corrino empire, including the Fremen, have been influenced by the Orange Catholic Bible, a document distilling the teachings of every old

Earth religion with more than a million followers. The Fremen have also been influenced by Judaic traditions from Salusa Secundus, Zen Buddhist traditions from the Zensunni Wanderers, and Islamic traditions from both Caladan and the Zensunni.

What's Wrong with Religion?

The people of the *Dune* universe weren't just unlucky that religion brought them such suffering. It's the nature of religion to become oppressive, at least according to the most insightful characters in the saga. As Leto II explains: "Religion always leads to rhetorical despotism."[11]

Even when religions begin well, they degenerate as institutions outlive their founding ideals, while retaining the authority of the divine. Chairman Toure Bomoko, who oversaw the composition of the Orange Catholic Bible, warned: "What is this shadow across the highway of Divine Command? It is a warning that institutions endure, that symbols endure when their meaning is lost."[12] The Preacher says, "I come here to combat the fraud and illusion of your conventional, institutionalized religion. As with all such religions, your institution moves towards cowardice, it moves towards mediocrity, inertia and self-satisfaction."[13]

Religion requires unquestioning acceptance of authority. According to the Bene Gesserit's Credo, "Religion is the emulation of the adult by the child . . . And always the ultimate unspoken commandment is "Thou shalt not question!"[14] Religion leads naturally to inquisition to crush unorthodoxy. Leto II notes: "In the shadow of every religion lurks a Torquemada."[15] By its nature, religion requires the deception of adherents. According to the Bene Gesserit *Instruction Manual of the Missionaria Protectiva*, there are "illusions of popular history which a successful religion must promote."[16]

Religion encourages people to believe that they already know everything of fundamental importance. According to the Inner Teachings of the Missionaria Protectiva, "All organized religions face a common problem, a tender spot through which we may enter and shift them to our designs: How do they distinguish hubris from revelation?"[17] Since any further revelation detracts from the religious authority of the establishment, religious establishments must regard revelation as complete. Such confidence is dangerous. Toure Bomoko warned that nobody should believe that they know everything vital. He insists "there is no summa of all attainable knowledge"[18] a conclusion repeated by Leto II.[19]

Those who believe they already know everything can't learn. Leto II explains: "This is the beginning of knowledge – the discovery of something we do not understand."[20] He advises, "Never attempt to reason with people who know they are right!"[21] Such certainty even kills the desire to gather more information. Leto II writes: "Religion suppresses curiosity. What I do subtracts from the worshipper."[22] Even among the technologically advanced

Tleilaxu, unbelieving foreigners are dismissed as foolish "Powindah," and their ideas condemned as "Powindah poison."[23] Doctrinal disagreements lead to conflict when a religion considers itself to be the only true religion. The purpose of the Orange Catholic Bible was "to remove a primary weapon from the hands of disputant religions. That weapon – the claim to possession of the one and only revelation."[24]

When religion is involved with government, it offers a pathway to political power and will attract those who want it. The Missionaria Protectiva *Text QIV* states: "All governments suffer a recurring problem: Power attracts pathological personalities. It is not that power corrupts but that it is magnetic to the corruptible. Such people have a tendency to become drunk on violence, a condition to which they are quickly addicted."[25] It's particularly bad when, as in the case of the Fremen, disobeying the law is a violation of religious duty. The ancient *Commentaries on the Orange Catholic Bible* warn: "When law and religious duty are one, your selfdom *encloses the universe*."[26] Muad'Dib explains further: "When law and duty are one, united by religion, you never become fully conscious, fully aware of yourself. You are always a little less than an individual."[27]

When a people's political and religious authorities are the same, it's dangerous for their neighbors, especially if the leader is considered holy. The Bene Gesserit have a saying: "When religion and politics ride the same cart, when that cart is driven by a living holy man (baraka), nothing can stand in their path."[28] The Bene Gesserit believe that religion is the unstoppable force of pent-up sexual energy; their military commander Miles Teg remembers, "This energy must have an outlet. Bottle it up and it becomes monstrously dangerous. Redirect it and it will sweep over anything in its path. This is an ultimate secret of all religions."[29]

Despite the dangers of mixing religion and politics, it can't be avoided when there's a religious orthodoxy. Muad'Dib warns:

> You cannot avoid the interplay of politics within an orthodox religion. This power struggle permeates the training, educating and disciplining of the orthodox community. Because of this pressure, the leaders of such a community inevitably must face that ultimate internal question: to succumb to complete opportunism as the price of maintaining their rule, or risk sacrificing themselves for the sake of the orthodox ethic.[30]

When religion and government mix, the state – believing it has divine support – becomes disastrously overconfident. Another Bene Gesserit saying about "religion and politics travelling in the same cart" is that "their movement become[s] headlong – faster and faster and faster. They put aside all thought of obstacles and forget that a precipice does not show itself to the man in a blind rush until it's too late."[31] Not even a holy leader can stop the headlong rush. Paul can't stop the holy war fought in his name – "Paul saw how futile were any efforts of his to change any smallest bit of this. He had thought to oppose the jihad within himself, but the jihad would be. His legions would rage out from Arrakis even without him. They needed only the legend he already had become."[32] After the death of Leto II, Atreides descendent Sheeana forbids building a new religion around her, arguing that "Religions are never really controllable."[33]

Religion in the Real World

The *Dune* saga presents us with a bleak analysis of the nature of religion. Is religion really so bad? In fact, there are many real-world parallels to all the major abuses of religion found in the saga.

Real-world religious figures have often required unquestioning acceptance. Breaks with orthodoxy have often led to death for being a heretic or apostate. Religions have often been used as a source of political power. Many rulers have claimed to have divine backing, so that a "whiff of blasphemy" arises from challenging their judgments. Some have justified their rule by insisting, like Paul, that they are God's appointed. Examples include the kings of Europe, caliphs and sultans of the Middle East, and emperors of China, among many others. Other rulers insisted, like Leto II, that they were themselves Gods, such as the pharaohs of Egypt, emperors of Japan, and some emperors of Rome. In the United States and most other modern democratic nations, politicians, particularly conservative politicians, routinely present themselves as being on the same side as God, and so by implication, as having God's support.

Religion has often been used to justify war. For example, the book of Exodus in the Jewish Torah and Christian Bible tells how God gave Palestine to the Jews, to take by force. In the Middle Ages, God would tell Christians to conquer the same territory in the name of Christianity, while He would tell Muslims to defend it with their lives. Often, the fighting has been worst among co-religionists who disagree over the specifics of doctrine, like Catholic and Protestant Christians or Sunni and Shi'ite Muslims.

Religion has often been used to justify empire building. "*Jihad*" is an Arabic term, and Muad'Dib's Jihad is obviously based on the Muslim conquests of the seventh to eighth centuries, begun by Muhammad and continued until Islamic rule extended from Spain to Mesopotamia. Similarly, the need to spread Christianity was one motivation for Europeans to rule over territories in North and South America, Oceania, Africa, Asia, and elsewhere. For example, in the fifteenth century, Pope Alexander VI authorized Spain to occupy the Americas in the interests of spreading Christianity.

Real-world religions always suffer from corruption, even when founded on lofty ideals. Jesus may have preferred helping the poor to getting rich, but people have been cashing in on his image since ancient times, from the selling of indulgences to extirpate sins to modern tele-evangelists working their audience for donations. Some depraved individuals have even used the priesthood as an opportunity to molest children, and then had the church cover for them.

Religion has often led people to believe that they know more than they really do, thus inhibiting learning. Scientific theories that have been rejected at some point on the basis of religious authority include the heliocentric model of the solar system, evolution, the view that diseases have natural causes rather than being triggered by sin, and man-made climate change.

Religion has often been used to justify oppression. Christianity has been used to justify exploiting the poor, enslaving Africans, subjugating women, beating children, persecuting Jews, burning heretics, prosecuting homosexuals, brutalizing criminals, conducting terror attacks, restricting the availability of sex education and contraception, and censoring art, just to name a few.

And there's nothing distinctive about Christianity in this. These and other injustices have been justified by other major religions. For instance, Hinduism has been used to justify widow-burning and the caste system; Islam to justify stoning adulterers, the Armenian genocide, and the destruction of Hindu and Buddhist cultural artifacts; Buddhism to justify state-sponsored violence against Muslims in Myanmar; both Buddhism and Hinduism to justify using past-life karma as an excuse to tolerate social and economic disadvantage; and Judaism and Islam to justify ritual genital cutting which, in the case of Islam, has sometimes included removal of the clitoris. Listing awful things done in the name of religion is as easy as finding sand grains in the deserts of Arrakis. Where holy texts directly encourage awful things, they can't even be revised and corrected, precisely because they are holy. Given all this awfulness, shouldn't humanity just give up religion?

In Defense of Religion

Maybe in the *Dune* universe, humans need religion. The religion of the Fremen people sustains them in their harsh lives. Bomoko writes: "Religion must remain an outlet for people who say to themselves, I am not the kind of person I want to be."[34] The Bene Gesserit seem to believe that society needs religion for social stability. When Reverend Mother Gaius Helen Mohiam meets young Paul Atreides, she advises him, "Grave this on your memory, lad: A world is supported by four things . . . the learning of the wise, the justice of the great, the prayers of the righteous and the valor of the brave."[35] Thousands of years after that, Bene Gesserit Mother Superior Darwi Odrade agrees that humans need religion. She thinks to herself, "Humans need us! Sometimes, they need religions. Sometimes, they need merely know their beliefs are as empty as their hopes for nobility."[36]

In the real world, religion satisfies powerful human desires. Like the Fremen, many rely on religion to help them cope with hardship. It gives them comfort to believe that they are under divine protection. Psalm 23 of the Hebrew Tanakh and Christian Bible promises, "The LORD is my shepherd; I shall not want . . . He restoreth my soul . . . Yea, though I walk through the valley of the shadow of death, I will fear no evil: for thou art with me; thy rod and thy staff they comfort me." The Qur'an 2:186 reads, "And if My servants ask thee about Me – behold, I am near; I respond to the call of him who calls, whenever he calls unto Me." Other religions offer similar comforts. There's evidence that these comforts help: studies have shown that religious belief correlates with better health, both physical and psychological.[37]

Religion has inspired evil, but it has also inspired good. Religious groups have founded many schools and universities, hospitals, orphanages, homeless shelters, and other helping organizations. Charity is an important element of all the major world religions, and religious individuals are more charitable, on average, than the non-religious. Many people have found religious inspiration to fight for social justice. All the evils that some Christians have justified in the name of their religion have been condemned by other Christians in the name of the same religion. Christian groups were fundamental, for instance, in organizing movements to abolish slavery and to fight for civil rights for African Americans. Other religions have likewise inspired adherents to fight for genuinely good causes. In the *Dune* saga, much killing is done in the name of Muad'Dib. Perhaps the saga would be more realistic if a few orphanages were founded in his name too.

It could be argued that many of the terrible things done in the name of religion would have been done even if religion had not been involved. People have often used religion as an excuse to do what they wanted to do anyway, as when Europeans enslaved Africans to save their souls. Wars and empire-building have often been given religious justification, but nations haven't needed religious motivation to fight wars or build empires. The non-religious have certainly proved capable of hatred, violence, and cruelty, just like religious folk. Many high-ranking Nazis were atheists, and other atheists have been instrumental in communist regimes in China, Russia, and elsewhere, regimes that have been as brutal and oppressive as theocratic states.

Of course, it's also possible that good things done in the name of religion would have been done without religion. Just as non-religious people are capable of hatred, violence, and cruelty, they are capable of love, peacefulness, and kindness. Perhaps those who have claimed that religion inspired them to campaign against slavery, or to fight for civil rights, would have fought just as hard against slavery, or for civil rights, if they'd had no religion. Perhaps schools and orphanages that have been funded by donations from churches would have been as well funded by civic groups if the churches hadn't been there. Strikingly, the Bene Gesserit, the faction in the *Dune* universe most devoted to the human good, are not religious.

Clearly, weighing up the likely positive and negative effects of religious beliefs is no simple task. What's more, we still haven't addressed the most important issue for deciding whether the likely impact of religion will be good or bad. It's an issue that the protagonists of the *Dune* saga consistently fail to mention when they consider the costs and benefits of religion: are the religious beliefs true or not?

The Ethics of Belief

In "The Ethics of Belief," English philosopher W.K. Clifford (1845–1879) argued that we have a duty to only hold beliefs for which we have sufficient evidence.[38] Holding beliefs based on insufficient evidence makes us more likely to believe false things, and believing false things makes us more likely to take the wrong actions. If Clifford is correct, then the question of whether or not we should hold religious beliefs is to be decided by whether or not we have sufficient evidence to hold them.

To argue that we have a duty not to hold beliefs on insufficient evidence, Clifford offers the example of a shipowner who forms the belief, without good evidence, that his ship is seaworthy. Because of this belief, he allows the ship to go to sea, putting at risk the lives of everyone aboard. To bring his example closer to *Dune*, imagine that you are a passenger on a Guild Heighliner. Let's further allow that the Guild mechanics responsible for maintaining the space-folding Holtzman engines decide to believe, for no good reason, that the engines are in perfect working order and no safety inspection is required. Thanks to the team adopting this belief, you are in danger of getting folded right into the heart of a sun, instead of arriving safely at Arrakis. Clifford would say that the maintenance team did something immoral by believing that the ship was safe without good evidence, since holding this belief endangered so many people. To take another example, imagine that a Suk doctor decides that you need a dangerous operation, but he makes his diagnosis not on the basis of medical science, but on the basis of beliefs he just made up. Clifford would say that it was immoral of the doctor to hold these beliefs with no good grounds, because such beliefs put patients in danger.

It's easy to see how false beliefs could lead to harm. If Thufir Hawat, Duke Leto's Master of Assassins, believed that you had betrayed the Duke to the Harkonnens, you'd be arrested in seconds and sent for interrogation (unless a hunter-seeker got you first). If some of the emperor's Sardaukar terror troops believed that you were an enemy combatant, you'd die with a kindjal up your sternum and a surprised look on your face. If a Fremen naib, like Stilgar, believed that you knew perfectly well how to use a stillsuit and didn't need to be shown, you'd dehydrate in the deep desert, leaving only a desiccated skeleton for desert mice to pick over.

It's also easy to see how false religious beliefs in particular could have terrible consequences. If I believe that it offends God if you don't recognize Muad'Dib as the Messiah, it could lead me to harm you in retribution. If I believe that the land you live on is holy, and that God wants my co-religionists to have it, it could lead me to dispossess you. If I believe that what you say spreads falsehoods that put people in danger of damnation if they believe them, then it could lead me to ensure that your opinions are never heard.

Of course, false beliefs can lead to good consequences as well as bad ones. If a Fremen mistakenly thinks you are a Fremen too, she'll feel bound by the Ichwan Bedwine to offer you help. If Leto II's Fish Speaker troops wrongly believe that you have faith in Leto's godhood, they'll suffer you to live. But just as we are safest while driving when we watch the road, so we are safest when acting while we see the real world. Or to put it another way, if you are taking a Guild Heighliner from Caladan to Arrakis, you might get there safely by punching buttons at random, but your chances are much better if you let a Guild navigator plot a course.

Some beliefs are more obviously dangerous than others. If I form the false belief that I sing well, I'm liable to do no more than annoy people, whereas if I form the false belief that I'm one of Muad'Dib's elite Fedaykin warriors, I might end up stabbing someone. It might be argued that our duty to believe only things that we have good grounds to believe extends only to beliefs that could be dangerous. Clifford is aware of this objection and isn't convinced. He argues that we can never be sure which of our beliefs might be dangerous, and so we have a duty not to believe *anything* on insufficient grounds.

It's easy to come up with cases where a belief that seems innocuous turns out to have surprising results. If I think that all Australians have the desert survival skills of Fremen, my belief is unlikely to harm anyone, but it could potentially lead me to leave an Australian in danger in the wilderness. If I think that I have the ability to foresee the future, I'm unlikely to do much more than lose money gambling, but the results could be much more dire if, say, I had a vision that you were going to assassinate the president unless someone assassinated you first.

False religious beliefs seem particularly liable to lead to unforeseen dangerous consequences. It's easy to become angry that others aren't doing what God wants, or are spreading false information about God. Many people have been killed over the millennia just for not sharing the religious beliefs of their neighbors. Beliefs that seem innocuous enough in themselves, such as the Catholic doctrine that the communion wine literally transforms into the blood of Christ, have led to much bloodshed between those who accept the beliefs and those who don't. The doctrine that holding false beliefs leads to damnation, a common view among Christians and Muslims, makes it particularly difficult to foresee what the consequences of holding any given religious belief will be. If the eternal fate of souls hangs on opinion, then any difference in opinion might end up being grounds for slaughter and oppression. What's more, the prospect of eternal reward in the afterlife can make death seem trivial. Killing is a minor harm when there are souls at stake. Indeed, martyrs may be just upgrading their lifestyle by moving to a better world.

The effects of religious beliefs are also particularly hard to predict because religious beliefs are rarely accepted or rejected individually, but rather as part of a whole bundle of beliefs that make up a religious creed. If you identify as Christian, then, unless you are extremely unorthodox, you commit yourself to many views about the nature of the universe, God, and morality. This complexity makes it hard to see all of the possible implications of your beliefs.

What's worse, the more extensive a doctrine is, the easier it is to interpret it in different ways. Books like the Bible and the Qur'an have become the holy text of groups with diverse beliefs. Even if we could predict the results of accepting a holy text under one set of interpretations, we couldn't possibly predict all of the different ways that people might interpret the text.

I think Clifford is too demanding in insisting that it's always wrong to hold a belief without sufficient evidence. Even in the case of religion, the need for truth might sometimes be outweighed by other factors. For example, if you were on the point of death and as your vital systems closed down, you began to see Muad'Dib smiling at you and beckoning you home, I wouldn't point out to you that you are likely hallucinating. Frankly, at that point, I'd be happy to agree with anything you say if it might make things easier for you on the way out, even if I'd be encouraging you to hold beliefs on insufficient evidence. You are welcome to do the same for me.

Nonetheless, in almost all cases, including religion, we have a duty to only believe what we have *good grounds* to believe. To do otherwise is to endanger ourselves and others through unforeseen consequences of our false beliefs. So to return to the question we began with, should humanity just give up religion? That depends on whether we have good grounds to believe that our religion is true or not. I won't attempt to resolve the issue here of whether there are grounds to believe that a given religion is right. I will note, though, that most religions are incompatible with most other religions, and so at the very least, humanity should ditch *most* religions. As for whether we should keep one or more, I'll leave that up to you. The Bene Gesserit Credo states, "Religion is the encystment of past beliefs: mythology, which is guesswork, the hidden assumptions of trust in the universe, those pronouncements which men have made in search of personal power, all of it mingled with shreds of enlightenment."[39] But perhaps you'll arrive at a more positive conclusion. Princess Irulan Corrino notes, "My father once told me that respect for truth comes close to being the basis for all morality."[40] He was no fool, the old Padishah Emperor Shaddam IV. So, think carefully and remember your duty to hunt the truth.

Notes

1. *Children of Dune* (New York: Penguin, 2019), 157.
2. *CD*, 3.
3. *CD*, 23.
4. *CD*, 59.
5. *CD*, 157.
6. *Dune* (New York: Penguin, 1990), 329.
7. *CD*, 72.
8. *God Emperor of Dune* (New York: Penguin, 2019), 84.
9. *Dune*, 326.
10. *Dune*, 341.
11. *GED*, 84.
12. *Dune*, 327.
13. *CD*, 125.
14. *CD*, 159.
15. *GED*, 85.
16. *CD*, 36.
17. *Heretics of Dune* (New York: Penguin, 2019), 304.
18. *Dune*, 327.
19. *CD,* 176.
20. *GED*, 120.
21. *GED*, 197.
22. *GED*, 148.
23. *HD*, 51.
24. *Dune*, 325.
25. *CHD*, 56.
26. *Dune*, 328.
27. *Dune*, 328.
28. *Dune*, 329.
29. *HD*, 440.
30. *Dune*, 261.
31. *Dune*, 249.
32. *Dune*, 314.
33. *CHD*, 409.
34. *Dune*, 328.
35. *Dune*, 20.
36. *CHD*, 362.
37. Paul S. Mueller, David J. Plevak, and Teresa A. Rummans, "Religious Involvement, Spirituality and Medicine: Implications for Medical Practice," *Mayo Clinic Pro*ceedings 76 (2001), 1225–1235.
38. W.K. Clifford, "The Ethics of Belief," at https://people.brandeis.edu/~teuber/Clifford_ethics.pdf.
39. *CD*, 159.
40. *Dune*, 134.

5

(Re)defining Masculinity and Femininity in Villeneuve's *Dune*

Edwardo Pérez

STILGAR: "Is he toying with him?"
LADY JESSICA: "No. Paul's never killed a man."

Paul's fight with Jamis is significant, especially in Denis Villeneuve's film adaptation of *Dune*. Throughout the film, Paul has visions of being killed by Chani; just before meeting Jamis, Paul sees the Fremen telling Paul in a vision that he will teach him the ways of the desert. As Jessica's observation to Stilgar points out, Paul hesitates to kill Jamis because Paul's never killed anyone. This is unlike Jessica, who methodically killed two Harkonnen warriors in the 'thopter when she and Paul were taken, and who could've easily killed Stilgar when she fought him prior to Paul's duel with Jamis. So, Paul's fight and his having to kill Jamis means something. It's not just about Paul and Jessica fighting to survive, nor is it just about Paul defending his mother. It represents a rite of passage for Paul, one that he doesn't easily embrace.

Earlier in the film we saw Paul hesitate to fight with Gurney Halleck, saying he wasn't "in the mood" to fight (he'd rather have Gurney sing a song). When Paul is tested by Gaius Helen Mohiam, we see Jessica standing outside the door, palpably terrified that Paul might be killed and letting out a sigh of relief the moment she sees that Paul survived the test. For Paul's part, he didn't just pass, he proved himself capable of matching wills with Gaius Helen Mohiam, as he eventually does with Jamis.

What's significant, then, is that Paul must learn not just to fight (whether he's in the mood to or not) but to kill, as indiscriminately and coldly as Jessica, Jamis, or any other warrior we see in *Dune*. On one level, this relates to Paul's prophecy and destiny – he needs to win the respect of the Fremen if he's going to lead them. On another level, Paul's fight with Jamis also offers an interesting glimpse into how Villeneuve represents gender in

Dune and Philosophy, First Edition. Edited by Kevin S. Decker.
© 2023 John Wiley & Sons, Inc. Published 2023 by John Wiley & Sons, Inc.

his version of *Dune*. Paul against Jamis is the culmination of Villeneuve's *Dune* part one, but as Chani says, "This is only the beginning," especially for Paul. Because in killing Jamis, Paul also metaphorically kills his own boyhood, initiating himself into manhood.

So, what does it mean to be a man or a woman in Villeneuve's *Dune*? How are masculinity and femininity defined? What roles are men and women expected to fill? Are men feminized and women masculinized? How is *Dune* gendered? Is *Dune* gender fluid? Does gender exist on a spectrum in the film? What does Paul's fight with Jamis really represent when it comes to gender and masculinity?

"Did you put on some muscle?"

Other than a film in the *Avengers*, *Fast and Furious*, or *Expendables* franchises, it's difficult to find a movie with more masculine men than Villeneuve's *Dune* (consider that Villeneuve essentially cast Poe Dameron, Thanos, Khal Drogo, and Drax[1]). Timothée Chalamet's looks may be as androgynous as a young Keanu Reeves but, to be fair, he goes for the head (or the neck) when he fights Gurney, he doesn't back down from Gaius Helen Mohiam, and he clearly proves himself fighting Jamis with a crysknife. Still, Chalamet's Paul doesn't exude the appearance of masculinity (or hypermasculinity) often associated with men, especially "chosen one" heroes like those who populate the superhero films that Martin Scorsese and Ridley Scott seem to abhor. So Duncan Idaho's teasing Paul about his thin frame speaks to the larger issue of how masculinity is (re) defined in Villeneuve's *Dune*.

Traditionally, masculinity is defined in a binary with femininity, as opposites. As Susan Hekman notes, "These opposites are always hierarchical and, most significantly, also gendered," adding that "the privileged side of the opposites that comprise the world is gendered masculine; the feminine is always the disprivileged 'other.' The masculine is the standard; entities defined as feminine are inferior."[2] At first glance, this tradition seems to be the standard in the Duniverse – Duke Leto is not only in charge, but Lady Jessica isn't his wife, she's his concubine, making her an "other" according to Hekman. Being a Reverend Mother of the Bene Gesserit sisterhood makes her even more "othered." Yet, Ferguson's portrayal of Lady Jessica and Chalamet's portrayal of Paul challenge the binary conception,[3] each offering a blend of masculine and feminine that reconfigures the terms from opposites to complements that can work together rather than in competition.

After Charlotte Rampling's Gaius Helen Mohiam tests Paul, she complains to Jessica. Not only should Jessica have had a daughter instead of a son, but the powers she's given to Paul are "wasted in a male." Later, Paul even laments his Bene Gesserit abilities to Jessica, calling himself a "freak." Yet, it's the combination of his "feminine" Bene Gesserit skills (if you will) and his "masculine" physical training from Duncan and Gurney that help to redefine the masculine/feminine binary. This new binary is a form that Jessica, and pretty much every woman in *Dune*, embodies too (no doubt, if she'd faced down the Sardaukar instead of Duncan, she'd have killed them all). This is an interesting reinterpretation of masculine and feminine that speaks to contemporary perspectives on to what extent gender is a spectrum, especially when we consider the fates of all the so-called "masculine" men in *Dune*.[4]

What Villeneuve's *Dune* seems to be suggesting is that, for a man to succeed, he must embrace the feminine (or at least not be afraid of it). Even Leto's treatment of Paul as the heir of House Atreides acknowledges this: after Paul asks, "What if I'm not the future of House Atreides?," Leto replies, "Then you'll be the only thing I need you to be . . . my son." It's a fascinating line that challenges the idea of traditional masculinity, in which men are expected not only to answer the call to leadership, but to seek it aggressively, not passively (as Aristotle first suggested, assertiveness is masculine and passivity is feminine). Oscar Isaac explains:

> This idea came up of having the Duke accept his son in whatever capacity. Because usually, the cliché is, "I'm building you into the leader I need you to be!" Instead, what you get, is him saying, "Hey, I get it. I understand if it feels like too much, and maybe it will be, and that's okay. But if there's something in you that can do it, know that I'm here to support you and I'm going to teach you everything that I know." I just thought that was a beautiful distillation of things that are implied in the book, but not said at all directly.[5]

Isaac's right, not just because the father/son dynamic subverts the masculine cliché, but because it helps redefine masculinity through a more feminine lens, one that alludes to what Carol Gilligan refers to as a "different voice," or the feminist ethic of care.

For Carol Gilligan, men and women engage in moral reasoning differently. As Gilligan explains:

> My research on identity and moral development led me to identify the ethics of care as a "different voice" – a voice that joined self with relationship and reason with emotion. By transcending these binaries it shifted the paradigm of psychological and moral theory. The ethics of care starts from the premise that as humans we are inherently relational, responsive beings and the human condition is one of connectedness or interdependence.[6]

This seems to be what Isaac alludes to when he describes Leto's perspective as a father to Paul. Taking a traditional masculine standpoint, Leto wouldn't offer Paul compassion and understanding, he'd likely order Paul to "Act like a man!" (as Vito Corleone bluntly put it in *The Godfather*). But as Isaac notes, his Leto wants to be supportive rather than authoritative, allowing Chalamet's Paul to find his own way.

"Honor requires that I be elsewhere"

Stilgar's visit with Leto offers another example of the ethic of care philosophy. The Fremen wastes no time with ceremony or formality when he meets Leto, which pisses Gurney off. Stilgar and Gurney engage in a typical masculine face-off: a test to determine the alpha male (with Gurney staring down Stilgar and giving him commands, while Stilgar all but ignores Gurney, barely giving him more than a glance). Yet, Duncan offers an option that portrays a feminized masculinity similar to Paul's. By thanking Stilgar, who spit on the table in front of Leto, for his gift of his body's water, Duncan is not only able to help defuse the situation, he's able to show the benefits of the ethic of care. By showing compassion and understanding, rather than barking commands and potentially creating an enemy rather than an ally, Duncan reinforces not just the ethic of care, but the different masculinity that Villeneuve's *Dune* works to portray.

Duncan isn't the only one who sees this. Leto sees it too, as does the Mentat Thufir Hawat; they both recognize that cultivating "desert power" will require, as Gilligan might say, a recognition of the Fremen as tightly interconnected not just with Arrakis, but with House Atreides too. A solely masculine perspective (which Gurney adopts, and which House Harkonnen completely embodies) sees the Fremen only as others. As Gurney remarks to Duncan when Duncan returns after spending weeks in the desert with the Fremen, "my god, man, you've gone native." Yet, through an ethic of care – or what I've referred to as a blend of masculine and feminine (a feminized masculinity) – the Fremen are not others, they're allies.

Gilligan's ethic of care explains how a woman's moral reasoning is typically different from a man's moral reasoning. Yet, Villeneuve's *Dune* seems to adopt something like this ethic of care, not as a way of showing how women and men are different, but to show how men can function within a different type of masculinity. Paul, Leto, Duncan, Thufir Hawat, even Stilgar all adopt a feminized masculinity to some degree in *Dune*, a perspective more productive of success and understanding than traditional masculinity. So what about the women? If a feminized masculinity is what men should embody in Villeneuve's film, should women embody a masculinized femininity?

"Our conversation ran short"

Women haunt Villeneuve's *Dune* – not just visually (Zendaya's Chani mostly appears in Paul's dreams), but narratively and aurally, from the vocal soloists featured on the soundtrack to "the Voice" employed to perfection by Lady Jessica and Gaius Helen Mohiam, to the wailing screams of the Shadout Mapes. For composer Hans Zimmer, the narrative of Villeneuve's *Dune* is driven by the female characters, so "the score is based on mainly female voices."[7] This creates an interesting aesthetic palate for Villeneuve, one that functions multimodally, blending layers of aural, visual, narrative, and visceral power through a feminine perspective. It's not just that the women drive the narrative, it's that they exude the most palpable power throughout Villeneuve's film, whether speaking, singing, wailing, or, especially, in their silence.

The effect, like the Brutalist-inspired visual aesthetic,[8] is a mixture of brutality and beauty – from Chani's hypnotic, angelic appeal to Jessica's various outfits to Liet-Kynes's quiet fierceness (not just in her steely, blue-eyed gaze, but in the mystery of her loyalties); it also extends to the formidable Bene Gesserit, who seem to lurk in the film's shadows. Every woman not only looks like they could walk the runway of a Jean Paul Gaultier fashion show (albeit one set in 10191), but that they could also best any man in battle without losing a thimbleful of sweat.[9] Paul might be the Lisan al Gaib, the "voice from the outer world," but the women's voices – at least in Villeneuve's film – are more powerful and significant than those of the men. For example, Leto gives an inspiring speech, and Gurney, Duncan, Stilgar, Jamis, Rabban, and the Baron all talk tough, but women in any chosen scene say more with their eyes and faces than any man does with words.

On one level, in Villeneuve's *Dune* women become empowered, while the men become emasculated.[10] Of course, Gilligan's ethics of care suggests that *Dune*'s message promotes a feminized masculinity for the male characters. But are the female characters really portrayed through a masculinized femininity? Perhaps this is so, since most of the women are badasses – especially when we consider these women's ability to kill, the very act that Paul struggles with not just in his fight with Jamis, but throughout the film.[11] However, another way to view the women of *Dune* is to see them as existing outside of the masculine–feminine binary.

"So much potential wasted in a male"

As Julia Kristeva and Hélène Cixous observe, the language of the binary is phallocentric, which means it privileges the masculine over the feminine. In such language, the feminine isn't just othered, the feminine exists, as Kristeva puts it, in an "absence of being."[12] Thus, women need to engage in what Cixous calls the "feminine imaginary,"[13] a term that references the work of French psychoanalyst and philosopher Jacques Lacan (1901–1981) and his concept of the imaginary. As Clara Juncker explains, in the Lacanian imaginary:

> Infants of both sexes merge with their mothers' bodies, with no sense of separation and no fear of castration. The imaginary is thus allied with bodily [impulses] and instinctive drives. At the Oedipal moment of separation,

however, the child enters into a symbolic system governed by the Phallus, Lacan's controversial term for the signifier of authority and "self-possession," of presence and absence, that is characteristic of language. The speaking subject is thus a gendered subject: while the male easily identifies . . . himself as a phallic "I," the female must identify herself with lack, with absence, and with negativity.[14]

So, engaging the feminine imaginary, what Cixous also refers to as *l'écriture féminine* (women's writing), reworks Lacan, focusing the imaginary through a feminine lens, requiring women to write for themselves rather than letting others write for them.[15] When they do they become free from the phallocentric, binary view, which, in Kristeva's view, provides women "with the radical potential to disrupt and transform discourse."[16] In other words, by recognizing that the male–female binary is constructed by phallocentric (Western modernist) language, women can learn to operate both within and outside such language, especially by engaging in "distinctively feminine writing,"[17] which, for Cixous, offers the possibility of transforming "social and cultural structures."[18] As Kristeva states: "women do not stop doing, and doing everything, because they do not fully believe in it – they believe that it is an illusion . . . to be remade."[19] Or, as Cixous puts it: "The woman who still allows herself to be threatened by the big dick, who's still impressed by the commotion of the phallic stance, who still leads a loyal master to the beat of the drum: that's the woman of yesterday."[20]

Isn't this what the women of the *Dune* film do? They're certainly not the women of yesterday – to the point that they seem to exist in a different realm than the men, especially the Bene Gesserit, who operate with their own set of rules; their rules allow them to exist within the phallocentric world, if you will, and also outside of it. Even Baron Harkonnen doesn't wish to upset the Bene Gesserit. Similarly, Leto's pleas to Jessica for the Bene Gesserit to protect Paul suggest that his status as Duke has no sway with the sisterhood – and Jessica's tepid reaction suggests that she's not certain of what the Bene Gesserit's response will be. But it's not just the Bene Gesserit who challenge the binary through a feminine imaginary; so do the individual female characters, like Jessica, Liet-Kynes, and Chani.

As Judge of the Change, Liet-Kynes exists on the outside, between the great Houses and the Emperor. She claims that she cannot take sides, but she's clearly on the side of the Fremen, who exist on the outside of the binary – at least as a group. Curiously, Liet-Kynes's existence is also binary, being both human and Fremen – though she claims to serve only one master, Shai-Hulud. She's female, yet her physical skills are clearly formidable; her character is something of an enigma, especially in her gender representation (it's worth remembering that Liet-Kynes was a man in Herbert's novel). Paul notes that she loved a Fremen warrior (and if Villeneuve's part two follows the lineage of the novel, Duncan-Brewster's Liet-Kynes would be Chani's mother). Yet, Liet-Kynes doesn't exude traditional femininity, at least not to the extent that Jessica does, given that we see Jessica garbed in formal dresses and we see her in maternal mode with Paul, teaching and "mothering" him throughout the film. Nevertheless, if Liet-Kynes is revealed to be Chani's mother, her influence over Chani seems clear, as Chani reflects the same quiet fierceness Liet-Kynes conveys in her every scene. Yet Chani, like Jessica, is feminized in traditional visuals, wearing dresses and being attracted to Paul. In *Dune*, sexuality doesn't seem to exist as an expression of affection, but rather as a necessity for procreation and the maintaining of familial lineage (and this is why the Bene Gesserit measure their progress in centuries) – though the Chani/Paul visuals seem to hint that the attraction between them may be more than perfunctory. In *Dune*, sexual love and desire also seem to function outside the binary. Isaac's Leto and Ferguson's Jessica seem to care for one another (and yes, they're expecting a girl!), yet we really don't see them acting "in love," do we?

For gender, it seems axiomatic that the masculine and feminine binary is rooted in the eventual union of the two opposites: the goal of the masculine is to pursue the feminine and the "duty" of the feminine is to surrender to the masculine. So, for feminized men and imaginary women, gender roles become blurred and sexuality becomes almost hidden – even for Baron Harkonnen.

"When is a gift not a gift?"

Examining gender in *Dune* would be incomplete without a look at Baron Harkonnen, who, in both Herbert's book and in David Lynch's 1984 film, is clearly depicted not just as gay, but as embodying a sort of deviant sexuality. He's an "an incestuous pedophile" who lusts after and exploits slave boys.[21] While Stellan Skarsgård's portrayal retains the Baron's grotesque physical appearance, we don't see any real evidence of the Baron's sexual predilections – unless having a naked (and heavily drugged) Oscar Isaac lying in a chair while the Baron eats dinner is sexual and deviant (which doesn't really compare to Kenneth McMillan's Baron ogling Sting's "Feyd, lovely Feyd"). The Harkonnen characters around Skarsgård's Baron give off a vampirish vibe and might look strange, but nothing overtly suggests that Baron Harkonnen is gay or entertains any deviant behaviors in Villeneuve's *Dune*; having Leto naked in a chair could simply be read as a way to embarrass the otherwise powerful Duke of House Atreides (and Feyd is never seen in Villeneuve's *Dune*, so we don't know what their relationship is like).

Again, it's as if sexuality just isn't important in Villeneuve's *Dune* – not like it was in his *Blade Runner 2049*, where Ryan Gosling's Joe clearly desired physical and emotional companionship with Ana de Armas's Joi.[22] So, it remains to be seen if sexuality will be explored further in Villeneuve's *Dune* narrative – for the Baron or anyone else.

"You have more than one lineage"

So, it appears that the traditional masculine/feminine gender binary is challenged throughout Villeneuve's part one, with many of the male characters embodying a feminized masculinity and with most of the female characters existing (writing themselves) within a feminine imaginary – to the point that *Dune*'s society borders on the androgynous. Is this the future Villeneuve wants us to imagine? Is the goal of humanity to transcend the binary: not just to exist outside it, but to reshape it into something else? Is this what Paul ultimately represents?

As Jessica reminds Paul when he's losing his mind during a vision: "You are your father's son. You are my son. You are the Duke Paul Atreides. You know who you are." Indeed, Paul is the embodiment of both masculine and feminine gender. In casting Chalamet and in portraying Paul as a visual and narrative balance of the masculine and feminine, Villeneuve further subverts the "chosen one" (or white savior) cliché, giving us a hero who exists not just outside the binary but outside the expectations of what we've been conditioned to see as masculine and feminine.

Notes

1. And these roles represent one of several "masculine" characters these actors have portrayed, especially Isaac and Brolin.
2. Susan Hekman, "Feminism," in Paul Wake and Simon Malpas eds., *The Routledge Companion to Critical Theory* (London: Taylor & Francis, 2006), 98.
3. And to some extent, Isaac's Leto, Jason Momoa's Duncan, and Javier Bardem's Stilgar also challenge this traditional binary, as do Sharon Duncan-Brewster's Liet-Kynes and Zendaya's Chani.
4. Most of the male cast don't make it to the end of part one, though some should return in the sequel.
5. David McGuire, "'Dune': Oscar Isaac Says the Father–Son Dynamic Between Paul and Leto Breaks Movie Tropes," *Collider*, October 27, 2021, at https://collider.com/dune-oscar-isaac-paul-leto-father-son-dynamic.
6. Carol Gilligan, "Interview on June 21st, 2011," *Ethics of Care*, June 21, 2011, at https://ethicsofcare.org/carol-gilligan.
7. Ryan Britt, "How Hans Zimmer Brought the Dune Soundtrack to Life," *Denofgeek*, November 2, 2021, at https://denofgeek.com/movies/how-hans-zimmer-brought-the-dune-soundtrack-to-life.
8. Jonathan Hilburg, "Desert Power: Designing *Dune* Required Mining the Past to Build Humanity's Future," *The Architect's Newspaper*, November 4, 2021, at https://www.archpaper.com/2021/11/designing-dune.
9. Duncan suggests that the Fremen are better than the finest warriors he's ever seen (that he even came close to death), yet Jessica easily defeats Stilgar, who, as Jamis points out, deprives Stilgar of being the leader. Thus, it seems that Jessica is perhaps the most effective warrior in Villeneuve's *Dune*.

10. This seems to be a recurring theme for Villeneuve – from *Sicario* to *Arrival* to *Blade Runner 2049*, the women in his films are ultimately more powerful than the men (especially when you cast Emily Blunt, Amy Adams, and Ana de Armas).

11. Especially as Paul contemplates the possibility of being a duke and confronts the history of his family and what it means to wear the family ring – because when your grandfather was a bullfighter and your father is an honorable leader who gives rousing, heartfelt speeches about answering "the call," you've got a lot to live up to.

12. Julia Kristeva, "Prelude to an Ethics of the Feminine," Speech at London Central Hall Westminister, July 24, 2019, at http://kristeva.fr/prelude-to-an-ethics-of-the-feminine.html.

13. Hekman, "Feminism," 99.

14. Clara Juncker, "Writing (with) Cixous," *College English* 50 (1988), 425–426.

15. And I take Kristeva and Cixous to mean not just literal writing or speaking but engaging in all aspects of society to challenge the patriarchal and phallocentric views that typically govern it.

16. Hekman, "Feminism," 98.

17. Hekman, "Feminism," 98.

18. Helen Cixous, Keith Cohen, and Paula Cohen, "The Laugh of the Medusa," *Signs* 1 (1976), 879.

19. Kristeva, "Prelude to an Ethics of the Feminine."

20. Cixous, Cohen, and Cohen, "The Laugh of the Medusa," 891–892.

21. Bessie Yuill, "*Dune*: Baron Vladimir Harkonnen and Queer Menace," *The Companion*, October 12, 2021, at https://thecompanion.app/2021/10/12/dune-baron-harkonnen-queer-menace-and-frank-herberts-homophobia.

22. Or how the sexual union of Harrison Ford's Deckard and Sean Young's Rachel was clearly significant, given that they were able to produce a daughter because they were in love.

ARRAKIS AWAKENING: SCIENCE AND ECOLOGY IN *DUNE*

6

Spiritual Realm Adaptation
Arrakeen Spice, Terrestrial Psychedelics, and Technique

A.M. *Houot*

I'll miss the sea . . . but a person needs new experiences . . . they jar something deep inside, allowing him to grow. Without change, something sleeps inside us . . . and seldom awakens . . . The sleeper must awaken.

Duke Leto Atreides

I stated that this book has a purpose; . . . to arouse the reader to an awareness of technological necessity and what it means. It is a call to the sleeper to awake.

Jacques Ellul

Drugs, and the states they induce, play central and interwoven roles in the *Dune* saga. Spice melange, the most valuable object in the known universe, is a cinnamon-scented, life-prolonging, mind-altering drug found only on the planet of Arrakis. Spacing Guild navigators arguably make the most important use of spice with its effect of prescience or foresight, to find the safest instantaneous route before their Heighliner spaceships fold space. Spice-enabled transportation is the backbone of the Imperium's network of planetary systems, from transporting goods and people to maintaining control over the Federated Great Houses of the Landsraad.

The Water of Life, another important drug found only on Arrakis, is the liquid exhalation of drowned sandworms. It allows select members of the Bene Gesserit Sisterhood access to the past lives of deceased Reverend Mothers. Reverend Mother Gaius Helen Mohiam tells Paul Atreides that melange is a Truthsayer drug, one that's dangerous but gives insight. The Water of Life gives this insight only to women, since all men who ever tried to neutralize the original lethality of the Water died.

In the real world of Earth, psychoactive drugs come in different types and produce varied effects: stimulants, depressants, and hallucinogens, to name just a few. Psychedelics, drugs in the hallucinogen class, share many properties with Arrakeen drugs. Drugs from both planets induce visions

Dune and Philosophy, First Edition. Edited by Kevin S. Decker.
© 2023 John Wiley & Sons, Inc. Published 2023 by John Wiley & Sons, Inc.

and can be lethal (depending on drug and dosage); both planets' drugs are native to niche biomes (*5-MeO-DMT* from the Sonoran Desert toad, *peyote* from southwestern United States and northern Mexico, *iboga* from western Central Africa). All have long-lasting effects, from visions to post-experience integration; and all are threatened by "biopiracy," that is, the practice of extracting or patenting organic materials used by indigenous peoples and not compensating them for their knowledge or ownership of said materials.

It's also intriguing that Imperial denizens refer to the universe's most valuable substance as "spice" and "melange." Spices are customarily used in meal preparation. Recipes sometimes tell us to add "salt to taste," meaning a pinch or two to the dish, to draw out the ingredients' natural flavors. On the other hand, the French verb *mélanger* means to mix, mingle, blend. We therefore have a visionary substance that seems to add a particular flavor to, draws something out of, or mixes with one's ordinary consciousness.

Oppositions found in *Dune* (animal vs. human, unconscious vs. conscious, asleep vs. awake) parallel the "before and after" of an exceptional, possibly visionary experience. Arrakeen and terrestrial drugs promise something new that might change potential users. Guild navigators and the Bene Gesserit, for example, take visionary drugs to generate psychic and physical changes. And while partaking in transformative experiences can be an end in itself, what happens next? Just as Paul and Lady Jessica truly face Arrakis's environment for the first time after the Harkonnen surprise attack, how might consumers of visionary substances survive the terrain of altered states once their consciousness changes? Paul and Jessica know from the outset that adaptation to the environment assures a greater chance of survival. But they are not alone; we as much as they *must* rely on technologies and techniques tailor-made to alien physical and non-physical environments.

"Increase and Multiply": Technology's Over-efficiency

Many high technologies are used throughout the Imperium: transportation technologies like Heighliners, shuttles, and Ornithopters; spice-mining technologies such as harvesters, spotters, and sandcrawlers. Oddly for such an advanced, space-faring civilization, there are no instances of artificial intelligence or something like quantum computing.

The reason for this lies in the *over*-efficiency of past technologies in the *Dune* universe. Computers, thinking machines, and conscious robots threatened humanity's *sovereignty* and humanity's *unique moral status*, particularly from a religious perspective. Space travel changed religious views in this universe, and "gave a different flavor and sense to ideas of Creation"; "Genesis was reinterpreted, permitting God to say: 'Increase and multiply, and fill the universe, and subdue it, and rule over all manner of strange beasts and living creatures in the infinite airs, on the infinite earths and beneath them.'"[1]

Fears of thinking machines and artificial consciousness culminated in the Butlerian Jihad (201 BG–108 BG). Humans not only destroyed their "god of machine-logic" but also billions of their fellow folk for two generations in its wake. The survivors concluded that "Man may not be replaced" and "Thou shalt not make a machine in the likeness of a human mind."[2]

Another feared technology, banned at some point during the *Dune* universe's long history, was the use of atomic weapons against human beings. During the Fremen assault on Arrakeen, Gurney Halleck expresses reservations about Paul's plan to blast the city's Shield Wall with atomics, citing the Great Convention's injunction. Here too we have a clue about a technology's over-efficiency. The use of chemical weapons during World War I, for instance, brought about the 1925 Geneva Protocol, effectively banning their use during times of war because they cause "agonizing suffering."[3]

There was something about these extremely efficient and advanced technologies, specifically, thinking machines and atomics, that did not sit well with the people of their times. Thinking machines impinged upon the human essence. In Herbert's fictional history, humans no longer wanted to submit to an environment dominated by machine-logic. They bristled at a technologized world for which humanity wasn't prepared. As for prohibiting the use of atomics against human targets, they probably felt the same way we feel about chemical weapons' ability to cause agonizing suffering. There is little chance of suffering from an atomic blast's direct hit, but what *really* causes suffering is the nuclear fallout and lingering radiation. Survivors live in pain for the rest of their lives. In addition, suffering is caused by the destruction of cultural and historical artifacts, not to mention environmental devastation. It's important to remember that these creations were threatening their creators in multiple ways; lacking the desire and possibly the competence to adapt to these technologies and the worlds they created, the Duniverse humans banned their use.

French philosopher Jacques Ellul (1912–1994) can shed some light on why these things happened. He said, "The machine tends not only to create a new human environment, but also to modify man's very essence. The milieu in which he lives is no longer his. He must adapt himself, as though the world were new, to a universe for which he was not created."[4]

Ellul doesn't explicitly say what the human's originary essence was and what its modified essence is. He does say, however, that the technologized world separates the human from their "living environment," a fabricated world in which the machine's dials replace human senses and wherein "mechanical time" replaces "nature's time."[5] Ellul intimates the defining characteristic of the human essence: we're *biologically* alive and connected to natural processes within ourselves and with other life forms that a machine could never *fully* understand.

Ellul contributed to the school of the philosophy of technology known today as *technological determinism*. The determinist believes that the overwhelming influence of technology allows technology to realize itself for its ends. Technology becomes autonomous like a runaway train with passengers along for the ride. Society and individuals must adapt *to it* and are adapted *by it*. Some philosophers, on the other hand, subscribe to the idea that technology can be controlled by humans. For example, they view technology simply as a neutral tool or advocate for democratic institutions to direct the design and preferred use of technology. Contemporary philosopher Andrew Feenberg asks, "Is the next step in the evolution of the technical system up to human decision-makers or do they act according to a logic inscribed in the very nature of technology?"[6] A difficult question to say the least. The events from *Dune's* early history might give us part of the answer. Ellul and others' techno-pessimistic view isn't the only way to interpret technological phenomena; however, it's a penetrating lens through which to extend our view of technologies in the *Dune* universe.

One of the core themes of Ellul's philosophy is *technique*, or the "totality of methods rationally arrived at and having absolute efficiency . . . in *every* field of human activity."[7] The main idea here is "efficiency" or "the one best way" to do something, whether machine or human activity. Ellul thinks that such efficiency and ordering is the "consciousness of the mechanized world."[8]

The pre-Butlerian "god of machine-logic" – with its hyper-efficiency, appeal to order, and omnipresence – may have sought to stamp out "less efficient" (read: humanly enjoyable) means of doing things. The people of that time may have objected to the logic of *the one best way* dictated by an unsympathetic machine consciousness. The likely explanation for the Great Revolt is that humans regarded their artificial creations as rivals seeking stewardship over the universe, including human affairs; in short, thinking machines robbed humans of their potential to think for themselves and decide their own future.

Yet the development of technique evidently has value, considering that schools like the Bene Gesserit, Spacing Guild, and Mentat emerged post-Revolt to "train *human* talents."[9] In the Duniverse, the exercise of technique by machine-logic *in a machine* is undesirable, but machine-logic *in a human being* is tolerable so long as that training doesn't violate the human essence, including the human capacity for suffering. The latter expression of Ellul's technique is a humanized or tempered version compared to the former.

Adapting to Dune

After years of forced migrations from planet to planet, the Fremen finally settled on Arrakis, becoming its indigenous population. Arrakis's environment is harsh: it's covered mostly by sand dunes and jutting rocks; intense heat, dangerous storms, sand-static, and enormous sandworms, the so-called Shai-Hulud or "makers," are a constant threat. Of greatest concern is Arrakis's lack of water.

The Fremen would have known about the over-efficiency of machines that caused the Butlerian Jihad. But unlike the over-efficiency rejected by Imperial citizens, the Fremen embrace the extremes of efficiency in order to survive, and even thrive, in one of the most unforgiving environments in the universe, one thoroughly unfit for humans. The Fremen depend on efficient techniques and technologies to survive on Arrakis, especially when it comes to water.

Fremen techniques include traveling at night, which is likely to expend less water in the form of perspiration (as well as avoiding Harkonnen patrols). In the open desert they cover as much of their body as possible. For example, Chani instructs Paul to cover his forehead to conserve his body's moisture and Jessica noticed that everyone under Stilgar's command traveled as a military company. The good discipline of the troupe is, according to Stilgar, the result of a strong leader who brings security and water.

Arrakis's environment forcibly preoccupied Jessica with water from the time of her arrival. The constant threat of not having enough water, compared to her previous home on Caladan, made Jessica realize that the Fremen were master technicians of *moisture-reclaiming*. As the watermasters emptied Paul's reward from the knife-fight with Jamis into the basin, Jessica observed not a single drop of water clinging to the meter trough. The Fremen are "perfectionists" when it comes to all-things water.[10]

This heightened awareness of water's crucial importance mobilized the Fremen to develop technologies that capture moisture. First, they draw out moisture from the air. Windtraps collect atmospheric moisture to be converted into water by means of precipitators, and dew collectors draw moisture out of the air to water outdoor plants. Personal moisture-capture technology takes two forms. The *stillsuit* reclaims bodily moisture from human waste, perspiration, and exhalation, and distills these secretions into potable water. But because techniques of conscious breathing – necessary for a Fremen to intentionally exhale through the nose into the stillsuit's nose tube – are not always possible, the Fremen create *stilltents* to capture exhaled moisture during periods of sleep.

As mentioned before, machines and technologies clearly exemplify the efficiency of Ellul's notion of technique. But Ellul reminds us that efficiency applied to technology is only the tip of the iceberg. Efficiency can also be applied to economics and politics, as well as what he calls "human technique," for instance, in matters of education, work, propaganda, amusement, sport, and medicine. In his usual pessimistic tone, Ellul laments the need for techniques to help humans psychologically adjust to their technologized, mass-society but acknowledges techniques' usefulness to survival. Thus, the application of efficient means is not limited to human-made devices but also to people. The common thread, according to Ellul, is adaptation of the human to a particular activity.[11]

Take assembly-line production as an example. For Ellul, it's important for vocational guidance counselors to help individuals find suitable kinds of work, jobs to which they can easily adapt and enjoy. Someone not suited to, or incapable of adapting to, the assembly-line's "rationalized industrial labor" may become neurotic.[12] Likewise, maladjustment to a particular job can be likened comparatively to an entire society's way of life. We know that some Fremen reject the desert life for the cities, or take non-Fremen partners; perhaps these nonconformists found Fremen efficiency and precision unbearable.

Naturalizing the Unnatural

The Butlerian Jihad represents the moment at which technology's over-efficiency alerted humans to the nature of a world for which they weren't created, one that assaulted the human essence and led to the eventual prohibition of technologies that caused the problem. By contrast, Fremen welcome technological determinists' views regarding efficiency and "the one best way" because this is the philosophy that allows survival in merciless environments.

Let's distinguish between "natural" and "unnatural" human environments. We can define the human's *natural environment* as any habitat that supports human survival and reproduction with a minimum of technology; this is the kind of habitat in which early humans most likely evolved. Such an environment would have plenty of water, abundant food sources, moderate weather, and could be imagined as a Garden-of-Eden-like habitat. Environments *unnatural* to human survival can be either (i) artificial, for example, the over-efficient and technologized world pre-Butlerian Jihad, or (ii) inhospitable or difficult to occupy such as Arrakis, particularly when compared to the human's natural/default environment. In the *Dune* universe and our own, technology can indeed "naturalize" or normalize unnatural environments, thus facilitating the presence of human life.

Another environment unnatural to humans is the spiritual realm. For example, Fremen believe in the *alam al-mithal*, "that metaphysical realm where all physical limitations were removed" and where "removal of all limitations meant removal of all points of reference."[13] The removal of all physical limitations and points of reference suggests that physically bound humans can and do interact with the spiritual realm through altered states of consciousness, although long bouts are unsustainable since humans must first and foremost attend to their continued physical existence.

Spice, the Water of Life, and psychedelics could be considered *spiritual technologies* because they are means to access spiritual realms. These drugs, however, might serve *merely* instrumental purposes: in the case of

Heighliners, for example, instantaneous travel from one point in space to another is made possible by ingestion of mind-altering drugs. During the Ceremony of the Seed when Jessica becomes a Reverend Mother, Chani says, "Here is the Water of Life, the water that is greater than water; . . . the water that frees the soul."[14] In other words, the Water of Life might be the means to simply get Jessica to the spiritual plane, whereas learned techniques enable Jessica to inspect, gain knowledge from, and ultimately survive the experience.

We can infer this from real-life experience: in the early 1990s, Dr. Rick Strassman and his team reignited psychedelic research in the United States with the first large-scale study on N,N-dimethyltryptamine (DMT). Study volunteers echo Paul's spice and Jessica's Water of Life experiences, describing ecstatic and intense states, contact with entities, movement, and near-death-like separation from one's physical body. A female volunteer reported, "When the patterns began, I said to myself, 'Let me go through you.' At that point, it opened, and I was very much someplace else . . ." One man said the DMT experience is "totally unexpected, quite constant and objective; . . . this is not at all a metaphor. It's an independent, constant reality. There is the real possibility of adjacent dimensions . . . It's not like some kind of drug. It's more like the experience of a new technology."[15] The specifics vary among the 60 volunteers' experiences, yet most of them reported going elsewhere, interacting with human or strange humanoid beings, or gleaning insights that lie just beyond normal states of consciousness.

Once we are transported via drugs to spiritual realms that lie on the other side of ordinary perception, what efficient means can we rely on to ensure survival in such an unnatural environment?

Enduring Spiritual Realms

Experiential knowledge will be an important teacher to someone without any prior technical or technological training in sustaining a presence in spiritual realms. Put another way, we can learn by doing. It's likely that the Fremen didn't create moisture-reclaiming technologies before arriving on Arrakis; instead, the desert environment prompted such inventions. Yet Paul didn't just learn by doing. Yes, he had to acquire skill in his initial encounters with spice-induced prescient abilities, and again later, with his god-like abilities as the Kwisatz Haderach. However, Paul had been primed his entire life not only with skills fit for a Duke's son, but also his mother's Bene Gesserit training (usually given to women only), in addition to his innate Mentat abilities (or so Jessica believed). Some of the Bene Gesserit mind–body practices in which Paul would be trained are the minutiae of observation; mnemonic blink; quick-sensing regimen; seeing and knowing things unnoticeable to others; registering a person; awareness-breathing;

the Voice; relying on non-visual senses; nerve-training (bindu-nervature); and controlling the body's every muscle and fiber (prana-musculature). Moreover, there's good reason to believe that all of Paul's training reinforced his ability to survive changing the Water of Life.

Paul feels Arrakis's spice-rich environment and diet changing him. He comes to the realization that his mother's teachings allowed him to experience the effects of spice in a *more efficient* or *enhanced* way than someone without proper training: "The spice changes anyone who gets this much of it, but thanks to *you*, I could bring the change to consciousness. I don't get to leave it in the unconscious where its disturbance can be blanked out. I can *see* it."[16]

Similar training for modern psychedelic users assists them in "surviving," or rather, successfully *enduring*, experiences of spiritual realms. Preparations before drug ingestion include addressing the potential resistance to unexpected or uncomfortable bodily and visionary phenomena; the practice of surrender or letting go to intense drug and non-drug experiences; and purposeful setting of intentions. In addition, there are non-drug methods and techniques that train the *refocusing of one's attention* such as meditation, yoga, controlled hyperventilation, singing, and dancing. More ordinary things like exercise, healthy diet, and stress reduction are also helpful before and after psychedelic experiences.[17]

The Fremen's blue-within-blue eyes are a sign of living in an environment where spice is in everything. Yet immediately after Jessica becomes the Fremen's Reverend Mother, Chani pulls Paul aside and tells him there's something frightening in him, that he makes her people see things. Paul says to himself, "They've a little of the talent, . . . but they suppress it because it *terrifies*."[18] A possible reason why spice-induced experiences and altered cognition terrify the Fremen is because they don't know how to drive their experiences. Instead, their experiences end up driving them, so they suppress them.

Ellul sees technique and technology as becoming autonomous and oppressive. By contrast, training in methods that embody the efficient, rationalized best practices of machine-like logic may enable psychoactive drug-users greater control of experiences, enhancing endurance of and adaptation to spiritual environments.

The Sleeper Is Awake: What Now?

Techniques and technologies change the people and societies that use them. Their use can also be restricted if they create a world with which humans no longer identify. As the examples of Paul, Jessica, and the Fremen show, though, the efficiency of machine-logic seems to have redeeming qualities for survival in unnatural environments. The Fremen figured out multiple ways to survive and endure Arrakis's environment, and training in mind–body practices prepared Paul to swim rather than sink in "race consciousness" and "trinocular vision that permitted him to see time-become-space."[19] Bene Gesserit sisters remind themselves too with the adage: "Survival is the ability to swim in strange water."[20]

Once someone awakens to a reality of normally unseen phenomena and altered thought processes, what's next? Efficient techniques and technologies aid experiencers in spiritual realm adaptation. At least two potential avenues exist.

First, there is *adaptation of the spiritual realm to the human*. For example, planetary ecologist Liet-Kynes carries on his father's mission to terraform Arrakis into an environment habitable to humans. According to Pardot Kynes, only 3 percent of the planet would need to be covered in green plants to produce enough carbon compounds to transform parts of the planet from sand dunes to prairies and forests. While the Kynes's and Fremen's bold plan to terraform Arrakis was working, it seems improbable (and maybe even unethical) to "terraform" or "humanize" the spiritual realm, that is, to make that environment fit for us. Little is known about that environment anyway, and what we do know comes from drug and non-drug altered states experienced by mystics, shamans, healers, and modern psychedelic users.

Second, there is *adaptation of the human to the spiritual realm*. For example, Staban Tuek, son of Esmar Tuek the smuggler, nicely sums up the general impression about living on Arrakis in a conversation with Gurney Halleck: "You're the only one of the Duke's lieutenants to escape, . . . Your enemy was overwhelming, yet you rolled with him . . . You defeated him the way we defeat Arrakis."[21] Proper training and methods make this second option more attainable.

The spiritual realm oftentimes threatens to overwhelm us, but it isn't an enemy to be defeated. Rather, Staban's comments teach us that no matter how uncontrollable or intense visionary environments can be, it is possible to develop the ability and know-how to "roll with" spiritual realms, to expect the unexpected, to make the uncomfortable comfortable. We can either adapt environments or adapt ourselves, but the path more in our control is adapting ourselves to physical and non-physical environments.

Both Duke Leto and Jacques Ellul speak of sleepers that must awaken. So, how might consumers of psychedelics be asleep? New and challenging experiences lead to change, which then leads to an awakening of something. For some people, psychedelics heal trauma; for others, they give insights to one's sense of self or the structure of material and immaterial realities. However, psychedelic users might be considered to be "asleep" when they're not applying efficient techniques and technologies to adapt better to spiritual realms. Dismissing or ignoring more efficient ways to experience visionary states might result in not making the most out of one's experience, essentially glossing over something that trained people *would* notice or be able to do, again, because they're adept in ways that further greater survival and endurance in non-ordinary environments.

We're clever enough as a species to figure out more efficient ways to occupy spiritual realms. Whereas physical technology in the twentieth and twenty-first centuries has pointed human beings on a trajectory toward outer space, psychedelic-induced experiences of spiritual realms are theaters of exploration that will require comparable means. Evolving humans didn't have to live in unnatural environments; it's much easier to settle in environments conducive to life. Likewise, people don't have to take mind-altering drugs. But if we're to endure and make sense of these spaces, we must adapt to them, not vice versa, and use anything and everything at our disposal to ease the process. We are guests who must learn how to roll with these host worlds.

Notes

1. *Dune* (London: Gollancz, 1965), 569–570.
2. *Dune*, 570, 596.
3. United Nations, "Chemical Weapons – Office for Disarmament Affairs," *United Nations*, at https://www.un.org/disarmament/wmd/chemical.
4. Jacques Ellul, *The Technological Society* (New York: Vintage Books, 1964), 325.
5. Ellul, *Technological Society*, 320–335.
6. Andrew Feenberg, "What Is Philosophy of Technology?" in John R. Dakers ed., *Defining Technological Literacy: Towards an Epistemological Framework* (New York: Palgrave Macmillan, 2006), 10–15.
7. Ellul, *Technological Society*, xxv.
8. Ellul, *Technological Society*, 6.
9. *Dune*, 11.
10. *Dune*, 359.
11. Ellul, *Technological Society*, 348.
12. Ellul, *Technological Society*, 358–359.
13. *Dune*, 432.
14. *Dune*, 399.
15. Rick Strassman, "The Varieties of the DMT Experience," in Rick Strassman, Slawek Wojtowicz, Luis Eduardo Luna, and Ede Frecska eds., *Inner Paths to Outer Space: Journeys to Alien Worlds Through Psychedelics and Other Spiritual Technologies* (Rochester, VT: Park Street Press, 2008), 60, 67.
16. *Dune*, 220.
17. Rick Strassman, "Preparation for the Journey," in Rick Strassman, Slawek Wojtowicz, Luis Eduardo Luna, and Ede Frecska eds., *Inner Paths to Outer Space: Journeys to Alien Worlds Through Psychedelics and Other Spiritual Technologies* (Rochester, VT: Park Street Press, 2008), 268–298.
18. *Dune*, 408.
19. *Dune*, 333.
20. *Dune*, 350.
21. *Dune*, 290.

7

Thinking Like a Desert
Environmental Philosophy and *Dune*

Zach Vereb

Liet-Kynes says, "The highest function of ecology is the understanding of consequences."[1] This often-repeated line from *Dune* implies that our thinking must be multidimensional: it must include not only the Arrakeen plants, people, sands, and skies, but also their interconnections across space and time. Philosophical ecology, put most simply, is the holistic comprehension of a *world* and its complexity, and Frank Herbert's *Dune* attempts this feat in an exceptional way. Beckoning us to think philosophically, *Dune* urges us to be citizens of the earth rather than consumers and conquerors.

The first *Dune* novel – which this chapter focuses on – is almost 60 years old! What about *Dune*'s world-building sci-fi speaks to us today? A story with ecological, ethical, and existential significance, Herbert's book speaks to *our own world* with its environmental pollution, global climate change, and political turmoil. Its sci-fi warning reminds us that we must cultivate – as planetary ecologists like Liet-Kynes do – a holistic mindset to survive and flourish.

Aldo Leopold's (1887–1948) "Land Ethic" will be our initial compass. A rugged, contemplative, and courageous naturalist, Leopold was not that different from the planetary ecologist Liet-Kynes. Not only was Leopold's pivotal work published only shortly before *Dune* (and likely influenced Herbert's themes), but its radical ideas on ecological stewardship will help us to appreciate *Dune*'s deeper philosophical dimensions. Let us then follow Leopold's vision. Using Kynes's lead, we shall begin to think like a desert!

Living Teachings, Left for Dead

After a devastating series of events culminating in his capture by the Harkonnens, Kynes is left for dead without life-support in the brutal Arrakeen desert. The Harkonnen plan, of course, is to rid themselves of the

Atreides accomplice without blood on their hands and with a pointed
irony: he is condemned to suffer his fate under the brutal conditions of a
world he tried to save. Kynes finds himself without a stillsuit: "The man
crawled across a dune top. He was a mote caught in the glare of the noon
sun. He was dressed only in torn remnants . . . his skin bare."[2] Despite this,
Kynes utters, in his desert loneliness, a re-affirmation of his ecological
vocation:

> "I am Liet-Kynes," he said, addressing himself to the empty horizon, and his
> voice was a hoarse caricature of the strength it had known. "I am His
> Imperial Majesty's Planetologist," he whispered, "planetary ecologist for
> Arrakis. I am steward of this land." He stumbled, fell sideways along the
> crusty surface of the windward face. His hands dug feebly into the sand. *I am
> steward of this sand.*[3]

Kynes begins to hallucinate from heat exhaustion: vivid childhood memories of his father, and of his ecological education, illuminate the epiphany
of his life's purpose. Kynes realizes, in that fatal moment, that he extends
beyond himself: he's a seed for a future, fertile world. Kynes now understands himself as a part of the land, embedded within it in life so also unto
death.

Why does Herbert let the rugged Kynes die so early? Is Kynes simply a
throw-away character? Hardly! His early demise is highly significant. As
many philosophers such as Plato and Lao Tzu are fond of reminding us, a
good death is important for making sense of a good life, and Kynes's
sacrifice is no exception. It is a reminder of the power of hope for future
worlds, and of the need for environmental stewardship. This is a topic that
Leopold can help us navigate.

A Sand County Almanac's Desert Outlook

Aldo Leopold was among the first American conservationists, and he
founded the field of wildlife ecology. More importantly, Leopold was an
environmental philosopher and naturalist who urged us to think in terms
of whole, dynamic systems, and not to embrace myopic human exception-
alism. When we remain stuck in our selfish, short-term ways, Leopold
writes, we fail to see the complexity, beauty, and diversity of nature. For
Leopold, this might involve seeing the harmonious balance, beautiful in its
own way, between predator and prey in an ecosystem. Wolves in Arizona
and New Mexico, for instance, keep deer populations in check. Short-
sighted hunters who cull these wolves for the ease of deer-hunting inadvertently transform the balance of those environments. Because environments
are dynamic systems, these changes go beyond wolves and deer, potentially
affecting all creatures and plants of the systems. Ecological tunnel-vision

can rob us of the chance to understand ourselves as biotic citizens embedded in an ever-changing ecological community. Leopold had hoped that we would one day work toward our place in nature as its stewards, maintaining the balance. Leopold's death, like his life, resembled that of Kynes: before publishing *A Sand County Almanac*, Leopold perished saving the land while putting out a neighbor's wildfire.[4]

For Leopold, the application of ethics constantly evolves: from women's suffrage to civil rights, and beyond. It was only natural and inevitable, Leopold thought, that we would expand our moral horizons to include not just animals, but the land understood as a dynamic system. The NASA scientist and environmentalist James Lovelock would later draw from this way of thinking with his "Gaia Hypothesis." Leopold and Lovelock want us to view the land as part of a larger Gaian system, a lot like an organism. Yet such a Gaian expansion, what Leopold calls an "ecological possibility and evolutionary necessity," would be paradigm-shattering.[5] It would be utterly alien to our present way of seeing things.

Kynes's thoughts and actions exemplify Leopold's philosophical outlook. For Kynes, "*The wealth of the planet is in its landscape, how we take part in the basic source of civilization – agriculture.*"[6] Leopold, like Kynes, agrees that we must stop valuing the land – whether mountain, forest, or sand – as a mere economic resource for wealth and power. As Leopold puts it, "the conqueror role is eventually self-defeating."[7] This profound statement will have important lessons for us when we consider Paul's development from prophet to conqueror.

Kynes's monologue continues: "The highest function of ecology is understanding consequences,"[8] a phrase that's repeated throughout *Dune*. Nature, for Leopold, is an interconnected, dynamic system worthy of respect. A classic example of these subtle but essential interconnections can be seen in the case of DDT, a pesticide developed primarily to get rid of pesky mosquitoes. Because humans failed to appreciate the connections and consequences inherent to ecological systems, DDT ended up wreaking havoc for humans and non-humans alike. By entering the water supply, for example, it affected humans, even becoming concentrated in mothers' breast milk. Failure to recognize these connections led to developmental issues in children and a quieting of nature: as the title of Rachel Carson's book *Silent Spring* attests, the long-term effects of a disrespectful use of pesticides creates a world with little wildlife. The birds and frogs become silent.

The standpoint of an Arrakeen planetary ecologist, like any wildlife ecologist of earth, embraces not individuals but relations. Kynes's father speaks forcefully on this in Kynes's death-visions:

"There's an internally recognized beauty of motion and balance on any man-healthy planet." [Pardot] Kynes said. "You see in this beauty a dynamic stabilizing effect essential to all life. Its aim is simple: to maintain and produce coordinated patterns of greater and greater diversity . . . The entire landscape comes alive, filled with relationships and relationships within relationships."[9]

The parallels between Leopold and Kynes's father Pardot are uncanny. To use Leopold's way of putting it, as we will see, these words take on the perspective of a mountain: "A planet's life is a vast, tightly interwoven fabric . . . our self-sustaining system."[10] The mind-altering awakening of spice allows some individuals to see the truth of this in a spiritual sense, as the Fremen grasp it in an intuitive sense. "Land," Leopold repeats – channeling spiritual, intuitive, and conceptual insight – "is not merely soil; it is a fountain of energy flowing through a circuit of soils, plants, and animals."[11]

Gaia's "energy pyramid" includes death in a cycle of balance with life. This cycle and its equilibrium create conditions for the possibility of human meaning, according to Leopold. A philosophical perspective on the meaning of life helps us to appreciate the weight and significance of the death that comes to all living things. The final moment of self-realization occurs to Kynes: "And I am a desert creature . . . You see me, Father? I am a desert creature."[12] In this moment of the eternal recurrence of life and death, Kynes reappraises himself and reaffirms his role. He is, both in life and now in death, a member and biotic citizen of the Fremen's Arrakis.

To Tame a Land? The Land Ethic on Arrakis

For the Atreides and Harkonnens, Arrakis is an "enemy" and "empty wasteland."[13] But the Fremen, like Liet, appreciate the harmony and equilibrium of their desert community. They see themselves in community with it while acting as stewards of greater diversity, integrity, and beauty. Consider, first, how the Fremen relate to animals. Besides sandworms, there aren't many animals in the first *Dune* novel, at least not until we are granted access to the Fremen standpoint. They appreciate the environmental contributions of all creatures, including bats, rodents, and birds. They respect the sublime worms as "Makers," seeing them as living symbols of the biotic cycle of life and death, with "each ring segment" of the Makers having "a life of its own."[14] Makers embody the wisdom of philosophical sages; each is "an old man of the desert. You must have proper respect for such a one."[15] The Fremen depend upon the Makers but do not exploit them, and this is precisely what Leopold argues for in our dealings with nature. For Leopold, as for the Fremen, we ought to strive for a "state of harmony between men and land."[16]

For the Fremen, even the smallest plant is worthy of tender care, and so their children are ecologically educated for the task of stewardship: "'Tree,' the children chanted. 'Tree, grass, dune, wind, mountain, hill, fire, lightning, rock, rocks, dust, sand, heat."[17] Leopold might explain this by saying, "The land ethic simply enlarges the boundaries of the community to include soils, waters, plants, and animals, or collectively: the land."[18] Paul has an epiphany in realization of this community: "It came to him that he was surrounded by a way that could only be understood by postulating an ecology of ideas and values."[19] Chani later reminds him, "You must think like a patch of sand . . . become a little dune in your very essence."[20]

Like Socrates, Leopold sees that philosophy is not about mere abstract ideas. Instead, philosophizing is about how we choose to live. The Fremen's environmental philosophy can be seen in how they emulate the land, at one with it rather than against it: "they must sound like the natural shifting of sand . . . like the wind."[21] The Fremen act as stewards of the land even though they know they will not see its full completion ("Our generation will not see it"[22]). Leopold points to the moral value of such action with his principle of integrity: "a thing is right when it tends to preserve the integrity, stability, and beauty of the biotic community."[23]

Further along in *A Sand County Almanac*, Leopold presents one of his most prescient images. He sketches the scene of a mountain ecosystem, with all its biotic and abiotic interconnections: plants, animals, soils, streams. Living creatures, over hundreds or thousands of years, come and pass. Behind it all, "only the mountain has lived long enough to listen objectively to the howl of the wolf."[24] The mountain thus symbolizes sagely wisdom. It encourages us to philosophize about our lives from expanded perspectives.

Instead of "thinking like a mountain," as Leopold puts it, *Dune* challenges us to confront the values of the Fremen, the Atreides, and the Harkonnen in "thinking like a desert" across the sands of time. This kind of thinking is particularly desirable today as we deal with global challenges like climate change. Climate change is a problem that exceeds the scope of mere individual action and requires thinking collectively across space and time, just as the Fremen do. Failure to change course puts us squarely on the path to a "hothouse earth" planet.[25] Such a world would have a more erratic nature, with unbearable heat, extreme weather events, mass extinctions, resource scarcity, and ensuing political conflicts. It would no longer be our familiar Earth, but, to use environmentalist Bill McKibben's phrase, would instead be "Eaarth." As world-building sci-fi, *Dune* predicted all this, even if hazily so. The story continues to remind us of our capacity for change, and of the power of changing perspectives. Maybe a Fremen-inspired "Desert Ethic," one that teaches us to think and see like a desert, is what we need to avoid an Arrakeen Eaarth for our grandchildren. But even a Desert Ethic requires us to turn inward. Without the inward turn, we would lack the motivating force to affect real-world change. After all, we need to understand *ourselves* before we can build a better world.

Paul's World-building *Bildung*

In the classic "coming-of-age" tale, the hero, through trials and tribulations, is tasked to become who she truly is. She learns how she came to be
and where she stands by facing her authentically chosen future possibilities. In literature, this sort of tale is known as a *Bildungsroman*. The
German word *Bildung* is hard to translate into English; among other
things, it suggests the process of personal growth, creativity, and self-
overcoming via self-building. *Dune* presents us with a sci-fi *Bildungsroman*
in the coming-of-age of Paul Atreides. But *Dune* is a story not just about
personal and social cultivation, but ecological formation. Paul slowly
comes to grasp the Fremen ecological wisdom: "Muad'Dib tells us in
'A Time of Reflection' that his first collisions with Arrakeen necessities
were the true beginnings of his education. He learned then how to pole the
sand for its weather, learned the language of the wind's needles."[26] For Paul
to become *ecologically* wise, he had to change his own self-conception, to
see himself embedded in a larger world, and to develop wider sympathies.

These *Bildungsroman* commitments also resonate in the real world:
developed by Arne Naess (1912–2009), "Deep Ecology" is a unique environmental philosophy that asks us to reconsider what it means to be
human. Deep Ecology, or "Ecosophy," forces us to step back from narrow
views of nature that see it as providing resources for human happiness.
From our deep self-reflections, we learn to challenge shallow ways of living
in which people treat each other and nature poorly. For the "shallow ecologist," science only teaches us to become better manipulators, not better
selves.[27] Deep Ecologists mobilize ecological self-understanding as the pre-
condition for practical political change, just as Paul learns from the Fremen
who he really is and what he can become. From this self-reassessment, Paul
comes to see how to lead the Fremen to a more sustainable future. This is
the Muad'dib of Deep Ecology.

A key idea in Naess's Deep Ecology is "wide identification." This concept is inspired by multiple traditions, including the pantheism of Baruch
Spinoza, the view of harmony with nature of Zen, and "attunement" to
our environment in the work of Martin Heidegger and Karl Jaspers. To
move beyond the narrow confines of the selfish ego, Naess tells us, we
must see ourselves as *beyond ourselves*. The world is not a collection of
stuff – of resources meant to be manipulated and consumed for short-term
benefit. Rather, it is an interconnected web. The selfishness of the shallow
ego is destructive and unsustainable; it only wants more and more. It does
not see itself embedded in that web. With a little change of perspective,
however, nature reveals the non-human parts as essential for our lives. For
example, microscopic phytoplankton in the ocean assist in the formation
of new clouds. Ample clouds, in turn, help block rays from the sun that
would otherwise heat the earth. When we continue to treat nature as a

mere resource and pollute the atmosphere, we contribute to the acidification of the oceans and global warming. Ocean acidification spells trouble for many of these phytoplankton, which are essential for keeping our planet cooler. Thinking about ecological consequences in this way shows us that we are dependent on the relations constitutive of that web, even the smallest parts.

These and related ecological relations sustain us. They allow us to be who we are in the first place. Undermining them with the shallow ego not only blinds us to our potential as humans, but creates conditions for our own ruin. Consequently, the selfishness of the shallow ego can never be satisfied, like the dark desires of the Harkonnens. If we understand ourselves more widely, as part of larger dynamic wholes, we can make sense of who we truly and most authentically are for Deep Ecologists: relational beings. This understanding gives us reason to protect those dynamic wholes. On this view, saving our oceans from acidification is not simply for ocean lovers and marine biologists. It is a moral act of self-defense! The same holds for the ocean-less desert world of Arrakis in Paul's awakening.

Paul, as Muad'Dib, finally comes to understand this in two ways. With his newfound abilities, he grasps the strands of time as a nexus with which he can identify *temporally*. He thus gains a new, intergenerational view of his world. And, with his wide ecological education from the Fremen, Paul begins to comprehend space differently, in terms of the importance of place: "*I must be part of the desert.*"[28] The shape of Paul's Ecosophy is related to us by Princess Irulan:

> There is in all things a pattern that is part of our universe. It has symmetry, elegance, and grace – those qualities you find always in that which the true artist captures. You can find it in the turning of the seasons, in the way sand trails along a ridge, in the branch clusters of the creosote bush or the pattern of its leaves. We try to copy these patterns in our lives and our society, seeking the rhythms, the dances, the forms that comfort.[29]

Paul is thus able to see the interconnections and harmony of all in one, one in all, connections within connections. He, himself, is a part of this living cosmic nexus.

Despite Paul's Deep Ecological awakening, he still succumbs – as all fallible humans can – to the unhealthy vices of control, domination, and imbalance. Like any good coming-of-age tale, there is a moral here as well: when we identify with the story, we see a mirror of ourselves. The mirror has cracks, and those cracks show the dangers of going too far. So let us conclude with *Dune*'s prescient warnings. These, curiously, hold even more weight today than they did in Frank Herbert's time, which further highlights his genius as a sci-fi writer.

Deadly Dedications and Dire Dangers

Take your copy of *Dune* and look at Frank Herbert's dedication: "To the people whose labors go beyond ideas into the realm of 'real materials' – to the dry-land ecologists, wherever they may be, in whatever time they work, this effort at prediction is dedicated in humility and admiration." Humility and admiration for ecology are the book's guiding virtues. What happens when we don't heed them? What are the vices of Ecosophy? If there is one thing that Herbert's *Dune* teaches us – through its subtle use of technology, multifaceted dynamical world, and compelling characters – it is that balance is vital. Balance in *Dune* appears in three ways: as moral balance, existential balance, and cognitive balance. Imbalances on each of these fronts promise deadly dangers, so we would be wise to be mindful of Herbert's dedication.

Ultimately, *Dune* cautions us about the dangers of excess. Consider Paul's over-identification with his people and his embrace of eco-fascist and authoritarian tendencies. Due to Paul's grandiose urge to become a great leader and Fremen savior, as well as his desire to live up to the expectations of his father, he begins to lose sight of who he is. Deep Ecology is valuable for reminding us of two things. First, we are relational beings embedded in larger dynamic systems. Second, we are still nodes in those systems. There is a tension between individual and whole that needs to be sustained. Over-identification with his role allows Paul to neglect the second aspect, and this enables him to see all obstacles – people included – as disposable. In other words, Paul's failure to recognize the value of balance and humility leads him to a distorted ecological vision where individual lives become expendable cells, to be sacrificed for a larger Gaian organism. If not carefully tempered, Leopold's own view might take us down this perilous route. On the other side, Baron Harkonnen's obsession with domination and the intellectual manipulation used by the Bene Gesserit (including Jessica) and the Mentats (including Thufir Hawat) treat people and nature as a mere means – as instruments for self-interested ends. They are blinded to the deep ecologies of *Dune* that are worthy of protection, appreciation, and respect. Jessica, unlike the Baron, learns this lesson toward the end of the novel as she witnesses Paul's transformation.

Clearly, philosophical reflections on *Dune* matter in real life. By inviting us to think like a desert – to reflect on the nature of the self, the dangers of excess, and the virtues of humility – *Dune* teaches us to be a little more like the Fremen with environmental resources. We can learn to be a little less Harkonnen-like when we think about the wide consequences of climate inaction and human arrogance. Liet-Kynes's stewardship approach to the land, paralleling Leopold's, presses us to reimagine what a motivated and educated humanity is capable of. And the philosophical teachings of Deep Ecology, like Paul's own coming-of-age experiences, show us how to connect the individual, social, and spiritual.

In fact, we must do so! A recent report by the IPCC reminds us that a *Dune*-like, water-scarce world might soon become more than fiction.[30] Maybe thinking like a desert, as *Dune* taught nearly 60 years ago, is just the spice that we need to avoid our own hothouse earth.

Notes

1. *Dune* (New York: Ace, 1990), 438.
2. *Dune*, 436.
3. *Dune*, 437.
4. Aldo Leopold, *A Sand County Almanac* (New York: Ballantine Books, 1986). For the best philosophical interpretation of Leopold for today, see J. Baird Callicott, *Thinking Like a Planet: The Land Ethic and the Earth Ethic* (New York: Oxford University Press, 2013).
5. Leopold, *Sand County Almanac*, 239.
6. *Dune*, 438.
7. Leopold, *Sand County Almanac*, 240.
8. *Dune*, 438.
9. *Dune*, 798.
10. *Dune*, 445.
11. Leopold, *Sand County Almanac*, 253.
12. *Dune*, 446.
13. *Dune*, 47.
14. *Dune*, 188.
15. *Dune*, 652.
16. Leopold, *Sand County Almanac*, 243.
17. *Dune*, 561.
18. Leopold, *Sand County Almanac*, 239.
19. *Dune*, 562.
20. *Dune*, 634.
21. *Dune*, 425.
22. *Dune*, 470.
23. Leopold, *Sand County Almanac*, 262.
24. Leopold, *Sand County Almanac*, 137.
25. Jan Zalasiewicz, Mark Williams, and Thomas Hearing, "Hothouse Earth: Our Planet Has Been Here Before – Here's What It Looked Like," *The Conversation*, August 13, 2018, at https://theconversation.com/hothouse-earth-our-planet-has-been-here-before-heres-what-it-looked-like-101413.
26. *Dune*, 551.
27. Arne Naess, "The Shallow and the Deep, Long-range Ecology Movement," *Inquiry* 16 (1973), 95–100, and Arne Naess, "Ecosophy T: Deep Versus Shallow Ecology," in Michael Tobias ed., *Deep Ecology* (Santa Monica, CA: IMT Productions, 1985).
28. *Dune*, 651.
29. *Dune*, 616.
30. Matt McGrath, "Climate Change: IPCC Report Is 'Code Red for Humanity,'" *BBCNews*, August 9, 2021, at https://www.bbc.com/news/science-environment-58130705?fbclid=IwAR0gUPbWjoNmM1N9aGcktcE9uDHNCp6i5rs51k4bQP-8cK46bcjWVE8LOGQ.

8

Humans, Machines, and an Ethics for Technology in *Dune*

Zachary Pirtle

Jihad, Butlerian: (see also Great Revolt) – the crusade against computers, thinking machines, and conscious robots begun in 201 B.G. and concluded in 108 B.G. Its chief commandment remains in the O.C. Bible as "Thou shalt not make a machine in the likeness of a human mind."

Terminology of the Imperium, appendix to *Dune*

The worlds of *Dune* forbid the creation of "thinking machines," due to an ancient war, called the Butlerian Jihad, which was fought to keep humans from using such machines. Frank Herbert's views on technology are some of the most famous and memorable parts of the book series. Beginning in the first pages of *Dune*, the dangerous ways in which humans can use technology to harm each other loom wider in the later books of Herbert's series.[1] The Butlerian Jihad, or the Great Revolt, resulted in new moral and religious values that determined which technologies were acceptable and which were not. Details of the technological values and motivations of the *Dune* universe are relevant to the ethics of technology in our own world. As we'll see and discuss, a particularly important topic in the philosophy of technology is the role of humans in directing changes in technology.[2] Do humans shape the future of technologies? Or do technologies evolve on their own and determine the course of human lives?

Social Construction versus Technological Determinism

The relationship between humanity and forbidden technology in *Dune* touches on two basic possibilities for the relationship of humans and technology: social construction of technology and technological determinism. The social construction of technology means that the use and development of a technology is deeply shaped by humans, with the presumption that political and cultural influences on a technology can matter as much as its

Dune and Philosophy, First Edition. Edited by Kevin S. Decker.
© 2023 John Wiley & Sons, Inc. Published 2023 by John Wiley & Sons, Inc.

underlying physics. Technological determinism, on the other hand, means that technology shapes our lives in ways that we can't control, inevitably influencing the political and cultural life of humans.

The ideas behind *Dune*'s Butlerian Jihad represent a nuanced worldview between social construction and technological determinism. Butlerians feared how technology might shape human lives, evoking worries about a lack of control. But the leaders of the Butlerian Jihad also embody the possibility of changing technology by fighting to change which technologies are permissible. The bans on certain technologies in the *Dune* universe epitomize social influence on how technology develops, but the bans themselves are driven by fear of technology's reach, which is a deterministic view. However, neither viewpoint fully captures the richness of how humans relate to technologies.

First, a definition: technologies are artifacts (or objects) in our environment that we can use to cause change in ourselves or our environment. Typically, these artifacts are created by humans, and many are designed and developed by engineers.[3] The philosopher-engineer Walter Vincenti defines engineering as "the practice of organizing the design and construction [and operation] of any artifice which transforms the world around us to meet some recognized need."[4] Technologies in our world range from spaceships, such as NASA's Space Shuttle or Orion spacecraft, to planes, to computers, but mundane objects like pencils and garbage trucks also count as technologies. Use alone may make an object a technology, as we can turn a branch into a walking stick or a pile of rocks into a fence. Many see food as technology – in that sense, the spice melange of *Dune*, similar to caffeine found in coffee beans in the real world, is a type of technology, as are the many poisons in the *Dune* universe. Technology has to be used by humans for some purpose, but that purpose can change over time.

Knives, Shields, Lasguns, and Feedback Loops

Now, consider technology in the *Dune* books. Life on Arrakis and under the Imperium is filled with technologies that range from the very realistic to the fantastical. Technologies that we can currently imagine as real include wind traps that collect moisture from the air, thumpers to create drumming noises on the ground, stilltents for capturing moisture, and the exotic paracompass, a guidance to mitigate the effects of Arrakis's uncertain magnetic field. Herbert shows some technologies that are ambiguous but fascinating: Ornithopters are used for air travel via "wing-beats . . . in the manner of birds," but it's unclear if they could be realized in the real world today.[5] The stillsuits of the Fremen provide the seemingly simple ability to retain moisture and process body waste, but they are far more efficient than similar real-world technologies today. Herbert also writes of atomic weapons. Paul uses atomics in a focused way, not to attack people directly, but to blast open the Arrakeen shield wall to allow worms and his Fremen army to attack the Emperor's Sardaukar soldiers. Whether or not the atomics of *Dune* are more powerful than our own nuclear weapons, they embody the Cold War concept of "mutually assured destruction." All the Great Houses and political leaders have foresworn use of atomics, with a pact to fight against any leader who uses them.

In light of these advanced technologies 24 millennia from now, it's strange that there are knives and sword-fighting in *Dune*. Yet it makes sense. Herbert's radical way of thinking about how technologies develop and grow in non-linear ways rests on the idea that there are *feedback loops* between technical innovations, humans, and other technologies.[6] We often talk about technologies developing in linear ways, with new technologies making old ones obsolete. The reality is much more complicated, though. For example, knives become necessary in the *Dune* future because of other, far more advanced technologies: defensive shields can be placed on individuals and buildings that repel fast-moving projectiles like bullets and artillery shells. The development of shields represents a feedback loop that made projectile weaponry obsolete.[7] Individual fighters equipped with shields must revert back to combat using slower-moving daggers and swords, hoping to win battles by penetrating an opponent's shield.

Herbert also creates lasguns, another fantastical technology, through a feedback loop that counters shields. These are basically lasers that cut through walls and body armor. Lasguns are incredibly powerful in the *Dune* world, but not as effective as their wielders might hope. If a lasgun strikes a defense shield, a fusion reaction is triggered, destroying both attacker and defender. Users of both shields and lasguns must take care to avoid shared destruction. *Dune* characters know this feedback loop exists, and so they change how they use the technologies as a result. Some characters exclusively use knives when they believe shields may be nearby, to avoid destructive feedback. Meanwhile, other characters find ways to cause trouble in desperate circumstances by setting a lasgun and shield against each other.

Just like real-world technical innovations, *Dune* technologies are used by individual people, who change the uses of their technology over time, based on new circumstances. The technologies don't develop in a linear, deterministic way, because feedback loops develop between technologies and the goals and desires of people.[8] Later, we'll see how spaceships in the *Dune* universe and other complex technologies always have a human "in the loop." This means the overall control, direction, and purpose of the machine is shaped by a person, not by forces outside our control.[9]

Technology: Cultural Prestige, or Everyday Life?

Philosophers of technology look both at the role of technology in society and at how a society's values shape those technologies. In *Dune*, even everyday technical devices get deep appreciation from key characters. So, after he realizes that people need stillsuits to endure everyday life in the Arrakeen desert, Duke Leto remarks that the "design and manufacture of these stillsuits bespeaks a high degree of sophistication," and he also expresses a strong interest in visiting a sietch factory.[10] Unfortunately, the novels never dig deeply into the inner workings of how specific technologies are created, but there must be a significant amount of work happening elsewhere in the *Dune* universe to make the technologies possible. In the scene where Paul realizes that his father has died, he reflects on the Fremen technology in front of them, saying "Think of all these special-application Fremen machines. They show unrivaled sophistication. Admit it: the culture that made these things betrays depths no one suspected."[11]

In fact, the main characters in Herbert's *Dune* universe may have a deeper appreciation of technologies than many of us do. Some real-world thinkers argue that western societies don't give enough attention to what it takes to engineer complex technologies.[12] (It would be great to have political leaders who sincerely appreciate factories for more than the number of jobs they provide!) In addition, we tend to glorify new innovations powered by science, while tending to ignore technologies used in everyday life.

Societies in the *Dune* universe tend to value a variety of everyday and cutting-edge technologies. But what about the technologies they eliminated? How could a society come to have ethical norms against thinking machines and related technology? What led to the Butlerian Jihad?

The Great Revolt to Set Humans Free

Understanding the reasons why some technology is forbidden in *Dune* depends on understanding how Herbert views human beings. The Reverend Mother Gaius Helen Mohiam's test of the gom jabbar on young Paul Atreides is a severe way to define "humanity," and this test greatly shapes Paul's sense of purpose. Mohiam uses a box that makes Paul believe his hand is in extreme pain; if he removes his hand from the box, then Mohiam will kill him with the poisoned gom jabbar needle. She calls this a "test for humans": true humans, unlike animals, will have the self-restraint to keep their hand in the box despite the pain. Paul passed the test but he was bewildered at the test's purpose. Mohiam explains that the gom jabbar "kills only animals . . . You've heard of animals chewing off a leg to escape a trap? There's an animal kind of trick. A human would remain in the trap, enduring the pain, feigning death that he might kill the trapper and remove a threat to his kind ... A human can override any nerve in the body ... Ever sift sand through a screen? We Bene Gesserit sift people to find the humans ... Pain's merely the axis of the test."[13]

Now, Herbert isn't trying to state that real humans should be able to suffer great pain. Mohiam says the goal of her hypothetical human is "to remove a threat to his kind." For her, the true "human" wants their kind – the human species and civilization – to continue, and is willing to undergo great pain and struggle to achieve it. Mohiam and the Bene Gesserit's vision for what it is to be truly human is based on serving a higher purpose for the good of humanity. Enduring pain, as with many kinds of struggle, serves as a test for whether a person really intends to support a higher purpose with action, or if they will only offer words.[14] Explaining how the Bene Gesserit sought to create continuity and order across the millennia, Mohiam says that they seek humans who will act for this higher purpose. But how does any of this apply to technology and the Butlerian Jihad?

The Butlerian Jihad's technological ethics are invoked in the very same discussion between Paul and Mohiam, where Herbert links his views on technology to his view of humans. Paul asks,

"Why do you test for humans?"
   "To set you free."
   "Free?"
   "Once, men turned their thinking over to machines in the hope that this would set them free. But that only permitted other men with machines to enslave them."
   "'Thou shalt not make a machine in the likeness of a man's mind,'" Paul quoted.
   "Right out of the Butlerian Jihad and the Orange Catholic Bible," she said. "But what the O.C. Bible should've said is: 'Thou shall not make a machine to counterfeit a *human* mind.' ...
   The Great Revolt took away a crutch," she said. "It forced *human* minds to develop. Schools were started to train *human* talents."[15]

There is so much hinted at here in so few words: religion, super-humans, and the history of technology and oppression! Let's tackle this in steps. First, the edict to not make a machine in the likeness of a human mind is based on an ethical and religious principle about technology. The OC Bible is the main religious document in *Dune*; it's a synthesis of many existing religious faiths and future ones that evolve in the next 24,000 years. The ethics of the OC Bible are treated so reverently by the cultures in *Dune* that its views on technology are an important element of *Dune*'s moral codes. This is similar to how we today might treat the significance of moral values from the Abrahamic faiths – Judaism, Christianity, and Islam. However, our society has very few deep ethical tenets about the nature of technology.[16]

Second, ending the use of certain technological "crutches" has created a new society dependent on enhanced humans. The book elaborates at length about enhanced humans, who play the role that computers do in our world today. In *Dune*, some people train their minds to become "Mentats," or human computers who strategize and collate large amounts of data together into calculations. (Paul himself was being trained to become a Mentat!) In other cases as well, the human brain in the *Dune* universe takes on some of the roles relegated to technological advancements: so instead of a computer guiding spaceships through faster-than-light travel (like warp drive or hyperspace), Guild Navigators have honed their minds to be capable of folding space, allowing travel throughout the galaxy.[17]

Third, Mohiam describes the causal role that thinking machines played in humanity's decline before the Jihad. In the distant past, many people allowed machines to do their thinking for them, and Mohiam says some bad actors used this fact to enslave the unthinking. The enemy was not thinking machines themselves, and so in this sense the edicts of the Butlerian Jihad are not necessarily anti-technology! Rather, they are about preventing the use of technology for oppression. It's implied that to be free as a human, we must think for ourselves with a higher power in mind.

The Forbidden "Thinking Machines"

What's the nature of the machines banned by the Butlerian Jihad? The epigraph that begins this chapter says that the Great Revolt banned computers, thinking machines, and conscious robots, all of which were believed to simulate ("counterfeit") a human mind. These types are generic, but we can make things clearer by examining each type of technology in turn. While ubiquitous now, computers were very different in 1965 when Herbert published *Dune*. Since then, computers have evolved far beyond performing targeted calculations using printed stacks of code. A simple calculator, probably what Herbert meant by "computer" in the 1960s, could even be considered something that simulates a human mind. It seems that part of what makes a technology a simulation of a human mind in *Dune* is the ability to solve complex equations.

Herbert provides fewer clues about what "thinking machines" might be. Perhaps these are supposed to be a subset of the kind of computers we just discussed. These would be programmed to run simulations, make models that predict the future of the world's climate or the economy. Recall that Mohiam said that humans turned over their mental process to thinking machines.[18] In the real world, it's common for us to make policy decisions about jobs or energy systems based on simulations. Some people obsess over computer simulations of political elections, to the point where the results of these simulations can even influence whether people vote or not. Maybe thinking machines are distinguished by the degree to which a human being can go back over the inputs, and understand the corresponding outputs of a simulation. It could be that thinking machines are different from mere calculators or simple computers in that they are far more opaque to the human mind.[19]

Defining the prohibited "conscious robots" is easier than "thinking machines," since conscious robots are based on the use of artificial intelligence. A technology that is artificially intelligent would be able to think and reason for itself. There are complex debates on what that means and if it is even possible. Science fiction is replete with examples of autonomous artificial intelligence that act and feel just like humans do, while others seem strange and alien in how they think. It's hard to know what Herbert intended, as his novels do not provide a detailed glimpse into the idea of fully autonomous robots. Thus the role of AI in the Butlerian Jihad remains unclear.

Regardless, Mohiam explained that some people relinquished their decision-making to "thinking machines," which are comprised of these three technologies, and said that others used this abdication to enslave the people who used those machines. Maybe the use of computerized analysis prediction with computers, thinking machines, or conscious robots helped some factions in the pre-Jihad society gain power and create wealth, resulting in unethical forms of control and oppression.[20] Mohiam's fear seems to rest on the fact that the exploiters took advantage of their fellows in ways they were not be able to resist.[21] The lesson of the Butlerian Jihad is that technology can create power imbalances that harm significant numbers of people. Mohiam's and the Bene Gesserit's mission to improve the collective human condition limits technology because it could be misused by humans.

This is another point at which we see that fiction can be entertaining, but may not offer real moral alternatives. If it's problematic that technologies can enable oppression of some humans by others, then shouldn't we also worry about the same from *Dune*'s enhanced humans, such as the Mentats? After all, people too often give up their duty to think for themselves by relying on other *humans* to do it for them. Maybe Herbert is implying that people will more readily push back against oppression if it has a human face rather than a machine one.

Herbert suggests that the best part of humanity is the ability to think for oneself. So the greatest risk in the use of technology is that it could replace our freedom of thought, our ability to decide our own path.

Freedom to Choose How We Want to Engineer

The cultures of the *Dune* universe place great cultural value on technology in its importance for everyday lives; like our technology, it develops in nonlinear feedback loops, shaping human preferences and raising or lowering the importance of other technologies. The Bene Gesserit embody the Butlerian preference against thinking machines and want to get humans to think for themselves, with a higher purpose in mind. How might we apply these insights to our own lives, suffused as they are with technology? We certainly shouldn't forbid the use of things like calculators. But we should think deeply about whether or not we use technology in ways that enable reflection and human prosperity. Does that mean reducing how much we rely on computer simulations, or limiting automated services in industries? Are there aspects of new technologies that might be more deterministic in shaping our lives? These are just some of the many topics in the ethics of technology that we should be thinking about in broadly public ways.

Carl Mitcham has laid out a vision for "the true grand challenge of engineering":

> In the words of the great Spanish philosopher José Ortega y Gasset, in the first philosophical meditation on technology, to be an engineer and only an engineer is to be potentially everything and actually nothing. Our increasing engineering prowess calls upon us all, engineers and nonengineers alike, to reflect more deeply about who we are and what we really want to become.[22]

Herbert's view is that we should think for ourselves, and in so doing articulate our own purposes in life. Developing technology that doesn't serve merely as a crutch is part of a vision for humanity. But there are many other ways we can debate what type of technological world we want to engineer.[23] Whatever we decide, we have to realize that unintended negative consequences often spring from technologies and it's hard to guarantee that our engineered systems will not be used for unjust purposes. Making individual humans think for themselves may require a new, democratic approach toward the governance of technology. Engineers should think through their democratic obligations, and make technologies that embody the desires and goals of the public.[24] The fact that *Dune* takes place more than 20,000 years from now should also be a humbling reminder to us of how much our current political and cultural norms might change over time.

Dune's ethics of technology is science fiction at its most provocative: a fascinating speculation about what kind of ethical values might shape human practices tens of thousands of years from now.[25]

Notes

1. For those who want to avoid spoilers for the later *Dune* books, I'll discuss this context in a footnote only. In a nutshell, the *Dune* series goes thousands of years after Paul Atreides, who himself comes almost 10,000 years after the Butlerian Jihad. Paul's son, the God Emperor Leto II, institutes a regime that deliberately squelches technological advancement for over three millennia. And 2000 years later, some type of thinking machines start hunting humanity for reasons Herbert never fully gets to explain. Reading the first book alone

doesn't give the full perspective on how the view of technology in *Dune* shifts across the series, although the first book is perhaps the most nuanced in its thinking on technology.

2. If you want to learn more about the philosophy of technology and engineering, check out the Forum on Philosophy, Engineering and Technology, which welcomes both engineers and philosophers. There's also the Society for Philosophy and Technology, which formed in 1976. A great resource is Diane P. Michelfelder and Neelke Doorn eds., *The Routledge Handbook of the Philosophy of Engineering* (New York: Routledge, 2020).

3. Herbert's world does call out engineers at several places in the book, in ways that recognize that science, technology, and engineering are related. Herbert also has a habit of using "engineering" as a very broad term to systematically enable change in something, with one of his recurring themes being about religious engineering, such as the mythology-making that paved the way for Paul and Jessica among the Fremen.

4. Walter Vincenti, *What Engineers Know and How They Know It: Analytical Studies From Aeronautical History* (Baltimore, MD: Johns Hopkins University Press, 1990), 6. This is a variation of the British engineer Thomas Tredgold's definition from 1828 definition.

5. *Dune* (New York: Ace, 2010), 850.

6. The philosopher of technology, Joe Pitt, articulated the notion of feedback loops in how technology shapes and adjusts our lives. See Joseph Pitt, "Afterword," in Andrew Wells Garner and Ashley Shew eds., *Feedback Loops: Pragmatism About Science and Technology* (New York: Lexington Books, 2020).

7. Or almost obsolete! Knowing that House Atreides soldiers would hide in caves, prepared to fight hand to hand with shields, House Harkonnen used ballistic artillery weapons to collapse the entrance to the caves, trapping the shielded Atreides inside. The Baron Harkonnen prided himself on his use of "ancient" weapons.

8. *Dune* famously was the first fiction book published by Chilton books, which was a long-standing auto-repair-manual publisher. The editor at Chilton had enjoyed reading the serialization of *Dune* so much that he reached out to Herbert, asking to expand and publish the book (Brian Herbert, *Dreamer of Dune*, New York: MacMillan Press, 2004). It seems likely that the heavily technological aspects of *Dune* made it an easier fit for Chilton as a publisher, though the editor at Chilton eventually lost his job when sales did not increase as quickly as planned.

9. It's possible that there are some computer algorithms that exist in the artifacts described above, just as our cars use algorithms and math to enable cruise control and anti-lock brake technologies. But such calculations would be about how an object functions and responds to its immediate environment, and would not be making broader calculations or simulations of the broader world. The technologies are still tightly linked to the human user's intentions.

10. *Dune*, 180.

11. *Dune*, 312.

12. Venkatesh Narayanamurti and Toluwalogo Odumosu, *Cycles of Invention and Discovery* (Cambridge: Harvard University Press, 2017).

13. *Dune*, 11, 13, 14, 15.
14. The larger narrative of *Dune* does focus on how pain can be used by others against the broader needs of humanity: the Harkonnen enemies of the Atreides seek their own benefit and power, and routinely inflict pain on others to manipulate them.
15. *Dune*, 17.
16. There are some instances where society views certain technologies as of questionable ethical values, such as those who view the existence of nuclear weapons as being undesirable. Others pass ethical restrictions on the use of stem cell technologies in research. There are also other examples of ethics applied to technology. The science and society scholar Jameson Wetmore has researched on how the Amish, a church fellowship group in the United States, have a set of moral values about what are acceptable technologies to use. But even for the Amish, the ban is not so much about inherent moral values of technology: "the foremost reason the Amish carefully regulate technology is to preserve their culture." See Jameson M. Wetmore, "Amish Technology: Reinforcing Values and Building Community," *IEEE Technology and Society Magazine* 26 (2007), 10–21.
17. Of course, such abilities are greatly assisted in *Dune* by use of the spice melange, which one could view as a technology that shapes human beings, enabling them to do it.
18. In the non-canon *Dune Encyclopedia*, Herbert said the "secret" of Butler was revealed: Jehanne Butler was a pregnant Bene Gesserit woman who lost her daughter because a machine from Richese had determined that the fetus was "too deformed to survive." They found that computer algorithms had been encouraging many unjust abortions, and more broadly that the "degree to which machines controlled the population of Richese, and had altered the emotional and intellectual characteristics of its inhabitants over centuries, was literally incredible." Butler found that religious priests took her anti-"thinking machine" vision much farther than she intended, with the Jihad so consisting of thousands of scattered commanders who were united by a "hatred for the machines they could neither understand nor replace." Willis Everett McNelly ed., *The Dune Encyclopedia: The Complete, Authorized Guide and Companion to Frank Herbert's Masterpiece of the Imagination* (New York: Berkley Books, 1984), 1, 138, 143.
19. Paul Humphreys has studied the "epistemic opacity" of simulations, or the way in which a simulation creates knowledge in ways that are unseeable ("opaque") to a human. Paul Humphreys, "The Philosophical Novelty of Computer Simulation Methods," *Synthese* 169 (2009), 615–626.
20. Conscious robots might wield great power, and we could imagine that humans want to mitigate them from taking power. But recall that Mohiam doesn't treat "conscious robots" as self-serving AI, like the Terminator, which humanity must fight. She's concerned about AI that enables other wrong-seeking humans.
21. I am not treating as canon the sequel and prequel books by Brian Herbert and Kevin J. Anderson, and have not examined them in detail. They shift the impetus of the Butlerian Jihad to focus on a "conscious robot"/artificial intelligence named Omnius, that was a much more Skynet-like evil AI, which sought to destroy humanity. They also walk back the moral prohibition

against simple calculator-like computers, attributing that to an overzealous follower of the Jihad, Rayna Butler. These changes seem contrary to Mohiam's views on the Jihad discussed here, and to me diminish the subtlety and value of *Dune* as a reflection on technology and ethics. Tying back to the earlier footnote on the non-canon *Dune Encyclopedia*, Herbert and Anderson also assumed that Butler lost a child as an impetus for the Jihad, although their machine's role in the death is much more intentionally evil.

22. Carl Mitcham, "The True Grand Challenge for Engineering: Self-knowledge," *Issues in Science and Technology* 31:1 (2014), at https://issues.org/perspectives-the-true-grand-challenge-for-engineering-self-knowledge.

23. I've offered some deliberations about what humanity's goals should be in exploring space, while others talk about what types of values we want to create through making everyday engineered artifacts. Pierre Bertrand, Zachary Pirtle, and David Tomblin, "Participatory Technology Assessment for Mars Mission Planning: Public Values and Rationales," *Space Policy* 42 (2017), 41–53. Shannon Vallor, *Technology and the Virtues: A Philosophical Guide to a Future Worth Wanting* (New York: Oxford University Press, 2016).

24. Zachary Pirtle and Zoe Szajnfarber, "On Ideals for Engineering in Democratic Societies," in Diane P. Michelfelder, Byron Newberry, and Qin Zhu eds., *Philosophy and Engineering: Exploring Boundaries, Expanding Connections* (New York: Springer, 2017), 99–112.

25. I appreciate significant comments and edits from Jared Moore, Ryan Britt, and Katelyn Kuhl. On the role of science fiction, see also: Malka Older and Zachary Pirtle, "Imagined Systems: How the Speculative Novel Infomocracy Offers a Simulation of the Relationship Between Democracy, Technology, and Society" in Zachary Pirtle, David Tomblin, and Guru Madhavan eds., *Engineering and Philosophy: Reimagining Technology and Social Progress* (New York: Springer, 2021), 323–340.

THE WISDOM OF MUAD'DIB: MIND, MEMORY, AND INTERPRETATION IN *DUNE*

9

"Thou Shalt Make a Human Mind in the Likeness of a Machine"

Imitation, Thinking Machines, and Mentats

Tomi Kokkonen, Ilmari Hirvonen, and Matti Mäkikangas

Alan Turing (1912–1954), the father of theoretical computer science, ended his important article "Computing Machinery and Intelligence" on an optimistic note: "We may hope that machines will eventually compete with men in all purely intellectual fields."[1] Frank Herbert's *Dune* novels show a fictional future universe in which Turing's dream turned out to be a nightmare. In *God Emperor of Dune*, Leto II explains to Moneo why people destroyed thinking machines in the Butlerian Jihad: "Humans had set those machines to usurp our sense of beauty, our necessary selfdom out of which we make living judgments."[2] Sadly, Herbert never reveals the specifics behind the Great Revolt; his scarce comments on the matter have led to different interpretations of the Jihad. After Herbert's death, his son, Brian, continued co-writing *Dune* novels with Kevin J. Anderson. In their prequel trilogy, the *Legends of Dune*, machines tried to enslave humankind, and this sparked the Crusade. However, a less literal, more metaphorical meaning of "enslavement" is worth looking into.

One way of reading Leto II's account of the Butlerian Jihad is through a legend told in Plato's (429–347 BCE) dialogue *Phaedrus*.[3] In this dialogue, Socrates (469–399 BCE) describes a discussion between two Egyptian gods: Theuth, the creator of writing, and Thamus, the king of the gods. Theuth praises writing, suggesting it will improve memory. Thamus insists that it will have the opposite effect: people will no longer need to remember things because they can rely on written signs and markings. Plato agrees with Thamus that we lose something significant when we outsource a crucial human characteristic like memory to technology. In Brian Herbert and Anderson's Duniverse, people were likewise enslaved by machines when they handed their thinking processes to their devices. Humans gave up their autonomy in an ironic turn.

Plato's and Thamus' view is supported by dialogue in *God Emperor of Dune*. Leto II discusses an Ixian machine with Siona. He asks, "What do such machines really do? They increase the number of things we can do without thinking. Things we do without thinking – there's the real danger. Look at how long you walked across this desert without thinking about your face mask." Siona responds that he should have warned her about the mask, to which Leto laconically replies: "And increased your dependency."[4]

The Butlerian Jihad sought humanity's independence from machines, but it wasn't necessarily true that the Great Revolt was sparked by the literal enslavement of people. When Reverend Mother Gaius Helen Mohiam tests Paul Atreides's humanity in *Dune*, she briefly mentions what lay in the background of the Crusade: "Once men turned their thinking over to machines in the hope that this would set them free. But that only permitted other men with machines to enslave them."[5] In other words, the machines didn't enslave humankind; they merely enabled slavery by letting some people seize power from others who had ceased to think for themselves.

The Imitation Game

Whatever the specific reason for the Great Revolt, it resulted in zealous opposition to artificial intelligence (AI). The Orange Catholic Bible (OCB), the key religious text in the *Dune* universe, forbids the creation of machines that imitate human thinking: "Thou shalt not make a machine in the likeness of a man's mind."[6] The OCB focuses on human mental abilities – especially computation, reason, and logic – that have a status that machines should not emulate. These abilities are what make humans special. They separate us from other animals and machines, giving us a unique status among all other natural beings. Creating a machine with human-like mental abilities would therefore endanger human uniqueness. The OCB's theological doctrine echoes the prohibition on creating images of God, or "idolatry" in Jewish, Islamic, and Christian spiritual traditions. The conviction is that humans should not strive to imitate or compete with God as a creator. In many religious traditions, worshipping an idol is not seen as giving reverence to a deity through the idol but rather replacing the deity altogether. The worry is that the idol becomes the object of worship rather than a mere representation. As physical objects, idols are fundamentally human creations. If an idol becomes an object of worship, humans would have essentially created God and given it a particular shape and form. In Herbert's universe, divine imitation and creation are presented in conflicting ways: on the one hand, they are strictly prohibited, on the other, they are aspirations for key characters.

Despite the prohibition on artificial intelligence in the Duniverse, there is still an obvious need for it. This problem has an ingenious solution: the Mentat. The aspiration to develop humans with machine-like intellectual capabilities – the training of Mentats – resembles what's called *imitatio Dei*, the drive to become more godlike by improving yourself. But what would it even mean for a machine to think? How would we know if we encountered an automaton with a mind like ours?

Herbert does not answer these questions. In looking for answers elsewhere, we could investigate how Alan Turing proposed a test for thinking computers. He calls it "the imitation game," also known as "the Turing test." The game goes as follows: in a room, there are two humans and a computer. One of the humans and the computer are hidden from the other person, who poses questions to both the hidden computer and the hidden human. The object of the game is to see if the question-poser can figure out which one of the other "players" is a human being and which is the computer. There are no restrictions on the questions that the interrogator can ask during the game.[7]

In a nutshell, the game is supposed to show us the circumstances under which we'd say that a machine thinks. Turing suggests that if a computer could imitate the answers of a human being so well that it would fool another human, then we could say, "Aha, these are the capabilities that we associate with thinking." Notice, however, that the test doesn't tell us whether a machine *does* think or even can *simulate* thinking; it just shows us what it means to say that a machine thinks. In fact, according to Turing, it's pointless to ask whether a computer can *really* think:

> The original question, "Can machines think?" I believe to be too meaningless to deserve discussion. Nevertheless I believe that at the end of the century the use of words and general educated opinion will have altered so much that one will be able to speak of machines thinking without expecting to be contradicted.[8]

Turing assumes that a computer's best strategy for winning the imitation game is to give answers that a human being would naturally give. Such a suggestion has raised several objections. Could a machine, for instance, behave in a manner that would convince us that it has fallen in love or that it has a sense of humor or has made mistakes and has moral convictions. Could a computer convince us that it has the ability to be creative, that it has enjoyed the taste of strawberries, understood poetry, and so on? It seems like a rather tall order to build a machine that could do such things or even persuade us that it could do them. Turing, however, is not convinced that it's impossible to create such a machine. For example, you could program a computer so that it occasionally seems to miscalculate to look more human. Most of the other possible shortcomings are, according to Turing, merely due to limitations in storage capacity. He believes that when computers' memory expands sufficiently, they will be able to fool us into thinking that they can perform these functions or even genuinely do them.[9] Only time will tell whether Turing is right or not.

Assessing the capacity to think by the behavior of a machine trying to appear human might sound odd. After all, isn't thinking an unobservable mental process? Turing doesn't deny that human thinking involves psychological processes. In fact, he agrees that there are many differences between brains and digital computers. But an explanation of *why something can think* is different from understanding *what we mean when we say* that something thinks. Suppose that machines take over some of the jobs that humans engage in when they think. Why wouldn't we extend the concept of thinking to include these machines? Current computers already serve as calculators and schedule planners but, perhaps in the future, they will perform more sophisticated tasks. They might even take over simple human jobs, such as the duties of a bank teller or a bus driver. Some have even suggested that machines could collect and analyze information or even do scientific research on behalf of humans. If we believe that these tasks require thinking and that future computers could take care of them, then surely we've got to admit that computers are capable of thinking in those situations.

Turing was not alone in thinking about thinking. For example, Ludwig Wittgenstein (1889–1951) also said that what was key was the observable standards for thought. However, unlike Turing, Wittgenstein did not consider it possible that machines could think. He even wrote: "Turing's 'machines.' These machines are *humans* who calculate."[10] Now, it would be easy to dismiss Wittgenstein as just being narrow-minded and forgive him for being unable to foresee the future of computer science. But this would be too hasty. Wittgenstein's criticism is not that we have a lack of evidence, but instead is about our concept of thinking itself:

> Could a machine think? – Could it be in pain? – Well, is the human body to be called such a machine? It surely comes as close as possible to being such a machine. But surely a machine cannot think! – Is that an empirical statement? No. We say only of a human being and what is like one that it thinks.[11]

Wittgenstein claims that saying a machine could think is a category mistake. In his mind, if it were possible to make a machine think, it would no longer really be a machine. A category mistake is committed when someone believes that a thing belongs to a category when it actually doesn't. For example, the question "How many in a dozen?" makes perfect sense since the answer is 12. But the question "How much is green?" is nonsensical because the word "green" does not express a quantity. Another way to make a category mistake is to say that a thing has a property that could not possibly belong to it. For instance, it would be ridiculous to ask someone to draw a circular rectangle simply because no angular shape can be round.

For Wittgenstein, thinking and other mental activities are *normative* – something like *following rules*. Thinking is not just a brain process in which certain inputs guarantee certain outputs. We don't say that our pocket calculators and laptops are "thinking," because they merely do what we (and their manufacturers) have programmed them to do.

Instead, reasoning is goal-oriented: a person thinking rationally tries to accomplish something, and they can fail in the attempt. When they are working right, computers act according to rules, but they are not *intentionally* following them. To understand the difference between intentional and unintentional action, it is good to remember that not all causal processes are deliberate actions. If, for example, there are domino blocks in a row, each of which knocks down the next, they are not acting intentionally. None of them is trying to knock down the block in front of it. Likewise, someone's actions may be in accordance with a rule, even if they are not trying to follow any rules. It is possible, for instance, that when someone starts to walk, they always take their first step on their left foot. The person in question might be totally oblivious about this. Therefore, they are not intentionally trying to follow the rule "take your first step with your left foot." It's merely something that they always just happen to do. Wittgenstein sees computers and other machines more like domino blocks. They don't have a specific rule in mind that they try to fulfil. Instead, they are merely part of a chain of causes and effects.

One thing that separates thinking from just manipulating symbols – what calculators do – is the possibility of making *mistakes*. A computer or a calculator can *malfunction*. But its malfunctioning is only wrong from our perspective, because the machine's failure to work properly stands in the way of our goals for using it. Whether functioning or malfunctioning, a laptop doesn't strive to do anything. It's simply part of a chain of input/output, cause and effect that starts with buttons being pushed and ends with symbols on a screen. Depending on what a computer user's intention is, something that would count as a malfunction from one perspective – for example, a computer virus – could be seen as proper functioning from another.

It's not just that computers fail to have goals or intentions. They also don't *justify* (that is, offer reasons) for their conclusions. If they seem to, this happens according to their programming. Thinking creatures – like human beings – can correct, check, and justify their actions by referring to rules. Besides this, Wittgenstein insists that thinking creatures will also behave in ways that make it possible for other thinkers to treat them as capable of a wide variety of other mental processes – like wishing or sorting through confusion. Turing doesn't agree with Wittgenstein's strict criteria for what we'd call thinking, and we don't believe that Wittgenstein's view is true about the minds of thinking creatures in Duniverse, either.

Opposing Thinking Machines

The world of *Dune* includes supernatural elements, but Herbert's perspective is mostly naturalistic – that is, compatible with the science of the time. Thinking machines are nothing magical. Machines in Herbert's universe may be technologically advanced, but they are always just tools. They're never used to do human cognitive tasks, no matter how trivial. But if they did, why would this be dangerous? And is the command "thou shalt not make a machine in the likeness of a human mind" just a religious taboo, or even superstition?

The Duniverse doesn't provide clear answers. But as artificial intelligence takes over more and more areas of our own lives, worries (and hopes) resembling those in *Dune* are emerging. Some worry about the abuse and control of people by AI. For instance, algorithms collect information about us on the internet and bias what we see in social media, search engines, and online shopping sites. This affects our thinking and behavior. It opens doors to manipulation for political or commercial purposes, as well as unintended consequences. As the application of AI technology expands, potential problems increase as well. Another source of concern is the lack of transparency in decision-making. If machines replace humans in, say, medical diagnosis or steering a car, we might not have access to the reasons behind these systems' decisions. Also, who's to be held morally accountable when things go wrong due to a decision made by AI? The Butlerian Jihad takes place in a future in which AI systems and machines controlled by them are vastly more advanced – and the potential problems are much more severe.

Paralleling the Butlerian Jihad, the fear that machines might replace humans arose during the first Industrial Revolution (1760–1840), which was accomplished with steam engines. Then, the Luddites – a group of British textile workers and weavers – sought to destroy machines that sped up production, not because of technophobia, but because of serious questions about the machines' social and economic impacts. Machines were seen to be replacing human skills in ways that transformed society for the worse. For instance, machines replaced highly skilled artisans, and those who had to operate the machines were forced to do tedious and monotonous work that lacked expressivity and personality. Humans needed to adapt to the machine world by becoming more machine-like themselves. Furthermore, industrialization lowered the number of people needed for production, and many people were marginalized, creating a new kind of impoverished underclass. The second Industrial Revolution (1870–1914, powered by electricity) and the recent third revolution (focusing on digitization) pushed the appearance of a machine takeover further, with increasing automation in both industries and in private life, eliciting cries from techno-pessimistic voices. The fourth revolution in AI and machine learning may transform the entire face of human society in ways that have machines taking over some functions of human thinking. While previous technological advances have taken over production industries and farming (in the sense that they have decreased the amount of human work needed), the AI revolution seems to be replacing humans in a more social sphere: service industries, hospitals (with care robots), and old people's homes, as well as entering our private lives in "smart homes" and "smart devices." In addition, AI algorithms have taken on analytical and even decision-making roles and functions in stock market trading and in analyzing scientific data.

These revolutions intensify the need to deal with new and difficult questions, some of them forward-looking. Do we have the right to create sentient beings? To treat them as slaves, as robots in science fiction often are? What are our moral duties toward them? What kind of social status should we give them? During the first industrial revolution, *Frankenstein* by Mary Shelley (1797–1851) posed such questions. Shelley warns about the hubris of becoming a creator and taking God's place. She forces us to consider the moral responsibility we have to a creation like Frankenstein's creature and whether we can live up to that responsibility, and what the implications of the creature having a will of its own might be. This is one fairly skeptical pole of attitudes toward human-created thinkers.

The other pole, we've already seen, is *imitatio Dei*. Humans could be seen as pursuing godlike qualities through the creation of ever-more sophisticated machines in their image. The desire to imitate the divine is rife in the Duniverse: take the mental capacities of Mentats, the Bene Gesserit (especially their program to create the superhuman Kwisatz Haderach), the Guild Navigators, and others. The prudential worry with sentient machines is what Brian Herbert and Kevin J. Anderson had in mind when they drafted the story of the Butlerian Jihad: machines built to be slaves would revolt and take over society.

The final reason for forbidding thinking machines is that transferring thinking from humans to machines diminishes humans. It is sometimes thought that the human mind, with its higher mental abilities, is the core of humanity and human potential, which distinguishes us from mere animals or machines. We can think, understand how things around us function, and we are in control of our own actions, not just reacting to immediate impulses, external or internal to us. Relying on intelligent machines externalizes parts of our thinking. It risks whether we really understand our own condition and takes away some of the autonomy of our action, making it conditional to externalized cognitive processes. Something like this is the reason for the Butlerian Jihad in the "semi-official" *Dune Encyclopedia*: using thinking machines as a substitute for developing one's own mental abilities.[12] This is also in line with how the Bene Gesserit see true humanity. According to them, humankind's dependence on thinking machines makes humanity inferior.

Now, humans are already dependent upon devices, as researchers into *extended cognition* have argued. This fact has led to extraordinary progress in human achievements. Even a small project like writing this chapter relies on books that store information, notebooks to extend memory, and pen and paper to enhance thinking and create more working memory. But all these are passive forms of extending the mind out beyond the brain. A calculator, for example, enables us to make calculations that we simply couldn't do otherwise. But it also stands in the way of actually understanding the mathematical principles that are part of its programming. Heavy reliance upon a calculator can result in the loss of instant recall of basic addition, subtraction, multiplication, and division facts.

Similarly, AI-based "smart home" devices may smooth the stresses of everyday living. At the same time, they are likely to increase our dependency on them and lessen humans' ability to control their own lives. Precisely because these devices make many things easier, they incentivize us to build routines around activities that machines are designed to be helpful with. They may end up structuring our life and putting us in the passenger seat. This kind of development is clearly similar to how humanity's relationship with machines is seen in the *Dune* universe.

Human Thinking Machines

But banning thinking machines, as the OCB dictates, creates a vacuum. A society built on thinking machines that abandons them must make up for the machines' lost functions or collapse. In *Dune*, humans fill that vacuum with schools that teach extraordinary mental skills and amplify existing ones. The Guild Navigators literally replace space flight computers by making complicated calculations that enable safe navigation in space. As it turns out, though, this is not a *replacement* but a *reversion*: in our world, "computer" initially referred to humans specialized in calculating (a use that goes back at least to the seventeenth century). Human computers were an instrumental part of doing science until machines took over the tasks and came to be called "computers" instead. Guild Navigators, with capacities enhanced by spice and training, are "computers" in the term's original, reverted sense. But with their limited functions, the Navigators are narrow-domain computers. Mentats, on the other hand, are all-purpose logical thinkers, universal computers. We could say that Mentats are the nearest equivalents to a Turing machine in Herbert's universe.

Mentats replace machines by use of hard, cold, logical thinking and reasoning with machine-like efficiency. Their capacities include extraordinary skills in memory and perception. Mentats are also trained to approach their target of analysis without preconceptions. They're typically disinterested servants who accomplish their master's goals as efficiently as possible. They are not advisors in the traditional sense but rather tools to impartially dissect a situation. They are not supposed to give subjective opinions and participate in an interactive deliberative process but to give objective knowledge and strategic advice of mathematical accuracy. It's ironic, then, that while Mentats possess nearly superhuman mental capabilities, they function effectively as machines devoid of human inclinations in their social roles, making them less than human. Some Mentats – such as Piter de Vries – were conditioned even further into "twisted Mentats." These Mentats could function wholly without ethical constraints, making them most like computers. So Mentats are the product of a curious piece of circular reasoning: humanity destroyed the thinking machines because they couldn't act within moral boundaries. This, in turn, gave rise to the need to create Mentats. When some Mentats are conditioned further, they more and more resemble the thinking machines that were banned in the first place.

Maybe more of a problem is the fact that the nature of a Mentat is akin to Frankenstein's creature. Society in Herbert's universe is feudal in character and lacks universal human rights. Mentats' role in this society is to be disinterested, thinking machines. They are not full subjects of their thinking, but instruments to extend their masters' thinking capacities, just like artificial thinking machines. They do not engage in thinking about a given subject out of their own goals and for their own reasons, and they don't act upon their own goals and motives, but that of their masters. Who we are, as humans, is partly due to what purposes we choose, what personal judgments we make, and how we think. Our external conditions may restrict our ability to choose to act in accordance with what we think, but it is not a Mentat's role to even decide what to think. Another way to say this is that the Mentat's superhuman skills come at the expense of their human subjectivity. Their thinking is powerful, but they don't think for themselves. They are artificial creatures composed of human capacities.

But it is Paul Atreides who most resembles Frankenstein's creature in *Dune*: he was created by the Bene Gesserit breeding program and Mentat conditioning, with the result that he is made a Messiah with little choice of his own. He also turned against his creators. Just as Frankenstein's creature is a hybrid composed of pieces of the dead, Paul is an interesting hybrid of thinking machine and superhuman Kwisatz Haderach.

In *Dune*, making a human mind in the likeness of a machine results in loss of agency and humanity. Mentats are trained to be disinterested servants, sometimes even to the extent that their capability for ethical reasoning is seen more as a hindrance than an advantage. The creation of humans with machine-like properties also poses questions to the creator: what ethical concerns arise from creating and treating individuals more like things, thinking machines, rather than free persons of equal worth? This relationship between man and machine has an inverse parallel in real life when we consider the possible moral status of beings with artificial intelligence. As the boundary between humans and thinking machines increasingly blurs, there are real-world consequences of how we conceptualize and treat thinking machines. As machines increasingly make decisions for us, humans have to be aware of how algorithms and technological inventions affect our emotions, decision-making, self-reliance, and social interaction. Are machines becoming more and more like humans, or vice versa?

Notes

1. A.M. Turing, "Computing Machinery and Intelligence," *Mind* 59 (1950), 460.
2. *God Emperor of Dune* (London: New English Library, 1981), 282.
3. Plato, *Phaedrus*, in *Plato: Complete Works*, ed. John M. Cooper (Indianapolis: Hackett Publishing Company, 1997), 274d–275b.
4. *GED*, 371.
5. *Dune* (London: Gollancz, 1965), 18.
6. *Dune*, 18.
7. Turing, "Computing Machinery and Intelligence," 433–434.
8. Turing, "Computing Machinery and Intelligence," 442.
9. Turing, "Computing Machinery and Intelligence," 435, 447–449.
10. Ludwig Wittgenstein, *Remarks on the Philosophy of Psychology*, vol. I, trans. G.E.M. Anscombe (Oxford: Basil Blackwell, 1980), §1096.
11. Ludwig Wittgenstein, *Philosophical investigations*, trans. G.E.M. Anscombe, P.M.S. Hacker, and Joachim Schulte (Oxford: Blackwell, 1953), §§359–360.
12. Willis E. McNelly, *The Dune Encyclopedia* (New York: Berkley Books, 1984), 195–196.

10

Herbert's Gholas
Mystical Legends and Scientific Inspiration

Jennifer Mundale

Frank Herbert's gholas are a curious twist on the *golem*, a creature inspired by Jewish theology and folklore.[1] Although Herbert's gholas differ in interesting ways from the traditional *golem*, the historic similarities can enrich and add to our appreciation of these creatures, especially *Dune*'s most famous and enduring ghola, Duncan Idaho. As is often the case with good science fiction, Herbert demonstrates remarkable foresight for many scientific and technological developments that had yet to occur when he wrote the *Dune* series. This chapter will explore Herbert's gholas from both of these perspectives; gholas as an extension of the *golem* tradition and as the anticipation of contemporary breakthroughs in biological science.

Golems

The original *golem* is a conceptually and metaphorically rich kind of creature that has featured in countless stories since the first use of the word "golem" in Psalm 139:16.[2] This Psalm, about the biblical creation story, uses the term *golem* to refer to the first human's state of being as unformed substance. This creature called Adam is brought to life and made fully human only when God breathes a soul into him.[3] The notion of a *golem* as an incomplete being, a proto-human substance, persists throughout ancient and medieval literature.

The "first record of a creation of a Golem by a human being"[4] is found in the Babylonian Talmud. Here, Rava (Abba Ben Rav Hamma, 299–353 CE), a learned merchant, makes a lengthy and extensive study of the Book of Creation (or *Sefer Yatsirah*), an early work of Jewish mysticism. He is guided in his study by a companion, Rabbi Zera, and after practicing the act of creation by making calf "golems," Rava finally creates a *golem* man, without any assistance from Rabbi Zera. The Talmudic account of this

Dune and Philosophy, First Edition. Edited by Kevin S. Decker.
© 2023 John Wiley & Sons, Inc. Published 2023 by John Wiley & Sons, Inc.

creation reads, "Rabha [Rava] created a man and sent him up to R. Zera. The latter spoke to him, and he did not answer. Exclaimed R. Zera: 'I see that thou wast created by one of our colleagues. It is better that thou shouldst be returned to the earth from which thou wast taken.'"[5] Rava's *golem*, though short-lived, is remarkable for existing at all, since it required the use of forbidden knowledge thought to belong exclusively to the divine.

One of the most famous *golem*s in Jewish lore is the "Golem of Prague," said to have been created in the sixteenth century by Rabbi Judah Loew. Its purpose was to protect the Jewish people against persecution stirred, in part, by "blood libel": false and inflammatory claims that Jews ritualistically consumed Christian blood. According to the legend, Rabbi Loew formed a giant man from clay (or in some versions, drew the form of a giant man in the mud of a riverbank) and brought it to life with secret, magical words and rituals. The animation of the clay depended on three Hebrew letters: *aleph, mem, tav* (which spells *emet*, the Hebrew word for truth) that Rabbi Loew inscribed on the forehead of the *golem* (or, in some versions, wrote on a piece of paper and inserted into the mouth). Now animated, the mute but obedient *golem* took up his duties as community protector, which, for a time, he performed well.

Eventually, it became necessary to deactivate the *golem*, either because he had served his purpose, or, in more commonly told versions, because the rabbi lost control and the *golem* became dangerously destructive. To accomplish this, all the rabbi had to do was erase the first letter, *aleph*, from the *golem*'s forehead (or tear the letter from the paper in the mouth), leaving only the letters *mem* and *tav*, which spell the Hebrew word for death, or *met*. This immediately stilled the *golem*. Similarly, *Dune*'s most famous ghola, Duncan Idaho, was also a protector; he too was killed, though he was reconstituted multiple times. More will be said about him below.

Just as the Prague *golem* was designed to serve a specific purpose, *golem* lore also tells of the creation of *golem*s for other purposes, such as for menial labor. Ruth Bienstock Anolik explains how the term "golem" came to take on a new, gendered association:

> Although the primary function of the golem is to save the Jewish people from danger, some golems also assist with homely household duties . . . These more mundane roles invite a reading of the figure of the golem as a veiled code for the woman in Jewish culture. In the Talmudic literature the word "golem" which literally means "unformed substance" is associated with women: "Thus an unmarried woman is called a golem, since her nature is not fully rounded until she is married" . . .; for similar reasons, the word can also "refer to a woman who has not conceived" . . . The golem is traditionally speechless like women in traditional Jewish culture . . .[6]

Anolik adds that the *golem* legend "works to limit the threat of female power by appropriating to the male rabbi the most powerful and thereby most anxiety-provoking act available to women in a traditional culture: the power derived from biology and sexuality to create life."[7] Golems are created, in part, through the use of magical language, but they are mute and so cannot wield it themselves. This, too, notes Anolik, is similar to the plight of the female in traditional culture. Women are prohibited from higher learning of any kind, especially knowledge of the arcane. They are banned from full participation in religious activities, and are themselves "ultimately subject to the linguistic power of the male rabbi."[8]

Beyond Talmudic legend and folklore, other *golem*-like creatures appear throughout myth and literature. One kind of story involves bringing a statue, puppet, or human-like mechanism to life. For example, one of the oldest myths of this kind is the story of an ancient Greek sculptor, Pygmalion, who renders his vision of a perfect woman in marble; with a kiss (and the divine intervention of Aphrodite), he brings her to life. Pinocchio is a modern example, as are his evil cousins who show up in contemporary horror shows featuring possessed or malicious dolls. These examples feature humanoid forms made of inorganic materials that are animated through the use of magic, divine intervention, or some other supernatural power.

Even more similar to Herbert's gholas are creatures made from organic tissue that is animated or reanimated, through either supernatural or scientific means. The main difference between such creatures and traditional *golem*s, of course, is the starting material: original *golem*s are made from earth, whereas these creatures begin with organic tissue. Examples of this kind are the zombies and mummies of classic horror and Frankenstein's monster. Like *golem*s, the mummies of fiction are brought (back) to life using magical incantations, often uttered unwittingly by unbelieving or ignorant explorers unaware that they are unleashing ancient magic once known to a privileged few. Frankenstein's monster, from Mary Shelley's 1818 *Frankenstein, or the Modern Prometheus*, lives up to the "modern" in the title: Victor Frankenstein was a man of science, not mysticism or superstition. His *golem*-like creature begins as an assemblage of cadaver parts reanimated by a bolt of lightning. In other respects, though, he echoes the *golem* legend, as many cultural and literary critics have noted.

*Golem*s and Gholas

*Golem*s in the Rava and Prague legends, as well as others common to early Jewish folklore, are created with word magic, and are ultimately controlled and destroyed with words. *Golem* creators are exclusively male; they have appropriated the female power to create life and carefully guard the secrets of this power. Their secrets are protected not just from females, but from any community outsiders. *Golem*s are often created for some purpose such as the defense of a community or menial labor. Finally, *golem*s of legend often escape the control of their creators, become destructive, and have to be destroyed.

Herbert's gholas, though existing thousands of years in the future, reflect all of these traditional elements. The creators of the gholas, the Tleilaxu, retain their closely guarded, highly secretive knowledge, just as the *golem* creators of the legends. The Tleilaxu are all male, and are a counterpoint to the exclusively female Bene Gesserit and Honored Matres. For millennia, the Tleilaxu are the exclusive creators of gholas, until the last book of the series, when the Bene Gesserit strike a bargain to pry the essential secrets of ghola creation from the last Tleilaxu master, a character named Scytale. During the process of ghola creation, the Tleilaxu insert a hidden command so that a ghola master can imprint the ghola, after its "birth," to respond to his vocalizations in the form of singing or whistling sounds. Gholas, like *golem*s, are created for a specific purpose – usually one that serves the political goals of the Tleilaxu.

Shocking details of how the Tleilaxu create gholas are only hinted at in the first books of the series. When Herbert reveals the true horror of the process in the last two books, ghola creators emerge as forceful examples of Anolik's point about the male assumption of female, life-creating power. As we know from the beginning, the Tleilaxu grow gholas in what they call "axlotl tanks."[9] Using as little as a single cell from the cadaver of the original, the ghola grows into a fully formed, physical copy of the original. As Herbert gradually reveals, these "tanks" themselves are alive. But what are they? In *Heretics of Dune*, Odrade, the Bene Gesserit Reverend Mother asks, "What if the axlotl tanks are not . . . tanks?" and "Who has ever seen a Tleilaxu female?"[10] Her suspicion that the tanks are the distorted remains of Tleilaxu females, forced into uterine surrogacy, is gradually confirmed, though never fully detailed, in *Heretics* and *Chapterhouse: Dune*. In the final book, memories of the axlotl tanks dimly float to the surface of the ghola Idaho's mind: "[Mother Superior Odrade's] question sent his thoughts into the misty probings that caused him to imagine strange things about the Tleilaxu – great mounds of human flesh softly visible to the imperfect newborn eyes, blurred and unfocused images, almost-memories of emerging from birth canals. How could that accord with *tanks*?"[11] Axlotl tanks seem to be living wombs that are controlled, manipulated, and exploited; we never learn how much, if any, of the original female being is left, apart from her womb. Perhaps the horror is more effective if left to the imagination. Certainly, though, this is a feature of gholas in which Herbert magnifies, rather than merely echoes, the legendary *golem*s.

Advanced Ghola Making: Duncan Idaho

Duncan Idaho appears in all six books of the original series, and Herbert develops his character more than any other ghola in the Duniverse. Idaho offers us the best glimpse of how Herbert conceives of these fascinating creations, and he also represents the pinnacle of ghola-making as a part of Herbert's futuristic vision of biological possibilities not yet realized.

In *Dune*, of course, Duncan appears as his human, non-ghola self. He's a sword master, pilot, and gifted fighter who serves House Atreides, and specifically, Duke Leto. He's also an ambassador to the Fremen of Arrakis and both mentor and guardian to the Duke's son, Paul Atreides (the future Muad'Dib, and the Kwisatz Haderach), whom he trains in different forms of combat and military strategy. At the end of the first book, Duncan is killed during an attack on Arrakis by the Harkonnens, but his sacrifice helps ensure the escape of Paul and his mother, Jessica. Since Paul's father was also assassinated in the midst of the attack, Paul becomes the new Duke and head of the House Atreides. It is only in the second book, *Dune Messiah*, that Paul's trusted friend Duncan Idaho returns, but as a ghola named Hayt. Idaho's body was collected by the enemy and found its way to the Tleilaxu, who made Hayt and gave him to Paul as a gift. This gift, however, was orchestrated by a group of conspirators, including the Tleilaxu, who seek to kill Paul. In Hayt's case, the conspirators programmed him to respond to the voice of a character named Bijaz, who is secretly a Tleilaxu Master. Using the special, singing vocalizations mentioned above, he controls Hayt and can order him to kill Paul – or so he thinks.

Hayt, at first, seems to be similar to what we today would call a clone. Except for his eyes, which are metallic, Hayt's appearance is identical to Idaho. When the Tleilaxu produced him, ghola technology had been in development for presumably thousands of years. Despite this, they had been unable to make a ghola who retained memories of their cellular donors. The Tleilaxu could, however, manipulate some features of the ghola while in the tank. They could enhance mental abilities, for example, and thus the first ghola of Duncan was made a Mentat, a sort of human computer with extraordinary thinking capacity. What truly set Hayt apart from other gholas was that he was the first to recover his memories of his human original, Duncan Idaho. This occurs as a result of conflicting impulses and trauma within Hayt after Bijaz orders him to kill Paul. In the end, it's his love and loyalty to House Atreides that win Hayt's inner conflict. The Tleilaxu fail in their assassination attempt, but succeed in their advancement of ghola technology. In each ghola incarnation of Idaho, the new creation had access to the memories of the original human. In a further development of the Tleilaxu's skill, the last Idaho of the series also had memories of all the other Idaho gholas, having been regenerated from cells secretly taken and stored, over millennia, from previous Idaho gholas.

At the end of *Chapterhouse: Dune*, we learn that the last Tleilaxu Master, Scytale, along with the most recent ghola of Idaho, a military strategist, have escaped in a ship that can't be tracked. Embedded in his body, Scytale carries a nullentropy capsule, a special preservation chamber with cells from all the major characters in the *Dune* series to that point. They can all be recreated. Although Herbert died before completing any further books in the series, it's not hard to see the parallels between the nullentropy capsule and the attempt to genetically sequence and resurrect extinct species through their last genetic records. Fictional parallels include *Jurassic Park*, where dinosaurs are cloned from cells taken from ancient dinosaur remains. Realistic examples abound in the popular news; scientists report projects to clone extinct creatures such as wooly mammoths from cells of bodies preserved in ice, or Tasmanian tigers from cells taken from the last known specimens.[12]

When *Dune Messiah* was published in 1969, genetic engineering, even of a primitive sort, was still four years away. There was, of course, the old-fashioned method of genetic manipulation through selective breeding, something that also plays an important role in the *Dune* series. Cloning *of a sort* occurred as early as 1885, when Hans Dreisch shook apart two-celled sea urchin embryos into single-celled embryos that each went on to develop into a fully formed sea urchin. By the time *Dune* was published 80 years later, scientists had cloned tadpoles by nuclear transfer, that is, by removing the nucleus from a cell taken from a tadpole, transferring it into a frog egg emptied of its existing nucleus, and growing that egg into a clone of the original tadpole. There was a glimpse of the future in these experiments. Yet it would not be until 1996, more than a decade after the last book of the original *Dune* series, that the first mammal, Dolly the sheep, was cloned from a sheep's *adult* somatic cell, as opposed to an embryonic stem cell. An adult somatic cell is just a cell of the body that is already specialized for whatever it's part of (skin, muscle, kidney, etc.). An embryonic stem cell is taken at such an early stage of development (just days after fertilization) that it is capable of becoming any kind of tissue: it hasn't specialized yet. Making a clone from an adult somatic cell is more difficult, but scientists have discovered how to shock the nucleus of the somatic cell back to an undifferentiated state that enables it to divide and grow into a clone of the original. Gholas are made from adult somatic cells, not embryonic stem cells, so Herbert's gholas were an intriguing fictional forecast in this respect. Whether science ultimately creates human clones (from adult somatic cells) or human gholas (from cadaver cells), it seems unlikely that either would be capable of recovering the memories of its human original through cloning alone. Yet, here, too, Herbert's imagination might not be so farfetched.

Flatworms and Caterpillars

Gholas make questions about personal identity and personal continuity through time more complex and more interesting. The *Chapterhouse* ghola of Idaho reveals his views on the matter in an exchange with the Bene Gesserit Mother Superior:

> Odrade said: "Tell me about those other lives."
> "Wrong. I think of them as one continuous life."
> "No deaths?"

He let a response form silently. Serial memories: the deaths were as informative as the lives. Killed so many times by Leto himself!
"The deaths do not interrupt my memories."
"An odd kind of immortality," she said.[13]

From Idaho's point of view, it's a mistake to think of his thousands of ghola incarnations as separate beings. They are all one, to him, because he remembers being all of them. This idea of continuity of memory as the basis for personal identity over time is famously associated with John Locke (1632–1704). In *An Essay Concerning Human Understanding*, in a chapter titled "Identity and Diversity," Locke wonders "what *Person* stands for." Locke writes that it "is a thinking intelligent Being, that has reason and reflection, and can consider it self as it self, the same thinking thing in different times and places." Further, "as far as this consciousness can be extended backwards to any past Action or Thought, so far reaches the Identity of the *Person*; it is the same *self* now it was then."[14] So it seems likely that Locke would agree with Idaho's self-assessment.

For modern biological research, Herbert's gholas have qualities that are much sought after; that is, a being in which both body *and* memory regenerate from cells of the original. In the humble, real-world flatworm (planaria), scientists actually find this possibility. In fact, Tal Shomrat and Michael Levin report that "planarians are the only molecularly tractable system in which memory and brain regeneration can be studied in the same animal."[15]

In the 1960s, studies began to appear that involved retained "memory" in planaria that self-regenerated after head amputation. Recent work by Shomrat and Levin is even more compelling. As they explain: "Nearly 55 years ago it was demonstrated that planarians could be trained to learn a task, and following amputation of the head, the animals regenerating from the original tail sections remembered the original training." These findings suggest that "some memory may be stored outside of the head and imprinted on the new brain during regeneration."[16] Their own research appears to support this claim. Though it is impossible to know how much of this early material Herbert may have come across, it was available, in its infancy, when he began to develop his unique brand of "golem."

Discoveries involving moths (Lepidoptera) are similarly intriguing. In 2008, Douglas J. Blackiston, Elena Silva Casey, and Martha R. Weiss demonstrated the continuity of memory between the late caterpillar stage and the fully formed moth.[17] In other words, a moth can remember some of what it learned as a caterpillar. The researchers trained a fifth-developmental-stage tobacco hornworm caterpillar with "an electrical shock associatively paired with a specific odor in order to create a conditioned odor aversion," with the result that the "larvae learned to avoid the training odor, and that this aversion was still present in the adults [moths]."[18] The associative learning they were looking for did not appear with caterpillars at a younger stage, suggesting that "post-metamorphic recall involves regions of the brain that are not produced until later in larval development."[19]

The late-stage caterpillar with which they worked was at the stage just prior to pupation, which is then followed by the emergence of the fully formed moth.[20] During pupation, the moth digests itself and liquifies. Metamorphosis from caterpillar into moth rebuilds the body from the level of cells and cell clusters in a process still not fully understood. Although unlike gholas with respect to the change in physical form, caterpillars are similar in their preservation of memory during regeneration. Current research suggests that, for these creatures, memory can be found at the level of cells or cell clusters.

Key to Herbert's ghola, as well as to flatworms and caterpillars, is the continuity of cellular substance, which produces continuity of memory (though only in primitive form in worms and moths). Duncan Idaho inspires us to ask questions about the nature of memory: where does it reside in the organism? And what counts as an actual memory (as opposed to an epigenetic change or hormonal influence)? The implications of research in primitive, real-world ghola-like creatures need to be drawn with caution and rigor, as this subject can be easily sensationalized. Nonetheless, in drawing inspiration from popular literature, maybe we can speculate more freely. For example, Duncan Idaho is both one and many beings at the same time. Until recently, continuity of memory from one physical body to another was not a realistic prospect. But now that it has been demonstrated in insects, perhaps it could be brought about in mammals. That would potentially raise weighty prospects for personal identity through time.

As we've seen, Herbert's gholas brilliantly include the essential elements of an ancient tradition that have been updated to include both scientific realities and technological innovations yet to be realized. Beyond that, the gholas of *Dune* serve as a stimulating thought experiment, suggesting further questions to ask about personal identity and further possibilities to explore.

Notes

1. Why Herbert uses the term "ghola" instead of *golem* is unclear. Ghola could be a purely *linguistic* evolution of the original *golem*, or it could be a unique name to reflect the evolution of a new kind of *creature*, or perhaps both; a deliberate variation on the original term to reflect a variation on the golem of antiquity. For the present purposes, it is not necessary to sort this out, as the similarities of historical *golem*s to Herbert's creation would invite comparison under any terminology.

2. Elizabeth R. Baer, *The Golem Redux* (Detroit: Wayne State University Press, 2012), 17; different versions of the Bible translate this Psalm somewhat differently. The Hebrew Bible, JPS (Jewish Publication Society) 1917 edition reads:

"Thine eyes did see mine unformed substance, and in Thy book they were all written even the days that were fashioned, when as yet there was none of them." The term "unformed substance," or "embryo" in other versions of the Bible, is the translation of the word *golem*.

3. Moshe Idel, *Golem: Jewish Magical and Mystical Traditions on the Artificial Anthropoid* (Brooklyn: KTAV Publishing House, 2019), 34.

4. Sherwin, *The Golem Legend*, 4, as quoted in Baer, *The Golem Redux*, 18.

5. *Babylonian Talmud, New Edition of the English Translation; Original Text Edited, Formulated, and Punctuated by Michael L. Rodkinson*, Section Jurisprudence (Damages) Tract Sanhedrin (Boston: The Talmud Society, 1918), Sanhedrin 65b.

6. Ruth Bienstock Anolik, *American Gothic Literature: A Thematic Study from Mary Rowlandson to Colson Whitehead* (Jefferson, NC: McFarland and Company, 2019), 237.

7. Anolik, *American Gothic Literature*, 237.

8. Anolik, *American Gothic Literature*, 237.

9. Axolotls are amphibians known for their impressive regenerative powers, able to regrow limbs, organs, and just about everything but their head, should it become lost or damaged. The name of these "axolotl" tanks (also sometimes spelled "axlotl," in the *Dune* series) is understandable, given the regenerative processes that occur in them.

10. Heretics of Dune (New York: Ace, 2019), 513.

11. Chapterhouse: Dune (New York: Ace, 2019), 85.

12. See, for example, Scott Neuman, "Scientists Say They Could Bring Back Woolly Mammoths. But Maybe They Shouldn't," *NPR Science*, September 15, 2021, at https://www.npr.org/2021/09/14/1036884561/dna-resurrection-jurassic-park-woolly-mammoth;
John Pickrell, "Tasmanian Tiger Genome May Be First Step Toward De-extinction," *National Geographic*, December 11, 2017, at https://www.nationalgeographic.com/science/article/thylacine-genome-extinct-tasmanian-tiger-cloning-science.

13. *CHD*, 87.

14. John Locke, *An Essay Concerning Human Understanding*, ed. Peter H. Nidditch (Oxford: Clarendon Press, 1979), 2.27.9.

15. Tal Shomrat and Michael Levin, "An Automated Training Paradigm Reveals Long-term Memory in Planarians and Its Persistence Through Head Regeneration," *The Journal of Experimental Biology* 216 (2013), 3799–3810.

16. Shomrat and Levin, "An Automated Training Paradigm," 3799–3810.

17. Douglas J. Blackiston, Elena Silva Casey, and Martha R. Weiss, "Retention of Memory Through Metamorphosis: Can a Moth Remember What It Learned as a Caterpillar?" *PLoS ONE* 3 (2008), e1736.

18. Blackiston et al., "Retention of Memory."

19. Blackiston et al., "Retention of Memory."

20. Curiously, given the present context, the word "pupa" comes from the Latin word for doll.

11

Psychological Expanses of *Dune*

Indigenous Philosophy, Americana, and Existentialism

Matthew Crippen

Like philosophy itself, *Dune* explores everything from politics to art to life to reality, but above all, the novels ponder the mysteries of mind. Voyaging through psychic expanses, Frank Herbert hits upon some of the same insights discovered by indigenous people from the Americas. Many of these ideas are repeated in mainstream American and European philosophical traditions like pragmatism and existential phenomenology. These outlooks share a regard for mind as *ecological*, which is more or less to say that minds extend beyond the brain into the rest of the body and the surrounding environment.

The cross-cultural strands in *Dune* tie closely to Herbert's life and interests. An outdoorsman born in the Pacific West, he had an abiding bond with a friend from the Quileute tribe, Howie Hansen. Herbert advocated for aboriginal rights and crafted well-intentioned if slightly stereotypical tales about indigenous characters, partly based on his visits with Northwest tribes.[1] Carl Jung (1875–1961), whose idea of collective consciousness echoes aboriginal views, was among Herbert's European influences.[2] So was existential phenomenology, especially as developed by Martin Heidegger (1889–1976). The names of characters in one of Herbert's novels – *The Santaroga Barrier* – in fact coincide with terms that Heidegger used to articulate how emotionally colored coping with our environment defines our existence.[3] Many indigenous philosophers have treated phenomenology and its American cousin pragmatism in approving ways. More than this, the ideas of North America's first inhabitants seem to have been absorbed by pragmatists and even earlier by transcendentalists like Ralph Waldo Emerson (1803–1882) and Henry David Thoreau (1817–1862).[4]

These different philosophies all advance a *place-based psychology*. Anne Waters, herself of mixed tribal heritage, generalizes the mindset of her

Dune and Philosophy, First Edition. Edited by Kevin S. Decker.

people this way: "American Indian consciousness, and hence American Indian identity is . . . interdependent with our land base."[5] Lee Hester, a Choctaw thinker, adds that practices – not mere beliefs – are most important for indigenous thought.[6] American transcendentalists and pragmatists, as well as European phenomenologists, similarly see hands-on practices and environmental interactions as the core of experience. Extending this a little, they sometimes suggest experience isn't individual but instead cultural. "Culture" is here understood as interactions within communities that define our worlds and experiences, as when we talk about the "French experience," "culture" or "world," or the "experience of parenthood."[7] This theme also shows up in American aboriginal outlooks.

Exploring the *Dune* universe, we find everything from land-based concepts of personal identity, to the idea of sharpening the mind through hands-on training, to collective notions of experience in cooperative tribes or through the genetic memory of central characters. The stories explore fate versus free will in cosmic contexts, introducing views from indigenous thought and the pragmatic philosophy of William James (1842–1910). Different forms of spiritualism mingle to shape minds and cultural mixtures around the globe, and the same occurs in the *Dune* series. The customs and personalities of characters fuse elements from Buddhism, Christianity, Hinduism, Judaism, Taoism, and especially Islam. The series not only highlights that religion shapes psychology, but also that faith connects to place, especially paralleling Judeo-Christian-Islamic desert faiths. In capturing these points, the *Dune* novels show that "our values, our lifestyles and even the ways we think and feel have been strongly influenced by our locations in history and geography. The study of the human mind is fundamentally the study of place."[8]

Place Is Where the Mind Is

Dune describes Paul Atreides's ancestral castle on the planet Caladan just before we meet him, linking personal identity to place. These connections are echoed in the names of characters. Duncan Idaho recalls the US state and the Scottish Highlands, evoking rugged unorthodoxy. Duke Leto shares his name with a Greek goddess who searched for a place to give birth, eventually finding the island of Delos. Herbert frequently uses words or variations of them from other languages, even if he doesn't keep their original meanings. His heavy reliance on Arabic words like Paul's Fremen name, Muad'Dib, brings to mind arid lands. In the novelized universe, the name means "kangaroo mouse," a creature admired by tribes on the desert world of Dune for its ability to survive the parched land. "Sihaya" means "desert springtime" and is Paul's intimate name for his beloved Chani; Herbert's son tells us that the word derives from Navajo.[9]

The *Dune* novels shadow Navajo worldviews and those of many other aborigines, who identify themselves according to their mountains, rivers, seas, stars, and animals – in short, their ancestral dwelling places.[10] Black Elk (1863–1950) of the Oglala Lakota spoke of the passage of time in terms of seasonal changes in the land, speaking of the Moon of blooming turnip, of black cherries, falling leaves, growing calf hair, popping trees, frost in tipis, and more.[11] The four directions plus earth and sky also have significance and provide a conceptual framework for religious practices, medicine, and reality itself. Ecological connections are reinforced by rituals like burying the placenta and umbilical cord to mark a covenant between a newborn and the land, or by the sharing of clan names with non-human animals and things like clouds and mountains,[12] which happens in *Dune* when Paul takes Muad'Dib as his Fremen name.

Pragmatists and phenomenologists did not develop land-based philosophies. But they did offer ecological psychologies stressing that we don't see the parts correctly outside of the whole.[13] So white cloth bathed in candlelight will appear yellow if you're peering at an isolated patch through a peephole. Similarly, emotions are only vague pangs if cut off from their sources, like the truck that swerved in front of you or the person you achingly love.[14] Pragmatist William James offered some advice: when inquiring into anything, "the living question always is, 'Where *is* it found?,'" so that "to know an object, is to lead to it through a context which the world supplies" and discern its "embedded character."[15] The first lines of *Dune* give the same guidance for understanding Paul Atreides: "take care that you first place him in his time" and "most special care that you locate Muad'Dib in his place: the planet Arrakis."[16] Just as we don't fully get what desert foxes are outside their habitats, we don't comprehend Paul without grasping Arrakis as essential to his identity – to who he becomes – after arriving from Caladan at age 15.

Desert Identities

Though the climate of the planet Arrakis – otherwise known as Dune – evolves over the 5000-year span of Herbert's novels, the desert is its key feature during Paul's time there. The arid climate shapes everything from vital water-preserving activities like dressing in stillsuits to rituals that reclaim moisture from the dead, which "belongs to the tribe," as the books repeatedly state. The world's vast desert bestows the main basis for the economy: the spice that is found there, valued for its mind-enhancing, life-extending qualities, and because it makes interstellar trade possible by giving Guild Navigators limited prescience so they can safely guide spaceships.

The sandworms make both the spice and the desert they need to survive. They in fact transformed a wet planet into the parched wastes of Dune after ancients introduced them from some other place, as Paul's son Leto II recounts, drawing on his genetic memory.[17] Sandworms can kill people, but are also transportation for the Fremen who ride them. Their teeth are fashioned into crysknives, which have religious significance and are the Fremen's main fighting weapon. Desert dwellers are addicted to the spice because it pervades their air and food. Consuming the spice essence that comes from drowning a sandworm in water, in combination with Paul's genetics, elevates his consciousness, giving him prescience. When the essence – sometimes called the Water of Life – is altered by a Reverend Mother like Jessica or her son Paul (the first male in history with that capacity), it ceases to be poisonous. The Fremen can then use it in spiritual rituals as a psychedelic that fosters a sense of oceanic oneness with the community.

The sandworms affect virtually all aspects of Fremen life and have religious significance, much as the buffalo did for the Lakota and other Great Plains tribes. The Fremen refer to sandworms as "Shai-Hulud," combining Arabic words that together mean "immortal thing." Sometimes they call Shai-Hulud "the Grandfather of the desert," mirroring indigenous customs of referring to important environmental beasts or forces as grandfather or grandmother.[18] Though not quite a deity, there's a sense that Shai-Hulud represents God. Invocation of the name "Shai-Hulud" accordingly shows up in religious rites such as death hymns, as well as everyday speech. This happens almost as frequently and in the same circumstances that Muslims use their many names for God – especially "Allah" – in phrases like *insha'allah*, *masha'allah*, *wallahi*, and *alhamdulilla* – roughly meaning "God willing," "blessings in God's gifts," "I swear by God," and "praise God." In Arabic and the languages of the *Dune* universe, divinely infused words, like language itself, are signposts synchronizing people with each other and their surroundings. Words are also a conduit that believers use to commune with spiritual realms; these realms have physical markers in the environment, whether in fictional sandworms, buffalo, mosques, the holy city of Jerusalem, or a sacred river. All of this together reinforces the identity in ecological philosophies between mind, knowledge, and place.

Bonding in Landscapes

It makes sense that Herbert begins *Dune* by saying that knowing Paul means locating him in his place. Arrakis is an organizing nexus for Paul's stories. It's the world that Paul's father dies on, and its deserts hide the surviving Atreides. It's where Paul gains the allegiance of the unmatched Fremen warriors and meets his love, Chani, among them. It's the source of spice and hence Paul's prescience, so it becomes a nucleus for his spiritual development, not to mention the religious movement that evolves around his person. Dune also forces on him habitual routines, from walking arrhythmically to escape sandworm detection, to Fremen customs of speech, to constant vigilance against assassins. In this way too, the planet sculpts Paul's behavioral tendencies – his personal disposition or character – for "habits are demands for certain kinds of activity; and they constitute the self,"[19] said the pragmatist John Dewey (1859–1952), echoing ancient Greek ideas.

This stress on habits hints at the importance of bodily actions for mental life, with a simple illustration being fingertips gliding across lacquered wood to bring smoothness into experience.[20] Most of our dealings are more complex because our actions are contextualized by social meanings: they involve contact with other people or with human-made things like clothes, chairs, and smartphones. For us, weekend-worlds and hence experiences of partying may come together around bottled beer, Tinder, and dancing. Likewise, the entire culture in the *Dune* universe coalesces around the value of spice.

Most things interest us based on their practical uses. William James said that what we're interested in affects what we see: a carpenter cares for wood and treats oil not as a mess to be cleaned up but as a wood darkener.[21] Heidegger adds that the Old High German word *thing* used to stand for a gathering to deliberate on matters of concern, and for him, these concerns gather worlds around them.[22] At "social gatherings," whether office lunches or the Fremen spice orgies, collectively desired goals gather people and coordinate their behavior. "Experience," for Dewey, is equivalent to culture because it unfolds in the world, and not just in our heads, and because it's forged in community activity.[23] "Experience" in Dewey's cultural sense arises in the communal beat of a concert, or public moods we find ourselves in because we're a member of an angry crowd, or in the collective rhythms of Fremen working in sync.

Indigenous people from the Americas and Africa also stress the collective dimensions of experience.[24] Tribal existence has levels of direct cooperation that make it hard not to celebrate and occasionally mourn the group aspects of life. So, Stilgar – who leads the Fremen clan that takes Paul in – repeatedly exclaims, "we work together!" before mounting a sandworm.[25] It's Paul's first time as the sandworm's mudir – Arabic for "the one in charge" – and he repeats Stilgar's assertion, even mimicking the Fremen leader's speech. For another example, think of when a Fremen fighter proposes joining his band's water with that of the Atreides by rendering the moisture from the dead of the House's troopers, which he says will be done with reverence. He stresses that the "wounded and unwounded must look to the tribe's future."[26] As if to affirm this, a few of his men crash their commandeered 'thopter into a troop carrier, killing themselves but also hundreds of enemies.

The Fremen philosophy is shaped by the unforgiving desert, making them more self-reliant than most. It also teaches the Fremen that those who look only to their own well-being doom themselves by endangering the tribe they need to survive. This echoes Henry David Thoreau, who defended radical individualism, on the one hand, yet, on the other, saw a heavy responsibility arising out of living in an interconnected world, obliging us to recognize that our actions affect people near and far.[27] Both these polarities may have arisen out of indigenous worldviews that provided models for human liberty without undercutting ecological entwinement,[28] outlooks Thoreau studied even while clinging to stereotypes of his day.[29] Like Frank Herbert, Thoreau had mixed cultural influences. He was particularly inspired by Hindu writings like the *Bhagavad Gita*,[30] which suggest that enlightenment brings oneness with the universe, an experience Herbert's Fremen have in their spice orgies and Paul has in his spice trances.

Working Together

Fremen settlements, like traditional tribal villages, embody interconnectivity. They are tightly packed cooperatives lacking soundproof walls and lock-and-key boundaries. The scorching desert leads the Fremen to bury themselves underground in cavern communities called sietches. These unmistakably recall the pueblos the Anasazi built into cliff alcoves in America's western deserts, dwellings which often had seep springs like the Fremen water stores. Ted Jojola of the Isleta Pueblo tribe calls such villages "the collective embodiment of the clanship experiences."[31] Groups within the pueblo contributed differing views that together formed the distinctive identity of the village, which in turn existed in the context of the larger cultural experience of the indigenous group. Fremen society likewise includes individuals and families within sietch villages that knit into the broader experience of the desert community.

Collectively working together remains paramount in clan experience, something Paul's son, Leto II, knows from his youth spent in a Fremen sietch; it appears to instill in him the conviction that "humans are a form of colony organism."[32] Still alive 3500 years later, Leto II repeats the same assertion about the genetically engineered Face Dancers and even himself. In calling himself a "colony creature," he testifies that, like his father, sister Ghanima, aunt Alia, and all the Bene Gesserit Reverend Mothers, he also carries ancestral memories.[33] He can even recall the times of Agamemnon in ancient Greece! Because his mind is composed of jostling personalities, his very identity requires the "solidarity of the colonial group" within him.[34]

By referring to himself as a colony creature, Leto simultaneously gestures to his future destiny. This ties to his past in the desert when he merged with baby sandworms called sandtrout. After covering his skin with them, he began transforming into a sandworm-human hybrid, which extended his life by millennia. Leto's reproductive stage interestingly coincides with his death. This happens when a bridge he's on is attacked, sending him into water below, which is deadly to sandworms and thus to him. Sandtrout, also described as having a colony existence, issue from his dying body, each carrying his psychological essence.[35] Now Leto literally splits into a colony of creatures – known as the "divided God" – spread over the land in an endless dream-consciousness that he has no control over.[36] At the time of his death, Dune had reverted back to a lush, verdant place, but the reintroduction of sandtrout and the sandworms they turn into begins the reversion into a desert planet yet again.

Leto, then, is fashioned by the planet Dune many times over: first, because he learned the desert habits of the Fremen in his youth; second, because he absorbed massive quantities of spice, changing his consciousness; and, third, because he merged with sandtrout. Leto also returns to the land as the divided God. His journey is an emblem for indigenous beliefs that not only see the land as living, breathing, and spiritually imbued, but also as something that supplies wisdom to the living and reabsorbs it upon their return to the earth in death. This is a reason why removing people from ancestral lands or destroying graves is so painful: it cuts them off from the lessons of those who are in the ground.[37] The distress is amplified because the indigenous connection to place is deeper than mere ownership. In an interview, a Navajo woman expressed the incomprehensibility of her removal from Big Mountain, Arizona, remarking: "If we are to make our offerings at a new place, the spiritual beings would not know us. We would not know the mountains or the significance of them. We would not know the land and the land would not know us."[38] As Chief Joseph (1840–1904) suggested, tribes and land belong to one another in the same way that family members do.[39] Accordingly, the land and its living things enter indigenous genealogies, telling people who they are and how they got to where they live.[40] This reiterates and enriches a theme found throughout *Dune*: that knowing something means locating it in its time and place, which also means knowing its wider history.

Fate, Will, and Worldbuilding

Near the beginning of *Dune*, Paul suffers an ordeal with the pain box, which convinces him his hand is being burnt off, even though he's unharmed. With a gom jabbar – a poisonous fingertip needle – readied at Paul's neck, Reverend Mother Gaius Helen Mohiam will kill him if he withdraws his hand. The choice is between enduring pain or dying to escape it, and the purpose is to differentiate between what the Bene Gesserit regard as animals and humans. An animal would act to escape the pain, even if it means destroying itself, whereas a human will look to the future and beyond immediate suffering. This last idea gets close to William James's observation that pursuing "future ends" marks "the presence of mentality."[41] Since passing the test means not being a slave to instinct, this scene also recalls James's claim that free will is "the sustaining of a thought *because I choose* to when I might have other thoughts."[42] The gom jabbar episode initiates a back-and-forth narrative about fate and free will that pervades all six novels in the series.

Much in the *Dune* novels weighs against free will. There's the Bene Gesserit's ability to rapidly appraise psychology and intone their voice in ways that people find impossible to disobey. Worse, the Honored Matres – remnants of the Bene Gesserit from the Great Scattering into the cosmos during the 15 centuries after Leto II's death – elicit addictive sexual ecstasy that completely enslaves victims. Then there's Paul, whose mind sees the future in minute detail, suggesting that events are preordained. His son Leto II is even more powerful, aware of virtually every place and time in the galaxy, over which he also exercises nearly omnipotent control.

But there's some wiggle room: Leto II is occasionally surprised, which typically delights him. This isn't just because he dislikes monotonous predictability, but because he has an entire program, executed over 3500 years, to create a human whose actions he can't predict. Siona, a relative of his long-dead sister, fulfills his project and also orchestrates his murder. As a result, anyone carrying Siona's genes is invisible to prescience, and this makes them freer than most others. After the Great Scattering into unknown cosmic reaches, humans diversify and spread so as to be beyond the control of the small number of surviving sandworms on Dune, which was Leto's goal. Events before this evolution were comparable to closely placed dominos, so that knocking down the first causes the rest to topple. Now events are like dominos packed in groups but with spaces between, so that one cluster can fall without impacting the rest.[43] Even so, the last book ends ambiguously with Daniel and Marty in a garden setting, two odd characters whose control over people in the universe is like a child's over an ant farm.

While we're left uncertain about whether there's free will, this doesn't destine *Dune* characters to inaction. The Fremen exemplify this. On the one hand, they see most things as fated, paralleling Muslims who hold that major events are decreed ahead of time. On the other hand and also like Muslims through history, the Fremen enact daunting agendas like attempting to transform Dune into a lush planet. Echoes of this pervade pragmatism, phenomenology, and transcendentalism, all of which say that we can craft both experiences and the places where we live. Emerson, for instance, wrote, "Nature is not fixed but fluid. Spirit alters, moulds, makes it . . . Every spirit builds itself a house; and beyond its house a world . . . Build, therefore, your own world."[44]

Emerson's proclamation is based on an idea that indigenous thinkers stress: humans aren't fundamentally separate from nature. In fact, the original people of the Americas cultivated everything from the rainforest habitats of Brazil to the Great Plains of Canada and the United States, paralleling ecological transformations that are repeatedly initiated on Dune.[45] Along comparable lines, the Fremen absorb Shai-Hulud into their customs even though sandworms aren't a native species. Inhabitants of the Great Plains similarly adopted non-native horses into their practical and cultural lives, so that the month of May became the Moon of shedding ponies and individuals took names like Crazy Horse and American Horse.[46] Anne Waters carries on this tradition. This is because she's also Jewish and incorporates this religion into her indigenous beliefs,[47] just as Black Elk found no contradiction between Lakota spiritualism and the Catholic faith he later adopted.[48] All of this together fits the indigenous idea, as Waters puts it, that "mind is part of an always changing nature, and hence is subject to all laws of nature," and at the same time, "thinking humans have the capacity to change nature, including human nature."[49]

So, regardless of whether we have free will, we can enact enormous change. It's a trope in the New Testament that faith can move mountains, and this is repeated by religious sages such as Mahatma Gandhi (1869–1948).[50] The theme reoccurs in a Taoist text, where an old man wants to move mountains to make way for a road. When chastised about the infeasibility of the task, he replies: "My descendants will go on forever, but the mountains will get no bigger. Why should there be any difficulty about levelling it?"[51]

This gets straight to the pragmatic point: we can move mountains, or end world poverty, or halt or accelerate climate change if we work collectively together long enough. Just think of the way the citizens of the Duniverse worked together to begin turning their planet back into a lush world, or consider Leto's 3500-year quest to shatter his own prescient grip on the galaxy. This is a core lesson that recurs throughout the *Dune* series.

Notes

1. See Brian Herbert, *Dreamer of Dune: The Biography of Frank Herbert* (New York: Tor, 2003).
2. Simon Guerrier, "The Sleeper Must Awaken: Inside the Mind of Dune," *The Lancet Psychiatry* 1 (2014), 264–265.
3. Martin Heidegger, *Being and Time* [1927], trans. John Macquarrie and Edward Robinson (New York: Harper and Row, 1962).
4. Scott Pratt, *Native Pragmatism: Rethinking the Roots of American Philosophy* (Bloomington: Indiana University Press, 2002); Bruce Wilshire, *The Primal Roots of American Philosophy: Pragmatism, Phenomenology, and Native American Thought* (University Park: Pennsylvania State University Press, 2000).
5. Anne Waters, "Ontology of Identity and Interstitial Being," in Anne Waters ed., *American Indian Thought* (Oxford: Blackwell, 2004), 155.
6. Thurman Lee Hester, Jr., "On Philosophical Discourse: Some Intercultural Musing," in Anne Waters ed., *American Indian Thought* (Oxford: Blackwell, 2004), 263–267.
7. See Matthew Crippen and Jay Schulkin, *Mind Ecologies: Body, Brain, and World* (New York: Columbia University Press, 2020), chapters 1–3.

8. Jesse Prinz, *Beyond Human Nature: How Culture and Experience Shape the Human Mind* (London: Norton, 2012), xi.

9. Brian Herbert, *Dreamer of Dune*, 189.

10. Roma Mere Roberts and Peter R. Wills, "Understanding Maori Epistemology: A Scientific Perspective," in Helmut Wautischer ed., *Tribal Epistemologies: Essays in the Philosophy of Anthropology* (Abingdon: Routledge, 2018), 43–78; Laurie Anne Whitt, Mere Roberts, Waerete Norman, and Vicki Grieves, "Belonging to Land: Indigenous Knowledge Systems and the Natural World," *Oklahoma City University Law Review* 26 (2001), 701–743.

11. Raymond J. DeMallie, *The Sixth Grandfather Black Elk's Teachings Given to John G. Neihardt* (London: University of Nebraska Press, 1984), 291–292.

12. Whitt et al., "Belonging to Land," 701–743.

13. For example, John Dewey, "The Reflex Arc Concept in Psychology," *Psychological Review* 3 (1896), 357–370; Maurice Merleau-Ponty, "Film and the New Psychology" [1947] in *Sense and Non-sense*, trans. Hubert Dreyfus and Patricia Dreyfus (Evanston: Northwestern University Press, 1964), 43–59.

14. John Dewey, *Art as Experience* (New York: Minton, Balch & Company, 1934), chapters 3–4; Merleau-Ponty, "Film and the New Psychology," 43–59.

15. William James, "The Sentiment of Rationality," *Mind* 4 (1879), 331; William James, "The Knowing of Things Together," *The Psychological Review* 2 (1895), 109.

16. *Dune* (New York: Ace, 2005), 3.

17. *Children of Dune* (New York: Ace, 2008), 39.

18. For example, DeMallie, throughout.

19. John Dewey, *Human Nature and Conduct: An Introduction to Social Psychology* (New York: Henry Holt and Company, 1922), 25.

20. See Maurice Merleau-Ponty, *Phenomenology of Perception* [1945], trans. Collin Smith (London: Routledge and Kegan Paul, 1962), 367–368; also see Matthew Crippen, "Enactive Pragmatism and Ecological Psychology," *Frontiers in Psychology* 11 (2020), 2598.

21. James, "Sentiment of Rationality," 319.

22. Martin Heidegger, "The Thing" [1949], in *Poetry, Language, Thought*, trans. Albert Hofstadter (New York: Harper and Row, 1971), 172.

23. For example, John Dewey "Syllabus: Types of Philosophical Thought" [1922–1923], in Jo Ann Boydston ed., *The Middle Works, 1899–1922*, vol. 13 (Carbondale and Edwardsville: Southern Illinois University Press, 1983), 351.

24. For example, V.F. Cordova, "The We and the I," in Anne Waters ed., *American Indian Thought* (Oxford: Blackwell, 2004), 173–181; Matthew Crippen, "Africapitalism, Ubuntu and Sustainability," *Environmental Ethics* 43 (2021), 235–259.

25. *Dune*, 509.

26. *Dune*, 268.

27. Henry David Thoreau, "Civil Disobedience" [1849], in Elizabeth Hall Witherell ed., *Collected Essays and Poems* (New York: Library of America, 2001), 203–224.

28. Charles Mann, *1491: New Revelations of the Americas Before Columbus* (New York: Knopf, 2005), 329–338; Scott Pratt, *Native Pragmatism: Rethinking the Roots of American Philosophy* (Bloomington: Indiana University Press, 2002), 269–275.

29. Lydia Willsky-Ciollo, "Apostles of Wilderness: American Indians and Thoreau's Theology of the Wild," *The New England Quarterly* 91 (2018), 551–591.

30. For example, Henry David Thoreau, *Walden* [1854], in Robert F. Sayre ed., *Thoreau* (New York: Library of America, 1985), 559.

31. Ted Jojola, "Notes on Identity, Time, Space, and Place," in Anne Waters ed., *American Indian Thought* (Oxford: Blackwell, 2004), 92.

32. CD, 269.

33. *God Emperor of Dune* (New York: Ace Books), 236.

34. *GED*, 581.

35. *GED*, 574.

36. *GED*, 303.

37. Whitt et al., "Belonging to Land," 701–743.

38. Whitt et al., "Belonging to Land," 702.

39. Young [Chief] Joseph and William Hare, "An Indian's Views of Indian Affairs," *The North American Review* 128, no. 269 (1879), 412–433; Whitt et al., "Belonging to Land," 701–743.

40. Whitt et al., "Belonging to Land," 701–743.

41. William James, *The Principles of Psychology*, vol. 1 (New York: Henry Holt and Company, 1890), 8.

42. William James, diary entry (April 30, 1870), quoted in Ralph Barton Perry, *The Thought and Character of William James*, vol. 1 (Boston: Little, Brown and Company, 1933), 323.

43. See Matthew Crippen, "William James and His Darwinian Defense of Freewill," in Mark Wheeler ed., *150 Years of Evolution: Darwin's Impact on Contemporary Thought and Culture* (San Diego: San Diego State University Press, 2011), 68–89.

44. Ralph Waldo Emerson, "Nature" [1836], in Joel Porte ed., *Emerson: Essays and Lectures* (New York: Library of America, 1983), 48.

45. Mann, *1491*, chapter 8.

46. See DeMallie, *The Six Grandfather Black Elk,* 292, 322.

47. Waters, "Ontology of Identity," 159.

48. DeMallie, *The Six Grandfather Black Elk*, 66–67.

49. Anne Waters, "Indigeneity, Self-determination, and Sovereignty," *APA Newsletters* 2, no. 1 (2002), 13, 14.

50. Mohandas Gandhi, "Prayer," *Young India: A Weekly Journal* 7, no. 39 (1925), 331.

51. *The Book of Lieh-tzu*, trans. A.C. Graham (New York: Columbia University Press, 1960), 100.

12

Thatched Cottages at Cordeville

Hegel, Heidegger, and the Death of Art in *Dune*

Kevin S. Decker

Maybe you've heard of this backwater, run-of-the-mill, "mostly harmless" planet called "Earth."

In the Duniverse – as in so many space operas set in the distant future – cultures and practices remind us of Earth, but also seem quite alien to it. Some of our best in-the-know authorities in the future of the Duniverse – Emperor Leto II in his *Stolen Journals* and Bene Gesserit Reverend Mother Darwi Odrade – agree that Earth is "gone," it's certainly uninhabited, and perhaps no longer exists, having been struck by a planetoid during the reign of Leto II. The Orange Catholic Bible survives, though. It is the most prominent synthesis of religious thought to have been handed down from Earth. Yet very few cultural artifacts from Earth remain – unsurprising, given that more than 26,000 years have passed since humans were relocated from Old Terra to Ceres. For a similar stretch of time, in the twenty-first century we would have to look back all the way to the Upper Paleolithic, prehistoric cave paintings in Europe and the *Venus of Willendorf*, one of the earliest works of human art. We can ponder the lives and imaginations of those anatomically modern humans who created and venerated this "Venus," but we stand as distant from them in the past as we do from the characters of *Heretics of Dune* and *Chapterhouse Dune* in the future.

It's in these late books by Herbert that we are surprised by the existence of a uniquely significant artifact from Earth's nineteenth century:

> The thing occupied a space on the wall of Taraza's morning room. Ixian artifice had preserved the painting in the finest hermetically sealed frame behind a cover of invisible plaz. Odrade often stopped in front of the painting, feeling each time that her hand might reach out and actually touch the ancient canvas so cunningly preserved by the Ixians. *Cottages at Cordeville*. The artist's name for his work and his own name were preserved on a burnished plate beneath

Dune and Philosophy, First Edition. Edited by Kevin S. Decker.
© 2023 John Wiley & Sons, Inc. Published 2023 by John Wiley & Sons, Inc.

Thatched Cottages at Cordeville (1890), Vincent van Gogh (public domain image: https://commons.wikimedia.org/wiki/File:Vincent_van_Gogh_-_Thatched_ Cottages_at_Cordeville_-_Google_Art_Project.jpg).

the painting: *Vincent Van Gogh*. The thing dated from a time so ancient that only rare remnants such as this painting remained to send a physical impression down the ages. She had tried to imagine the journeys that painting had taken, the serial chance that had brought it intact to Taraza's room.[1]

Two German philosophers, Georg W.F. Hegel (1770–1831) and Martin Heidegger (1889–1976), help us to understand why artworks establish a connection between audience and history, similar to the way in which Odrade experiences perhaps the only human painting left in the universe. Both Hegel and Heidegger would find the lack of art in Herbert's distant future more disturbing than merely the loss of technique and beauty. It signals, in a sense, the loss of, and inability to recover, a deeply meaningful way of being – it signals the end of a world.[2]

Where Words Are Unable to Explain

By today's standards, we might think that the ancient Greeks got it wrong about art. Plato (ca. 429–ca. 347 BCE) thought that arts were just imitation (*mimesis*) of nature; his ideal city-state in the *Republic*, founded on laws informed by direct access to the truth, had little place for art.[3] Aristotle (384–322 BCE) was more inclined to accept the value of art, but still thought it was just mimicry – even arts like dancing, flute playing, and lyre playing represent human emotions and actions outside the world of art. By contrast, most modern philosophers have agreed that art is not about *representing* people, animals, landscapes, and other things. After all, if representation is all that matters, a *perfect* picturing of, say, Duke Leto's head and shoulders would just be a photograph – or worse, a Xerox. And as Robert Pippin comments, "A person who travels to Florence to see Michelangelo's *David* in order to see what David looked like has missed something."[4]

The history of aesthetics – philosophy that asks deep questions about art – hasn't led to a clear consensus about why art is special. What, for example, turns a painted canvas into a portrait? Infamously, what changes a toilet into a "Fountain," the name that Marcel Duchamp gave to a urinal that he displayed at a 1917 New York art show? Paul Muad'Dib has weighed in on this, with an emphasis on how meaningful patterns and beauty in nature help us understand the attractions of art:

> There is in all things a pattern that is part of our universe. It has symmetry, elegance, and grace – those qualities you find always in that which the true artist captures. You can find it in the turning of the seasons, in the way sand trails along a ridge, in the branch clusters of the creosote bush or the pattern of its leaves. We try to copy these patterns in our lives and our society, seeking the rhythms, the dances, the forms that comfort.[5]

Paul's sense of what the "true artist" captures resonates with a lot of non-Western art – as well as some minority Western views, like John Dewey's (1859–1952) sense that writing about fine art ought to "restore continuity between the refined and intensified forms of experience that are works of art and . . . everyday events, doings and sufferings . . ."[6] Dewey is in the minority here, for from the late eighteenth to the early twentieth century, a crucial aspect of our authentic experience of genuine art was "distance," a certain lack of personal interest in the work of art.

This sounds paradoxical. We've already seen how Robert Pippin warned us that we're not experiencing Michelangelo's *David* as art if we're curious about what David looked like. Similarly, we're not interested in art *as* art if we're considering buying a particular sculpture as an investment, or if we're mainly interested in a painting, as comedian Steve Martin once joked, for its "heft and smell." To get in touch with something as *art*, we have to achieve "distance" from it by adjusting our attitude: our practical needs and desires can't get in the way of the appreciation of the architecture, poetry, or sculpture before us. How exactly we might adjust our attitude is complex, but we can sum it up for now by saying that people capable of achieving aesthetic "distance" from works of art have *taste*, while others do not. "Taste" here means the ability to judge art as better or worse; as achieving an effect on our senses and our emotions convincingly or not.

A great example of what many people understand to be tasteless works of would-be art are grouped under the name "kitsch" (*Velvet Elvis*, *Dogs Playing Poker*, and others). "Kitsch art" even exists in the Duniverse, and it'll be no surprise to find that it's a product of the Harkonnens. When Miles Teg escorts the Duncan Idaho ghola into one of the Harkonnen's abandoned no-globes on Gammu, Duncan finds himself hard-wired to loathe the clocks he finds there. "It was an antique, a round face with two analog hands and a digital second counter. The two hands were Priapean – naked human figures: a large male with an enormous phallus and a smaller female with legs spread wide. Each time the two clock hands met, the male appeared to enter the female."[7] Young Duncan may not be able to tell what art is, but thanks to his buried original memories, he knows what he hates.

Truth and Art

While Plato was critical of the role of art in society as mere "shadows" or images that distracted people from pursuit of truth, Georg W.F. Hegel turned this criticism upside down. Art, he said, was as important as religion and philosophy for getting to the core truths of life and experience. Each of these three pillars of human culture, though, approaches truth differently: "Through art, truth can be *enjoyed* without the severe discipline of philosophy or the personal urgency of religion, as the fruit of our own creative activity."[8] For Hegel, the truth that great art expresses is found in themes of unity, reconciliation, and harmony explored in different styles by each artist in their distinctive way.

What's common to all artists, for Hegel, is not that they imitate or represent nature or the human body, but rather that they *idealize* the subject of their art. Ironically, artistic geniuses create the illusion of reality in marble or on a canvas in order to let the truth of their subject "shine forth," manifesting as beauty. There are many ways to experience this beauty, and not all of them require "taste" or formal experience interpreting art. If there is truth in the saying that we can see a person's soul in their eyes, then, Hegel says, "art makes every one of its productions into a thousand-eyed Argus, whereby the inner soul and spirit is seen at every point."[9] The different ways of interpreting the meaning embodied in the artwork are, in other words, limitless.

The experience of truth through art is to see the elements of the artwork – for example, the sky, trees, and also the lane and bungalows of *Thatched Cottages at Cordeville* – not with the same eyes as if we were walking by this scene in person. Van Gogh, through choices about color, line, and form, lifts this scene from the rural outskirts of Paris out of the ordinary, giving it new life. The thick use of paint (impasto) and waving motion that runs through all the elements of Van Gogh's study turn typical French dwellings into something out of a fairy tale.

The point of *Cottages at Cordeville* – the Duniverse version of this painting owned by Taraza, Mother Superior Odrade, and then Sheeana – as revealing a truth beyond understanding is highlighted in its brief appearance in *Chapterhouse: Dune*. After the destruction of the surface of Arrakis by the Honored Matres, the Bene Gesserit are attempting to "desertify" the planet Chapterhouse to support a new population of sandworms.

> Odrade went through her sitting room to her sleeping cell, where she stretched out on her cot fully clothed. One glow-globe bathed the room in pale yellow light. Her gaze went past the desert map to the Van Gogh painting in its protective frame and cover on the wall at the foot of her cot. *Cottages at Cordeville.* A better map than the one marking the growth of the desert, she thought. *Remind me, Vincent, of where I came from and what I yet may do.*[10]

The wheel of time turns yet again. The "desertiforming" of Chapterhouse inverts the greening of Arrakis started by Paul Muad'Dib. And while Odrade values her planetary map that shows the growth of the sandtrout-supporting deserts, she values *Cottages at Cordeville* more because it presents a reconciliation of past, present, and future that the Mother Superior longs for. We can imagine she sees the fields and shacks as a poignant scene from a home world long lost – yet also a new home that can be created at the end of the changes made to Chapterhouse.

Hegel's philosophy of history says that when we look at art, just like looking at any evidence of a past culture, this "takes place in a specific historical context with its own historical presuppositions."[11] This means that, strictly speaking, it's impossible for someone in the distant future like Darwi Odrade to experience the truth of *Cottages at Cordeville* in the same way we do – but then again, in terms of Hegel's view of history, even *we* don't experience it as the people of Van Gogh's time did. This means that our ability to take inspiration from the truth and beauty in art is limited by where and when we live.

In a series of lectures from 1823, Hegel says that the making and appreciation of art is similar to the making of meaning in religions and in philosophy: all three aim at expressing the freedom of the human spirit. Beyond this, he explains that there has been an historical progression of periods of art: Symbolic (ancient cultures from Egypt to India), Classical (Greek and Roman cultures), and Romantic (art of the "Christian era," from the Middle Ages to Hegel's own nineteenth century). His explanation for how art succeeds or fails in each of these periods is remarkably similar to what Odrade seeks in the Van Gogh painting: inspiration and freedom. In philosophy, religion, and art, Hegel writes, human consciousness sees different patterns of its own rational workings and in doing so,

> liberates itself from the cramping barriers of its existence in externality, by opening for itself a way out of the contingent affairs of its worldly existence, and the fine content of its aims and interests there, into the consideration and completion of its being in and for itself.[12]

Hegel's jargon is a lot to take in, but upon closer inspection, we can see that this is Hegel drawing the consequences of what happens when we see art with the kind of "distancing" mindset mentioned in the last section. Great art makes it possible for us to leave aside "the contingent affairs" of "worldly existence," liberating our senses and imagination from the limits of our body's and natural world's "externality." Besides the "positive delight and enjoyment" we can get from engaging with great art, for Hegel, "the highest value of art, and what makes art great, is its ability to afford us an aesthetic experience of freedom and reconciliation."[13]

For Hegel, this sense of reconciliation – our sense of individuality reconciled with our social nature, our mental life reconciled with our lived bodies, our emotions reconciled with our rationality and self-interest – is where truth is found. And despite the existence of powerful *Dune* characters with prescience like Leto II, the action in Herbert's novels is mostly animated by people – like Sheeana, Miles Teg, and Darwi Odrade in the later novels – working to secure a better future based upon merely partial truths. It's no surprise in light of the terrifying power of the Honored Matres that Odrade – and later Sheeana, who escapes Chapterhouse in a no-ship with *Thatched Cottages* – might find solace in a work of art that demonstrates a reconciliation between an idyllic French setting and its artist's turbulent, if creative mental illness.

Memory Work

By the time of *Hunters of Dune* by Brian Herbert and Kevin J. Anderson, the continued survival of the painting that Odrade took from Mother Superior Taraza, preserved in turn by Sheeana's theft after Odrade's death, seems like a miracle. Sheeana – a figure of mystical religious power on both Rakis and Chapterhouse – treats *Thatched Cottages* as if it has a protective aura of magic:

> The Van Gogh painting hung on a metal wall of Sheeana's cabin. She had stolen the masterpiece from the Mother Superior's quarters before escaping from Chapterhouse. Of all the crimes she had committed during her flight, taking the Van Gogh was her only selfish and unjustified act. For years, she had drawn comfort from this great work of art and everything it represented . . . *Thatched Cottages at Cordeville* had survived the atomic destruction of Earth ages ago, the Butlerian Jihad and ensuing dark ages, then Muad'Dib's Jihad, thirty-five hundred years of the Tyrant's rule, the Famine Times, and the Scattering. Without doubt, this fragile piece of art was blessed . . .
>
> One day she would show the painting to the ghola children.[14]

Hegel would approve of Sheeana's thoroughly historical approach to this last remaining fragment of old Earth, as would Martin Heidegger in the twentieth century. However, Heidegger's philosophy of art is touched with an unmistakable nostalgia, the feeling that despite the survival of great works of art – paintings, Greek temples, poetry – something has been lost.

Heidegger's thoughts about art are situated within his answer to "the question of Being" in his book *Being and Time*. Humans, trees, books, and sandworms are beings, but what is Being itself? The problem Heidegger's readers face here is that Being is similar to the *Dao* of Chinese Daoism – the more you say about Being, the farther away from it you get. Heidegger offers clear criticisms of those who attempt to understand Being in too-restrictive ways. For example, the ancient thinker Pythagoras believed that Being was mathematical in nature: if something could be measured or quantified, then it existed. But Heidegger shoots back: "Calculation refuses to let anything appear except what is countable. Everything is only what-ever it counts."[15] Any attempt to think about Being by only considering parts of it (so, by excluding things that aren't countable, like thoughts about the new *Dune* film or the beauty of a sunset) will be a success, but nowhere near a *complete* success. Heidegger names the root of our desires to quantify, order, categorize, and scientize Being as "the forgetting of Being."

Heidegger tries to show that before philosophy as we know it was kicked off by Socrates and Plato, ancient Pre-Socratic Greek thinkers like Thales and Heraclitus struggled to put into words their own encounters with Being. Heidegger treats ancient Greek terms like *aletheia* (truth) and *ousia* (being) very seriously, since their original meanings capture a way of seeing – and being – that he believes disappeared during the golden age of Greek philosophy. In fact, "Heidegger . . . saw history as little more than the unfolding of a slow decline whose roots harken back to the Greeks in the constant forgetting of Being."[16]

In his lecture "Origin of the Work of Art," Heidegger confronts a puzzle. We have already asked about some traditional philosophical questions about art works ("what is a piece of art, and how do we tell it from non-art?") and their creators ("what does the placement of human forms in this painting signify?" and "what emotions was the composer trying to express in this symphony?"). But for Heidegger, the artwork is also the "origin of the artist." Artwork and artist both belong in the "art world" because of their relationship to a third thing – "art." Now, as so many other chapters in this book also show, one of the best ways to apply philosophy to the Duniverse is to marshal the resources of its "environmental" or "ecological" ways of thinking.[17] Heidegger's thought – as Kristin Lund showed in her chapter in the original philosophical anthology on *Dune* – is a perfect example of this.[18] In looking at art, then, Heidegger avoids making two mistakes: he doesn't put much emphasis on the artist as "genius creator of novelty," but he also says we can't ignore the historical and social context of the artwork by considering it in abstraction from the context of its creation and intended audience.

Cruel Shoes

So Heidegger views great works of art along lines similar to the way Odrade and Sheeana look at *Thatched Cottages at Cordeville*. In fact, to make a few important points, he uses another Van Gogh picture, *A Pair of Shoes* (1886), a painting that ultimately became much, much more significant than its subject matter:

> In 1886, van Gogh visited a Paris flea market and came across a pair of worn-out shoes. He bought them and brought them back to his atelier in the city's Montmartre district. It's not clear why he bought them, but it could be simply that he needed a new pair of shoes. Apparently, he did try to wear them and found the fit impossible. Instead, he decided to use them as a prop for painting, and the shoes soon became the most celebrated footwear in the history of modern art.[19]

Heidegger thinks the way Van Gogh painted these shoes conveys a sort of truth about the world in which the shoes played an essential role on the feet of hard-working peasants. He writes:

> The peasant woman wears her shoes in the field. Only here are they what they are. They are all the more genuinely so, the less the peasant woman thinks about her shoes while she is at work, or looks at them at all, or is even aware of them . . . [But] from Van Gogh's painting we cannot even tell where these shoes stand. There is nothing surrounding this pair of peasant shoes in or to which they might belong – only an undefined space. There are not even clods of soil from the field or the field-path sticking to them, which would at least hint at their use. A pair of peasant shoes and nothing more. And yet—[20]

And yet we must read more into the painting, and doing so will help us understand two important ideas for Heidegger: *earth* and *world*.

> From the dark opening of the worn insides of the shoes the toilsome tread of the worker stares forth. In the stiffly rugged heaviness of the shoes there is the accumulated tenacity of her slow trudge through the far-spreading and ever-uniform furrows of the field swept by a raw wind. On the leather lies the dampness and richness of the soil. Under the soles slides the loneliness of the field-path as evening falls. In the shoes vibrates the silent call of the earth, its quiet gift of the ripening grain and its unexplained self-refusal in the fallow desolation of the wintry field . . . This equipment belongs to the *earth*, and it is protected in the *world* of the peasant woman.[21]

On full display here is the mysticism of Heidegger's later philosophy. "Earth" here doesn't mean "dirt," nor does it mean "the home world of humanity"; it is this philosopher's new way of referring to Being as the primitive and inexhaustible – but also ultimately incomprehensible – source that life, nature, meaning, and yes, art spring from. For Heidegger, stressing the

existence of an unbridgeable gap between "earth" and what can be quantified, understood, named, and labeled is to give Being its proper due. And for
this peasant woman, who likely lived and died having never read philosophy
nor having seen a great painting, her shoes are part of a complexly
interconnected web of meaning and significance that is mostly unseen and
unremarked on. The "world" of the peasant woman is a world of "equipment" – shoes, scythes, hats, rakes. This equipment, far from merely being
tools for doing jobs, gives her life the meaning it has while also uncovering
new possibilities – no matter how limited – for what her life might become.

We might worry that Heidegger has read far too much into this painting.
To some, it might sound as if he's romanticized the peasant lifestyle.
Marxist critic Frederic Jameson would agree. Jameson agrees that the
painting reveals a "truth," but suggests another interpretation of *A Pair of
Shoes* which will sound more like common sense: it represents the world
of "agricultural misery, of stark rural poverty, and the whole rudimentary
world of backbreaking peasant toil."[22] Jameson also challenges Heidegger's
arcane-sounding terminology. Heidegger's notion that "the work of art
emerges within the gap between earth and world" is one that Jameson prefers to translate as "the meaningless materiality of the body and nature and
the meaningful endowment of history and of the social."[23]

Jameson is at his most helpful when he says that both his and Heidegger's
readings of *A Pair of Shoes* are "hermeneutical." The "hermeneutic"
approach to art is that "the work in its inert, object form is taken as a clue
or a symptom for some vaster reality which replaces it as its ultimate
truth."[24] Hermeneutics – not a common word in anyone's vocabulary – is
the branch of study dealing with how we interpret texts. Historically, hermeneutics emerged in the nineteenth century in controversies over interpreting the Bible. A hermeneutical view of art takes great works as "cultural
paradigms" that "collects the scattered practices of a group, unifies them
into coherent possibilities for action, and holds them up to the people,"
producing a shared understanding.[25]

According to Jameson's definition, it seems clear that Hegel is also a hermeneutic philosopher when it comes to art. And whether the people of the
Duniverse see *Thatched Cottages at Cordeville* as really portraying France
in the nineteenth century or not, it's clear that Sheeana and Odrade find
something like Hegel's "aesthetic experience of freedom and reconciliation" in the painting. They may not know a lot about art, but they know
what sets them free.

The Bad News

Despite their pioneering views on the philosophical importance of art and
their remarkable combination of history with the artistic value of truth,
neither Hegel nor Heidegger painted a particularly rosy picture of the
future of art. It may be surprising to hear that Hegel believed that art was

already dead by 1823, when he first delivered his lectures on aesthetics. Because his theory of art stresses its function of reconciling conflicts and opposites, Hegel found that the Romantic art of his own period had gone astray. Hegel was disturbed by the emergence of irony in the work of Romantics like playwright Heinrich von Kleist, who committed suicide while still young in 1811 and who was a later inspiration to Franz Kafka. For this and other reasons, Hegel believed that the art of his time was, effectively, no longer art.

For different reasons entirely, Heidegger believed he had seen the death of art. Pessimistically, Heidegger pronounced in the introduction of "Origin of the Work of Art": "Art – this is nothing more than a word to which nothing real any longer corresponds. It may pass for a collective idea under which we find a place for that which alone is real in art: works and artists."[26] Heidegger's pessimism is philosophical but also cultural. According to François Dosse, "Heidegger never stopped reiterating his Cassandra-like warning against the decline (*Verfall*) in which the West was inexorably becoming mired: 'The spiritual force of the West eludes us and its edifice trembles, the dead appearance of culture crumbles.'"[27] Dosse helps to explain Heidegger's rural celebration of *A Pair of Shoes* when he points out that the solutions to the problems of the fragmented techno-scientific West were to be found in "the strength of rootedness, tradition, and country."[28] Heidegger believed that most of humanity was too alienated from the sources of Being – "earth," nature, a world without straight lines – to relate to artworks in the way he described with *A Pair of Shoes*. It's not difficult to guess that he would have had nothing good to say about modern abstract art. While viewing the Van Gogh in 1930, he might have come across the distinctly non-representational art of Kandinsky, Mondrian, and Paul Klee and wondered if these productions were just what passed for "art" in a society ordered and categorized by math and science.

The Good News

The fate of art in these German philosophers mirrors developments in the Duniverse. Like Hegel's Romantics, Paul Atreides, traveling a more or less conventional hero arc in *Dune*, becomes the blind, raving "Preacher" of *Children of Dune*. The Preacher, ironically, rails against many of the same philosophies that Paul had used to become Emperor and Messiah. And like Heidegger's warnings that art dies when humans are alienated from history and the "earth," Liet-Kynes and his daughter Chani take radical action in defense of Arrakeen ecology when Harkonnen technological superiority threatens.

In their aesthetic philosophies, Hegel and Heidegger make curiously little mention of the dramatic play as an important form of art. Surely the epic saga of the Duniverse, viewed from the audience's perspective, is one vast drama, sometimes comedic, while often also tragic. With Brian Herbert and Kevin J. Anderson's decision to continue and conclude Frank Herbert's space opera in the books *Hunters of Dune* and *Sandworms of Dune*, we are introduced to the next generation of the Duniverse – the inheritors of *Thatched Cottages at Cordeville* – the young gholas of Paul, Chani, Lady Jessica, Thufir Hawat, and even the traitorous Dr. Yueh. Despite Hegel and Heidegger's bad news that "art is dead," these gholas and their destinies make it seem as though the vast cycle of the play called *Dune* is ready to begin yet again – surely good news.

Notes

1. *Heretics of Dune* (New York: Ace, 2020), 151–152.
2. Hegel and Heidegger have also been connected with *Dune* in the context of alt-right, neo-fascist interpretations of Herbert's work; this isn't my intention, and I find these readings both reprehensible and unsustainable. See Jordan S. Carroll, "Race Consciousness: Fascism and Frank Herbert's 'Dune,'" *Los Angeles Review of Books,* November 19, 2020, at https://lareviewofbooks. org/article/race-consciousness-fascism-and-frank-herberts-dune.
3. For more details on *Dune* and Plato's *Republic*, see the chapter in this book by Galipcan Altinkaya and Mehmet Kuyurtar (Chapter 21) and Greg Littmann's chapter on the Bene Gesserit (Chapter 13).
4. Robert B. Pippin, *After the Beautiful: Hegel and the Philosophy of Pictorial Modernism* (Chicago: University of Chicago Press, 2014), 91.
5. *Dune* (New York: Ace, 2005), 481.
6. John Dewey, *Art as Experience* (New York: Perigee, 1980), 2.
7. *HD*, 257.
8. Stephen Houlgate, *An Introduction to Hegel: Freedom, Truth and History*, 2nd ed. (Malden, MA: Blackwell, 2005), 211.
9. G.W.F. Hegel, *Aesthetics: Lectures on Fine Art*, trans. T.M. Knox, vol. 1 (Oxford: Clarendon Press), 153–154.
10. *Chapterhouse: Dune* (New York: Ace, 2020), 182.
11. Houlgate, *An Introduction to Hegel*, 218.
12. Hegel, *Aesthetics*, 94.
13. Houlgate, *An Introduction to Hegel*, 219.
14. Brian Herbert and Kevin J. Anderson, *Hunters of Dune* (New York: TOR Books, 2006), 201–202.
15. Martin Heidegger, "Postscript to 'What Is Metaphysics?'" in William McNeill ed., *Pathmarks* (New York: Cambridge University Press, 1998), 235.
16. François Dosse, *History of Structuralism*, vol. 1, trans. Deborah Glassman (Minneapolis: University of Minnesota Press, 1997), 367.
17. For example, see the chapters in this book by Zach Vereb (Chapter 7) and Matthew Crippen (Chapter 11).
18. Kristian Lund, "Wiping Finite Answers from an Infinite Universe," in Jeffery Nicholas ed., *Dune and Philosophy: Weirding Way of the Mentat* (Chicago: Open Court Publishers, 2011), 149–160.

19. Scott Horton, "Philosophers Rumble Over Van Gogh's Shoes," *Harper's Magazine*, October 5, 2009, at https://harpers.org/2009/10/philosophers-rumble-over-van-goghs-shoes.

20. Martin Heidegger, "The Origin of the Work of Art," in *Poetry Language and Thought*, trans. Albert Hofstadter (New York: Harper & Row, 1971), 33.

21. Heidegger, "Origin of the Work of Art," 33–34.

22. Frederic Jameson, "The Deconstruction of Expression," in Charles Harrison and Paul Wood eds., *Art in Theory 1900–2000*, new ed. (Malden, MA: Blackwell, 2003), 1046.

23. Jameson, "The Deconstruction of Expression," 1047.

24. Jameson, "The Deconstruction of Expression," 1047.

25. Hubert L. Dreyfus, "Heidegger on the Connection Between Nihilism, Art, Technology, and Politics," in Charles B. Guignon ed., *The Cambridge Companion to Heidegger*, 2nd ed. (New York: Cambridge University Press, 2006), 354.

26. Heidegger, "Origin of the Work of Art," 17.

27. Dosse, *History of Structuralism*, 368.

28. Dosse, *History of Structuralism*, 368.

THE LENS OF TIME:
FREEDOM, HISTORY, AND
EVIL IN *DUNE*

Should the Bene Gesserit Be in Charge?

Greg Littmann

"The Great Revolt took away a crutch," she said. "It forced human minds to develop. Schools were started to train human talents."

"Bene Gesserit schools?"

She nodded. "We have two chief survivors of those ancient schools: the Bene Gesserit and the Spacing Guild. The Guild, so we think, emphasizes almost pure mathematics. Bene Gesserit performs another function."

"Politics," he said.

"Kull wahad!" the old woman said. She sent a hard glance at Jessica.

"I've not told him. Your Reverence," Jessica said.

The Reverend Mother returned her attention to Paul. "You did that on remarkably few clues," she said. "Politics indeed . . ."

Dune

At the opening of *Dune*, we find humanity in a political mess, having reverted to a "feudal trade culture" with a hereditary emperor in the form of Shaddam IV of House Corrino.[1] Reverend Mother Gaius Helen Mohiam explains: "We've a three-point civilization: the Imperial Household balanced against the Federated Great Houses of the Landsraad, and between them, the Guild with its damnable monopoly on interstellar transport."[2] On the planetary level, humanity serves lesser hereditary nobles like the Atreides Dukes of Caladan and the Harkonnen Barons of Giedi Prime. Duke Leto Atreides claims that the Great Houses have suffered a "melancholy degeneration," and House Atreides is no exception.[3] It's said that

Dune and Philosophy, First Edition. Edited by Kevin S. Decker.
© 2023 John Wiley & Sons, Inc. Published 2023 by John Wiley & Sons, Inc.

Duke Leto himself "rules with the consent of the governed," but since he's a hereditary Duke, the supposed reliance on consent can extend only so far.[4] By the Duke's own admission, his "propaganda corps is one of the finest."[5]

Since nobles are born into the job, it's easy to end up with a leader who is unsuitable, like the cruel and avaricious Baron Vladimir Harkonnen. Indeed, the Baron plots to seize the Golden Lion Throne and might have become emperor himself. After him, the emperor could have been the impulsive glory-hound Feyd-Rautha, or the "muscle-minded, tank-brain" Rabban.[6] As for the Spacing Guild, it seems to care only for its own wealth and safety, not the wellbeing of humanity. The guild is content as long as the spice flows and wealth flows in.

By *Heretics of Dune*, the Bene Gesserit are directly ruling in the remnants of the old empire. Maybe the Bene Gesserit should have been in charge all along! They seem uniquely suited to the job. Politics is their area of specialization, and only those who have the intellectual gifts needed to study and understand politics are admitted. They are rigorously trained for their duties from earliest childhood, gaining extraordinary control over their minds and memories. Reverend Mothers learn to access memories from their female ancestors. Bene Gesserit are trained to read people's psychological states. Some, trained as Truthsayers, can detect any lie.

Self-discipline is the cornerstone of Bene Gesserit training. They distinguish two types of people: "humans" and "animals." Someone who has overcome instinct has become fully human, which is a state Bene Gesserit must achieve. Paul proves himself "human" to Reverend Mother Mohiam by being able to resist removing his hand from a box that causes agonizing pain. She explains: "A human can override any nerve."[7] According to Jessica, her first lesson as a Bene Gesserit was "Humans must never submit to animals."[8] Appropriately, Rabban, who is a slave to his passions, is reviled as "Beast Rabban."

As if that isn't enough to recommend the Bene Gesserit as rulers, their training instills extraordinary dedication to the human good. Their motto is "We exist only to serve" and they seem to live up to it.[9] It's remarkable that no Bene Gesserit has ever sold out because of personal ambition and blabbed Bene Gesserit secrets. What favor might Princess Irulan have gained with her father, the emperor, if she'd shifted her loyalty from the order to him? Reverend Mothers are so dedicated that they resist the temptation to use their powers to extend their lives by thousands of years, for the good of the order – "[I]f one did it, sooner or later all would try it. There could be no concealing such an accumulation of ageless women."[10] The only striking exception to Bene Gesserit fidelity is Lady Jessica, who defies the order to bear Duke Leto a son, and then sides with that son when he declares himself Messiah.

It may be that in the universe of *Dune*, an all-female organization is particularly suited to rule. Men and women are consistently presented as being psychologically different. Leto II explains why he uses an all-female army, the Fish Speakers, to control his empire. "Men are susceptible to class fixations. They create layered societies. The layered society is an ultimate invitation to violence."[11] Women never do this, according to Leto, "unless they are almost completely male dominated or locked into a male role model . . . [because w]omen make common cause based on their sex, a cause which transcends class and caste. That is why I let my women hold the reins."[12] Women in the *Dune* universe *can* be violent and brutal, as demonstrated by the vicious Honored Matres, who return from the Scattering to invade the old empire after the death of Leto II. But women seem to have a better chance of being dedicated to the common good.

The Principle of Specialization

The earliest written Western political philosophy we have comes from Plato (428–348 BCE). In *The Republic*, he argues that a society will flourish best if every job is undertaken by the individuals best suited for that job, while everyone else keeps out of it. This is known as the "Principle of Specialization." For example, if a Guild Heighliner is to make a trip from Caladan to Arrakis, it makes sense that the person given the responsibility to navigate the journey be a Guild Navigator, who has the appropriate specialist training. It wouldn't make sense to let Dr. Yueh do it, or to hand the job off to a foot soldier or a Pundi Rice farmer. After all, none of them have the relevant expertise. Doctors should stick to healing, soldiers to defense, and rice farmers to growing rice. Likewise, if a noble has been poisoned by chaumurky in their spice coffee, it makes sense to send for a Suk doctor at once. It would make no sense to have a Guild Navigator examine them instead, or to send for a troubadour or a Truthsayer. After all, it's the doctor who has medical expertise. The others should stick to their own areas of expertise, navigating, playing music, and Truthsaying respectively.

Plato argues that just as navigating should be in the hands of the best navigators, and medical work in the hands of the best healers, so government should be in the hands of those best suited to governing. He thinks that monarchy is a bad system of government because authority is assigned by birth, not ability and character. Similarly, democracy is a bad form of government because it places authority in the hands of people who have no expertise in governing. Allowing every farmer, foot soldier, and desert survivalist to have a say in government is as crazy as giving them a say in navigation or medicine. They need to stick to their own areas of specialization and stay out of government, leaving it to the government specialists. If Plato is right, then it seems that the Bene Gesserit *should* be in charge of the *Dune* universe.

Asking whether the Bene Gesserit should be in charge of the *Dune* universe isn't just an intellectual exercise. In the real universe, we must decide to what degree we should concentrate political power in the most capable and dedicated hands, as well as which hands would likely be the most capable and dedicated. Considering the best role for the Bene Gesserit in the *Dune* universe should help us decide what to say about the real world.

The Bene Gesserit and Plato's Guardians

Over the centuries, many thinkers have wanted to see power concentrated in the hands of a guardian class of political experts, something like the Bene Gesserit. In Western philosophy, this tradition begins with Plato. In *The Republic*, he describes an ideal city-state, organized along lines radically different from anything previously tried. Since *The Republic* is a description of a theoretical society, it arguably qualifies as the first work of science fiction.

While the Bene Gesserit classify people as either animal or human, Plato identifies three types of people based on what dominates their soul: rationality, spirit, or appetites. The rational soul is driven by reason. Plato believes that reason tells us to be good, so the rational person will be a moral person. Since there is no more to self-discipline, in Plato's view, than being ruled by one's rational faculties, the rational person will be supremely self-disciplined. They will have the sort of awareness and self-control that the Bene Gesserit would describe as "human." An example might be a principled, disciplined intellectual like Paul or Jessica. Spirited souls are dominated by the desire for honor and glory. They are driven by emotion rather than being ruled by reason. A fanatical Sardaukar or Fedaykin might be archetypal examples of the spirited soul. Finally, appetitive souls are ruled by base desires. They yearn for money, food, sex, and all sorts of luxury. Driven by instincts, they are the clearest counterparts to what the Bene Gesserit call "animals."

Plato argues that people with rational souls should be in charge of the rest. His society is organized into three classes: guardians, the military, and workers. The guardians, made up of the rational people, run the state. Below them is the military class, made up of the spirited people. Like Sardaukar, they are born into their military careers and trained to fight from earliest childhood. At the bottom are the appetitive people, who do the work. They grow food, build ships, heal the sick, and take on all the other jobs that don't come down to administration or war. Nobody is born into the ruling class. Rather, the most capable, moral, and dependable young people from the military class are promoted to the guardian class for further intensive training.

The education system of the military and ruling classes is the foundation of the state. It not only provides practical skills, but hones the student's reasoning ability, self-discipline, and moral character. Because the ruling class have been taught to be guided by reason, they will be almost incorruptible and will not be "money-loving, slavish, a boaster, or a coward . . . [or in any way] unreliable or unjust."[13] To help keep them incorruptible, Plato reverses the traditional relationship between power and wealth. Guardians are banned from having money or owning private property; instead, the state will provide what they need to live the simple healthy lifestyle appropriate for a "warrior athlete." This is in striking contrast to the opulence Bene Gesserit like Lady Jessica and Princess Irulan enjoy!

A common element of the education of a Bene Gesserit and the education of a member of Plato's guardian class is the emphasis on physical training. Future guardians, along with other children of the military class, are given intensive exercise and kept in peak physical condition. The Bene Gesserit are taught prana-bindu, giving them control over their nerves and muscles. Likewise, Plato's guardians spend their youth being drilled to be highly capable soldiers. The Bene Gesserit are trained to be supreme martial artists, able to use the "weirding way" to overcome opponents. They are so effective in combat that Jessica easily defeats Stilgar when she and Paul first encounter him in the desert.

Whereas the Bene Gesserit prefer to influence events subtly, society under the rule of Plato's guardians is highly authoritarian, with the condition of ordinary citizens comparable to slavery. The character of Socrates, speaking for Plato, explains: "to ensure that a [normal citizen] . . . is ruled by something similar to what rules the best person, we say that he ought to be the slave of that best person . . . It isn't to harm the slave that we say he must be ruled . . . but because it's better for everyone to be ruled by divine reason."[14]

Like the Bene Gesserit, the guardian class manipulate ordinary citizens through religious lies. These include a mythological tale of the founding of the state and false prophecies concerning the disastrous results of disobedience to the state. Also like the Bene Gesserit, the guardian class oversees breeding. One of the Bene Gesserit's most important functions is, as Reverend Mother Mohiam tells Paul, "separating human stock from animal stock – for breeding purposes."[15] Plato's guardians make sure that "stock" is improved and that only those of good stock rise to positions of power. The character of Socrates explains: "It follows . . . first, that the best men must have sex with the best women as frequently as possible, while the opposite is true of the most inferior men and women, and, second, that if our herd is to be of the highest possible quality, the former's offspring must be reared (as guardians) but not the latter's."[16]

Strikingly, membership in Plato's ruling class is much more open to women than the Bene Gesserit are to men. Plato believed that women were, in general, inferior to men in all ways. However, he recognized that some women are highly capable, and thought that these unusual women should be given work and authority suitable to their abilities. All jobs open to men – including the highest levels of government – are open to women. Females in the military and guardian classes receive the same education as males on the grounds that they will be doing the same kinds of work.

Forerunners of the Bene Gesserit
in Speculative Fiction

Plato was not the last thinker before Frank Herbert to imagine society being guided by a class of guardians composed of experts in politics. Nor was Plato the last thinker to believe that we should place government in the hands of such a guardian class.

For example, in *Utopia* (1516), English statesman Thomas More (1478–1535) responds to Plato with his own account of a fictional utopian society. As in *The Republic*, government is in the hands of those who have studied politics, and the ruling class is drawn from the most astute scholars. Also, as in *The Republic*, society is authoritarian. The state organizes people's work, food, and housing, restricts non-essential travel, and oversees public morals. The people are so dedicated to the common good that, like Plato's ruling class, they have no private property, but take what they need from a common store.

In *Gulliver's Travels* (1726), the Irish Anglican priest Jonathan Swift (1667–1745) offers his own response to Plato. Swift's ideal society, the Houyhnhnm, are a race of intelligent horses. Like the Bene Gesserit, they breed in accordance with eugenics, not love, to keep the stock strong. There are two distinct social classes, based on stock, with the ruling dark-coated strain being superior in intelligence. The two classes never intermarry. Diet is strictly controlled to maintain health, and young Houyhnhnm of both sexes are given a thorough education in practical matters and rigorous physical training.

Like Plato, Swift explicitly rejects democracy on the grounds that it makes no sense for people with no expertise in government to form opinions on matters of government. Gulliver, speaking for Swift, blames the tendency of ordinary folk to expound on politics on "a very common infirmity of human nature, inclining us to be most curious and conceited in matters where we have least concern, and for which we are least adapted by study or nature."[17]

In *A Modern Utopia* (1905), English writer H.G. Wells (1866–1946) likewise lays out plans for an ideal state, in response to Plato. Much as Bene Gesserit identify two kinds of mind, and Plato identifies three kinds of soul, Wells identifies four types of mind. Poietic minds are creative; kinetic minds are active but not creative; dull minds are unimaginative; and base minds have no moral sense. The poietic minds provide society with its "voluntary nobility," the "Samurai." Like Bene Gesserit, the Samurai are characterized by dedication and self-discipline. They are restricted to a simple, healthy lifestyle, with lots of exercise, few luxuries, and no alcohol or tobacco. The Samurai are not permitted to buy or sell on their own account and may not have servants. Women have the same rights as men and may be Samurai. The state practices limited eugenics, forbidding motherhood where it would lead to "the reproduction of inferior types."[18]

In *Walden Two* (1948), American psychologist B.F. Skinner (1904–1990) proposes a utopia achieved through the study of psychology. Democracy is rejected because it only serves the majority and, as in *The Republic*, because it is rule by the unqualified. Instead, Planners are appointed as a guardian class. Planners are rigorously educated and psychologically conditioned, and their conditioning ensures that they will never be corrupt. Like all members of the community, Planners must live modestly. The Board of Planners is usually composed of three men and three women.

Other writers have viewed the presence of a guardian class as a recipe for dystopia. In *Brave New World* (1932), by English writer Aldous Huxley (1894–1963), society is ruled by the Alphas, who ensure that citizens enjoy life and have a high material standard of living. Rather than controlling breeding to produce the best stock, Alphas oversee a system in which citizens are physically and psychologically conditioned, even before birth, to fulfill a role in one of four social classes: Alphas, Betas, Gammas, and Deltas. Each of these classes is less intelligent and educated than the last. Though the populace is happy, they are denied the chance to flourish as human beings because society takes complete control of their thoughts and actions.

In *1984* (1949), by English writer George Orwell (1903–1950), the citizens of Oceania are ruled by the Inner Party, an elite group trained in politics since early childhood. But though the Inner Party theoretically serve the interests of all citizens, in fact, they hoard luxuries to themselves and assure themselves of their own power by making others suffer. Like the Bene Gesserit, they routinely lie to the populace to control them.

Not every forerunner of the Bene Gesserit comes from a work with a political agenda. In the *Foundation* saga (1942–1993), American writer and biochemist Isaac Asimov (1920–1992) was exploring ideas rather than offering a blueprint for society. Asimov introduces two guardian classes for his galaxy-spanning civilization. The First Foundation specializes in the study of the physical sciences, while the Second Foundation specializes in the study of politics. Both use lies and deception to control others. Like the Bene Gesserit, the First Foundation manipulates religion. The Second Foundation develop telepathic powers reminiscent of Bene Gesserit Truthsaying and Voice. The First Foundation eventually grows corrupt and authoritarian, but the Second Foundation remains in the hands of idealists dedicated to the good of humanity.

The Danger of the Bene Gesserit

So much for the theory. If we want to decide whether it's a good idea to concentrate power in the hands of a guardian class, we should take a look at how guardian classes have worked out in practice. The historical record is dismal. Kings and nobility have often been looked on as the caretakers of the ordinary people. For instance, the ancient Babylonian ruler Hammurabi (1792–1750 BCE) boasted in his law code, "I am the guardian shepherd whose scepter is just and whose beneficent shadow is spread over my city. In my bosom I carried the people of the land of Sumer and Akkad; under my protection they prospered; I governed them in peace; in my wisdom I sheltered them. In order that the strong might not oppress the weak . . . and to give justice to the oppressed." Fine words, but how has nobility worked out? Nobles have exploited and ripped us off, executed us, starved us, tortured us, made us fight their wars, and generally treated us more like lambs for the slaughter than a beloved flock under their benign protection.

Imperial and colonial guardianship has just as black a record. For instance, when Europeans decided it was their duty to "take up the white man's burden" to bring civilization and Christianity to other peoples, their stewardship tended to result in exploitative empire. Even slavery was sometimes justified as being in the slave's best interest. In communist states, when power is concentrated in the hands of the party, authorities have tended to use that power to exploit and oppress ordinary citizens. Male-dominated societies, in which men are given authority over women, have tended to exploit women. In short, guardian classes have tended to rule badly.

The Bene Gesserit *Missionaria Protectiva Text QIV* states: "All governments suffer a recurring problem: Power attracts pathological personalities. It is not that power corrupts but that it is magnetic to the corruptible."[19] There's been a recurring hope, since the time of Plato, that we could minimize corruption if only the right people were appointed to power, with the right training. But to date, we've never hit on an education system that reliably makes people good, nor a selection process that reliably weeds out the corruptible.

If the Bene Gesserit were real, perhaps they actually would be an organization to which we could safely hand over the running of society. The rules of real-world politics need not apply to the inhabitants of a science-fiction universe, who have powers far beyond our own. But if the Bene Gesserit *were* put in in charge of humanity, there are several traditional ways that they could fail as a guardian class.

First, there would be the natural temptation to favor their own interests over those of the people they rule. Whatever it is that might entice a Bene Gesserit – knowledge, power, glory, favor for her family, or so much melange that her eyes turn blue – it would be there for the taking. It would be tempting, too, to overlook abuses by members of the order against outsiders.

What's worse, it would be tempting for Bene Gesserit to favor those who are like them. So, for instance, just as all-male authorities have historically tended to favor men over women, we could expect an all-female authority to tend to favor women over men. Even more significantly, Bene Gesserit tend to live as one of the rich. Some are nobles in their own right, like Princess Irulan. Others are wives and concubines of important men. Nobles like Shaddam IV, Duke Leto, and Count Fenring have Bene Gesserit spouses, as do high-ranking professionals like Dr. Yueh. When a guardian class is composed of the rich, they traditionally favor the rich.

Even when members of a guardian class act with the best of intentions, it's traditionally been easy for them to be ignorant of the needs of those they protect. The Bene Gesserit know that they have things to learn from the experiences and knowledge of men. After all, they engage in a millennia-long project to produce a Kwisatz Haderach, a male Bene Gesserit who can access both male and female ancestral memories. Likewise, important experiences and knowledge are possessed by all others who are not Bene Gesserit.

Often, pride will lead a guardian class to form negative stereotypes of those who are unlike them. In *A Modern Utopia*, H.G. Wells has a character explain the danger: "[S]tupid generalizations have been believed with the utmost readiness, and acted upon by great numbers of sane, respectable people. And when the class is one's own class, when it expresses one of the aggregations to which one refers one's own activities, then the disposition to divide all qualities between this class and its converse, and to cram one's own class with every desirable distinction, becomes overwhelming."[20] So men have caricatured women, Europeans have stereotyped peoples of colonized lands, and the rich have belittled the poor. In the *Dune* saga, the all-female Honored Matres, who rule vast territories, stereotype men as unfit to command women. They are shocked to encounter Miles Teg, military commander of the more insightful Bene Gesserit: "Teg's dominance was not lost on the Honored Matres. They glowered at him as they obeyed Haker's invitation. Men ordering women about!"[21]

You'll recall that Skinner criticized democracy in *Walden Two* as being a system that only serves the majority. There's something to this criticism. Since groups in power tend to do what serves them best, if you put the majority in power, they will tend to do what serves the majority best. But concentrating power only tends to make the problem worse, as the class being served grows smaller.

The Limits of Democracy

Given the terrible historical record of guardian classes and the lack of Bene Gesserit in the real world, we shouldn't place a guardian class in charge of society. Plato is right that democracy is rule by the unqualified, but the corruption of guardian classes has been so harmful that keeping power with the unqualified masses is a better bet, in general, than concentrating it in the most capable hands. Having said that, it would be too simplistic to try to be as democratic as possible.

There are many limits we place on democracy, and rightly so. In the US, we are bound by a Constitution, limiting what voters can do. It's possible for voters to change the Constitution, but it's difficult, and not possible with a mere majority. Even proposing a change requires a two-thirds majority vote in both the House of Representatives and the Senate or a constitutional convention called for by two-thirds of the State legislatures. Another limit on democracy is that we don't usually vote directly on issues, but on representatives. Generally, we think that we are voting for people who know more about government and the relevant issues than we do. Given modern information technology, there's no reason why we couldn't vote directly on issues a lot more than we do rather than delegating decisions to a representative, but it isn't clear that the voter should be given such responsibility.

Likewise, outside the legislature, we often rightly concentrate power in the hands of experts rather than distributing it as widely as possible. We appoint police officers to apprehend suspects, judges to sentence criminals, academics to decide when medical students are qualified to be doctors, building safety inspectors to ensure architecture is sound, and generals to direct the army. In all of these cases, opportunities for corruption arise from the concentration of power, and yet, in all these cases, it's better to concentrate power in the hands of experts than to give everyone equal say.

As for the Bene Gesserit, even if they don't belong in charge of the *Dune* universe, at the very least, power should still be concentrated to a more limited degree in the hands of individual members of the order. Truthsayers could serve in courtrooms, prana-bindu experts could provide therapy for injury victims, and Reverend Mothers, with the memories of generations, might be professors of politics and history, or holders of elected political office.

Plato isn't entirely wrong, then. He's right about the problems of democracy and the need to place power with experts, even if he overestimates the degree to which power should be concentrated. The great problem we face is how to get the balance right between distributing power widely to limit corruption and concentrating power in the hands of the best individuals. I have no easy answers for you. In fact, I think this is the most fundamental, and toughest, problem in political philosophy. But as our favorite worm-emperor Leto II said, "This is the beginning of knowledge – the discovery of something we do not understand."[22]

Notes

1. *Dune* (New York: Penguin, 1990), 16.
2. *Dune*, 15.
3. *Dune*, 68.
4. *Dune*, 60.
5. *Dune*, 68.
6. *Dune*, 153.
7. *Dune*, 15.
8. *Dune*, 29.
9. *Dune*, 129.

10. *Children of Dune* (New York: Penguin, 2019), 54.
11. *God Emperor of Dune* (New York: Penguin, 2019), 155.
12. *GED*, 155.
13. Plato, *The Republic*, in D.S. Hutchinson ed., *Plato: Complete Works* (Indianapolis: Hackett Publishing Company, 1997), lines 486b–c.
14. Plato, *The Republic*, lines 590c7–d3.
15. *Dune*, 8.
16. Plato, *The Republic*, lines 459d–e.
17. Jonathan Swift, *Gulliver's Travels* (Ware: Wordsworth Classics, 1992), 123.
18. H.G. Wells, *A Modern Utopia* (Project Gutenberg, 2004), chapter 5, at https://www.gutenberg.org/files/6424/6424-h/6424-h. htm.
19. *Chapterhouse: Dune* (New York: Penguin, 2019), 56.
20. Wells, *A Modern Utopia*, chapter 10.
21. *CHD*, 336.
22. *GED*, 120.

14

Prisoners of Prophecy
Freedom and Foreknowledge in the *Dune* Series

William Peden

> Prophecy and prescience – How can they be put to the test in the face of the unanswered questions? Consider: How much is actual prediction of the "waveform" (as Muad'Dib referred to his vision-image) and how much is the prophet shaping the future to fit the prophecy? . . . Does the prophet see the future or does he see a line of weakness, a fault or cleavage that he may shatter with words or decisions as a diamond-cutter shatters his gem with a blow of a knife?
>
> "Private Reflections on Muad'Dib" by the Princess Irulan

Among the special abilities of characters in the Duniverse, prescience – the ability to see into the past, present, and future – is both the most isolating and the most strange. Guild Navigators use spice to acquire the foresight needed for safe interstellar travel. Paul attains an extraordinary level of prescience, even compared to the Navigators. His sister Alia as well as his children, Leto and Ghanima, possess these abilities to a phenomenal degree. Leto's foresight and its consequences dominate the *Dune* books from *God Emperor* to *Chapterhouse*. Some other characters, like Mother Superior Darwi Odrade and Siona Atreides, have relatively limited prescience.

Why is prescience isolating for its possessor? As Paul finds when talking to Stilgar, he cannot explain it to those without the power: it's beyond their comprehension.[1] The deceptive strangeness of prescience in *Dune* is typical of Herbert's ideas.[2] At first, it seems like magic, but Herbert is taking something familiar to our modern perspective – the ability to make predictions – and making it strange. We can't prophesize like Paul, but we can "see" the future, sometimes with great accuracy, using scientific knowledge, common-sense reasoning, consulting experts, and so on. The ancient Babylonians were able to systematically predict astronomical events, but contemporary astrophysicists can forecast distant events beyond the Babylonians' wildest dreams.

Dune and Philosophy, First Edition. Edited by Kevin S. Decker.
© 2023 John Wiley & Sons, Inc. Published 2023 by John Wiley & Sons, Inc.

Herbert describes the prescience of characters like Paul as a hyper-awareness of possibilities and probabilities given certain choices, rather than being able to examine a fixed future. The course of time is not entirely predetermined. Paul and Leto II must confront a nightmare in which all their possible choices involve horrific events. The only paths they can see for avoiding human stagnation and extinction involve tyrannically suppressing humans for millennia and then unleashing a cultural reaction against that despotism. Their prescience is not magical, but instead an unimaginable ability to anticipate the outcomes of present choices. That's an amplification of what we can already do – for instance, we can model the global climate and estimate outcomes of various environmental policy choices, but after that, we must choose how to act given this information. Of course, Herbert doesn't give us all the details of how prescience works; if that knowledge were public, characters in the Duniverse wouldn't see the powerful predictors as a messiah or a God Emperor.

There are two areas of real-world research especially relevant to the questions of prescience that Herbert explores. First, there is decision theory, which combines ideas in philosophy, economics, psychology, and other fields. Decision theorists study how we make choices and which choices are rational. Second, there is the philosophy of action, which is about the puzzles and insights surrounding our abilities to choose, to will, and to succumb to temptation, among other actions. Philosophy of action intertwines with psychology, neurology, the philosophy of causation, and other areas. For our purposes, it's the area in which questions about the relation between freedom and foreknowledge fall.

The Prisoner's Dilemma

Common sense suggests that prescience should help us live together better. For example, you're faced with uncertainty if you come across a stranger on a dark night in an unfamiliar country. Preparing for trouble (like going into a fighting stance) might make them nervous, escalate the situation, and lead into a spiral of violence. If you knew that the stranger wouldn't harm you, then you wouldn't have to risk this reaction and its consequences. Many wars would never have been declared if their outcomes had been foreseen.

However, decision theorists can show that the foresight of Paul and Leto II creates traps that ordinary people might escape. One of these is the "Prisoner's Dilemma." To understand this trap, let's first make it clear what decision theorists mean by "rationality": your beliefs and desires, whatever they might be, should fit together coherently. A simple example: you shouldn't believe both of two statements that contradict each other. So if you believe that you have ten fingers, it's irrational to also believe that you have eleven fingers.

This sense of "rationality" differs from our everyday sense of the word. It's "formal" rationality, which decision theory understands through the logical and mathematical relations among a person's beliefs and preferences, rather than what those beliefs and desires are about. In contrast, we often talk about "rational beliefs," "irrational desires," and so on. For example, if someone desires the short-term pleasures of a drug knowing about the long-term suffering that it will cause, then we might say that their desire is "irrational." But this judgment is not something we reach by looking at formal rationality.

For the Prisoner's Dilemma, this formal sense of "rationality" entails this: if you regard all the possible results of an action A_1 as more desirable than the possible results of another action A_2, then you should choose A_1 rather than A_2. So, if Leto II believes that the Golden Path will *inevitably* be better than any alternative, then it is rational for him to lead humanity in that direction.

The Prisoner's Dilemma can be interpreted in different ways, but the basic logic is always the same. It is what decision theorists call a "game," again a word with a technical meaning. A game is any interaction between decision-makers involving strategies. A "strategy" is a plan of action. Poker is a game, but battles, trade negotiations, and even romantic dates can also be seen as "games." In the Prisoner's Dilemma, we assume that the interacting "players" are formally rational. We also assume the players each have only two possible actions; that they know the outcomes of these actions; and that they know that both players are rational.

The Prisoner's Dilemma is an imaginary interaction between "prisoners," but it actually might make more sense with prescient characters from the Duniverse. The trap is that rational strategic behavior by the players leads to what decision theorists call a "suboptimal" outcome: consequences that aren't the best possible results. Imagine that Paul is interacting with the prescient being developed by the Bene Tleilax in one meeting that will be their only interaction. This prescient being is mentioned in *Dune Messiah* and called "Thallo" in *Paul of Dune*. Departing from the books, let's assume that Thallo has identical abilities to Paul. These two prescient beings can choose between fighting and cooperating. They'll make their choices simultaneously. Furthermore, with their prescience, they can predict the consequences of their choices. If they both fight, *Galactic Conflict* occurs with unpredictable ultimate results. If either chooses to fight while the other tries to cooperate, then the player who chooses to fight will win. Finally, if they both choose to cooperate, then they rule jointly, and we assume that, despite the uncertainties involved, they prefer *Joint Rule* to *Galactic Conflict*. We can lay out the possible choices and consequences using what decision theorists call a "payoff matrix" (Figure 1).

Figure 1

	Thallo Fights	Thallo Cooperates
Paul Fights	*Galactic Conflict*	*Paul Rules*
Paul Cooperates	*Thallo Rules*	*Joint Rule*

To create a trap, all we need is to assume that Paul and Thallo have these preferences:

a. Paul prefers *Paul Rules* to *Joint Rule*, both of those to *Galactic Conflict*, and *Galactic Conflict* to *Thallo Rules*.
b. Thallo prefers *Thallo Rules* to *Joint Rule*, both of those to *Galactic Conflict*, and *Galactic Conflict* to *Paul Rules*.

Notice how both players prefer *Joint Rule* to *Galactic Conflict*; both realize that *Galactic Conflict* is not the best-case scenario. Now, decision theory says that a rational player will make a decision that is one of their best choices, given other players' decisions. When all players reason this way, we have a "Nash equilibrium," named after the economist John Forbes Nash (1928–2015) who developed the idea. In the Prisoner's Dilemma, there is only one Nash equilibrium. We can find it by elimination. It can't be *Joint Rule*, because if Paul is cooperating, then Thallo better satisfies his preferences by fighting, and vice versa. It can't be *Paul Rules*, because if Paul is fighting, then Thallo prefers fighting as well. And it can't be *Thallo Rules*, because if Thallo is fighting, then Paul prefers fighting as well. Therefore, the Nash equilibrium is *Galactic Conflict* – what Paul and Thallo would choose if they are deciding rationally.

The Prisoner's Dilemma paradoxically shows how rational choices can lead to suboptimal outcomes. As strange as this might seem, it happens in the real world. For example, imagine a very crowded bar. Suppose that the optimum outcome is that everyone talks at a moderate level: the different groups in the bar can't hear each other perfectly, but still fairly well. However, it could be individually rational for each group to raise their voices slightly to hear each other better, then slightly more when the other groups do the same thing, until it's almost impossible for anybody to hear each other. Again, rationality leads to a suboptimum outcome. Economists call such situations "market failures," but they also happen in situations that we don't normally call "markets," like politics.[3]

Foreknowledge and the Iterated Prisoner's Dilemma

It's possible to modify the Prisoner's Dilemma to avoid a market failure. Imagine now that Paul and Thallo must repeatedly choose between fighting and cooperating – the "iterated" Prisoner's Dilemma. If they don't know how many times they'll play this game, then choosing to cooperate can be rational, because this makes it possible to avoid the other player choosing to punish you in the future.

One rational strategy is called *tit-for-tat*: cooperate in the first game, and in future games only choose to fight ("defect") if the other player fought you in the previous game. Additionally, *tit-for-tat* requires cooperating if the other player cooperated in the previous game. *Tit-for-tat* swiftly punishes defecting, but also rewards the other player for switching to cooperation. If both Paul and Thallo start out with this strategy and stick to it, then they will start with *Joint Rule*, and keep choosing it. Also, if Paul chooses *tit-for-Tat*, then there are a lot of other strategies that Thallo could choose where they will ultimately end up cooperating. Iterated interactions can offer one escape from the trap of rational suboptimality.

Yet iterated Prisoner's Dilemmas can still trap the prescient. Imagine that there are exactly ten Prisoner's Dilemma interactions between Paul and Thallo. Suppose that, before the tenth game, both of them can foresee with certainty that this game is their last together. Assuming that their preferences fit the pattern (a) and (b) above, it's rational for both of them to choose to fight in the tenth game, because they can't punish each other. Now, imagine that the end of the interactions is foreseeable just before the ninth game. Both Paul and Thallo know that fighting will be the rational choice for both of them in the tenth game; there's no incentive to cooperate together in the ninth game, because they can't be rewarded for cooperation in the tenth game. The same reasoning works whether the end becomes foreseeable on the ninth game, the eighth game, and so on, up to and including the first game. Therefore, if Paul and Thallo have powers of prescience that enable them to identify the end of their interactions, they will be trapped in rational suboptimality. So prescience is not always a gift; it can be a trap. Since our own knowledge of the future is just a weaker version of what Paul and Thallo can do, it's possible that our own foresight can lead us into similar disasters.

Here is one of the many places where philosophers can add something insightful to decision theory. Common sense suggests that it is rational to achieve optimal outcomes. Does the Prisoner's Dilemma imply a contradiction between decision theory and common sense?

I've been using "rationality" in the formal sense, implying the coherence of preferences and beliefs but not restricting what our beliefs or preferences are about. Philosophers have developed stronger senses of "rationality," though. Aristotle (384–322 BCE) argued that being rational requires having the right kinds of preferences: a rational person desires to perform their family roles well, to be a good friend, to be a good citizen, and so on. A rational person, for Aristotle, prefers to be a good person, and so rational people will prefer not to benefit at the expense of others, as occurs in *Paul Rules* and *Thallo Rules*. If both Paul and Thallo know that they have these preferences, then they know that they will both prefer *Joint Rule* to ruling, and thus avoid a Prisoner's Dilemma. Similarly, the philosopher Immanuel Kant (1724–1804) argued that rationality requires acting according to a rule that everyone else could follow in the same situation (similar to the Golden Rule: do unto others as you would have them do unto you). This would exclude the outcomes *Paul Rules* and *Thallo Rules*, so Kantian rationality would achieve the optimal outcome of mutual cooperation.

If Aristotle and Kant are closer to our everyday concept of rationality, then there may be no genuine conflict between decision theory and common sense: both can be useful for different purposes. We just need precision in how we define "rationality."

Prediction and Rationality

Adding to the problems with prescience, it can paradoxically cause conflict between two intuitive rules for rational decision-making:

> *Maximization*: A rational decision-maker acts to maximize the sum of how much they prefer (or dislike) each foreseeable outcome of each action, weighted by (a) the strength of their preference and (b) how probable they think each outcome will be, given that action. This sum is called "expected utility."
>
> *Dominance*: If one action A_1 is better than another action A_2 under some foreseeable circumstance and A_2 is not better than A_1 under any foreseeable circumstance, then it is rational to do A_1 rather than A_2.

In a puzzle called Newcomb's Paradox, these principles seem to conflict. Suppose that you are playing a game with a Guild Navigator. Their prescience is imperfect, but you know they can reliably predict your choices. The Navigator's aides have put money in two boxes. You can see into Box A, which has $1000 inside, while you can't see into Box B. You are offered two possible choices, One-Box (choosing just Box B) or Two-Box (choosing Box A and Box B) (Figure 2). If the Navigator predicted that you will pick Two-Box, then they left Box B empty. If the Navigator predicted that you will pick One-Box, then they will have put $1,000,000 in it. You won't know their prediction until after you've chosen.

Figure 2

	Navigator Predicts One-Box Choice	Navigator Predicts Two-Box Choice
One-Box	$1,000,000	$0
Two-Box	$1,001,000	$1000

You can choose one of two strategies, One-Box and Two-Box, and let's assume that the strength of your preference corresponds to the amount of money you win. The principle of *Maximization* suggests that you should choose One-Box, because you know that the Navigator is an extremely reliable predictor, and the expected payoff of One-Box is about $1,000,000. However, Two-Box always gives a higher payoff than One-Box: $1,001,000 vs. $1,000,000 in the first column, $1000 vs. $0 in the second column. Therefore, the principle of *Dominance* recommends Two-Box.

Decision theorists disagree about which choice is most rational. One approach is Causal Decision Theory (CDT), in which the aim of rational action is not to maximize an action's expected utility, but instead the utility of the action's consequences. The Navigator isn't directly observing the future, so their choices aren't *caused* by your decision. So reasoning in terms of *Maximization* doesn't work: you can't cause the Navigator to predict that you will One-Box, and so you can't cause your winnings to increase by choosing it. In contrast to CDT, Evidential Decision Theory (EDT) says to maximize your expected utility *given your evidence*, and this is achieved by choosing One-Box, since it gives you evidence that the Navigator predicted this choice.

Neither supporters of CDT nor of EDT have yet found any definitive arguments for their preferred theory. Since both CDT and EDT seem plausible, we might worry that these paradoxes reveal a fundamental incoherence in our concept of formal rationality. However, in recent years, a third position has developed, which argues that when we specify the details of such paradoxes precisely (more precisely than I've done) then EDT and CDT give the same recommendations.[4] If this view is successful, then there might be little or no real disagreement between EDT and CDT. In general, little details in a scenario's formulation can make a big difference in decision theory.

Self-knowledge and Freedom

One of the most curious things about prescient beings like Paul or Leto II is that they know things about *their own* future behavior. Yet, in this sense, we all have some foreknowledge. I can predict that I'm not going to become an early riser tomorrow, although I might desire that. A psychology student learns more about her own future behavior as she studies. In neither case is the foreknowledge absolutely certain: it's conceivable, though extremely unlikely, that I might knock my head on a door tonight and become an early riser. Paul and Leto II really only differ from us in their self-knowledge's extent and reliability.

It might seem that, as knowledge of our future behavior expands, our sense of our own freedom contracts. Leto II can see that there are certain plans that he cannot complete: they are psychologically impossible for him, because they are too ruthless or painful. The knowledge itself doesn't restrict him, but should he feel less free? Assuming we want to feel free, is this kind of self-knowledge a curse?

Stuart Hampshire (1914–2004) argued that self-knowledge tends to have the opposite effect – that it makes us freer.[5] If Leto II knows that he can't follow a plan, then he can avoid making commitments he can't fulfil. In this way, he'll be able to accurately plan his life, and this is part of what it is to be free. Hampshire also argues that if we believe that we have *any* choice in a situation, an increase in our self-knowledge from science or other sources doesn't stand in the way of our sense of freedom. No matter how much we know in such a situation, we can always step back and ask, "If these are the actions that are possible based on my psychological features, which action will I choose?"

Hampshire's view of action builds on Francis Bacon's (1561–1626) argument for scientific research: knowledge is power. According to Hampshire, self-knowledge is also power. But what if we lived in a theocracy where we'd be imprisoned if we discovered certain facts? Even in that case, it's the theocrats who are responsible for our loss of freedom, not the self-knowledge. Self-knowledge from prescience could be uncomfortable for Paul and Leto II (they might discover nasty truths about themselves, like a potential for great cruelty), but it's actually the opposite of a trap.

What about learning that we never had any freedom? Hampshire surprisingly says that we would see that we do not decide at all – in fact, we would learn that we do not think, because thinking presupposes making decisions. Can't we predict what others will decide? Yes, Hampshire says, but until we make a decision we can only learn the boundaries of our choices, not what we will choose. And to "know what we will do" is to decide, not to predict.

At least in the Duniverse, prescience can work with this view. Prescience is a vastly expanded understanding of possible and probable consequences given information and choices, not the observation of a fixed future. Having examined their possible futures, Paul and Leto II can still ask, "What shall I do?" This sort of prescience seems empowering, not entrapping.

We started with the question, "Is prescience a trap?" It definitely can be, as the Prisoner's Dilemma reveals. However, Duniverse prescience need not rob Paul or Leto II of their sense of freedom, if Hampshire is right. Does self-knowledge suggest that our concept of rationality is incoherent? That depends on the answer to puzzles like Newcomb's Paradox and other exciting debates between philosophers, economists, psychologists, and others. Fortunately, none of us are prescient enough to foresee their results.

Notes

1. *Dune Messiah* (New York: Ace, 2020), 62.
2. Consider also the Voice and the imprinting powers of the Bene Gesserit and the Honored Matres. Herbert takes familiar abilities (verbal manipulation, sexual manipulation) and considers their improvement by over 20,000 years of refinement.
3. David Friedman, *The Machinery of Freedom* (Scotts Valley, CA: CreateSpace Independent Publishing Platform, 2014), chapter 53.
4. Wolfgang Spohn, "Reversing 30 Years of Discussion: Why Causal Decision Theorists Should One-box," *Synthese* 187 (2012), 95–122; David H. Wolpert and Gregor Benford, "The Lesson of Newcomb's Paradox," *Synthese* 190 (2013), 1637–1646.
5. Stuart Hampshire, *Thought and Action* (Notre Dame, IN: Notre Dame University Press, 1959) and *Freedom of the Individual* (Princeton, NJ: Princeton University Press, 1975).

15

Time versus History
A Conflict Central to Herbert's *Dune*

Aaron Irvin

George Santayana famously wrote, "Those who cannot remember the past are doomed to repeat it."[1] This idea of historical recurrence – that past events repeat themselves throughout time – is central to the Western idea of what History is. In fact, it goes all the way back to the establishment of History as an academic subject. In his fifth-century history of the Greco-Persian Wars, Herodotus (ca. 484–ca. 425 BCE) claimed that History was a continuous cycle driven by the gods. Societies began by being small, impoverished, and insignificant, then became great, then proud and decadent, and finally were overthrown by a different small, impoverished people, with the cycle beginning anew. Frank Herbert endorses Herodotus' cyclical view of empires in his presentation of the history of the Imperium. Take the example of the Butlerian Jihad, a religious movement opposed to technology that established the feudal society of Dune and that is referred to in the *Dune* Appendices as "The Last Jihad." This name turns out to be ironic, since *Dune* and its sequels focus on yet another jihad – unleashed by Paul Atreides's religious movement – and its aftermath, the reign of Leto II.

Herbert's historical universe in *Dune* is bound within a series of ever-repeating cycles. But this cyclical history clashes with Herbert's picture of Time as constantly shifting, unpredictable, its surface "impermanent as that of the windblown kerchief."[2] Paul, and later Leto II, are able to see that Time and space grant humanity an endless array of choices and options. But their access to Other Memory shows them a History in which humanity is unable to make new choices and repeats the same cycles. This conflict between cyclical History and open-ended Time is central to the unfolding of the first four novels. "Time versus History" forms the basis for Herbert's themes about human action, fatalism versus free will, and the repetition of religious motifs across vast distances of space and time.

Dune and Philosophy, First Edition. Edited by Kevin S. Decker.
© 2023 John Wiley & Sons, Inc. Published 2023 by John Wiley & Sons, Inc.

Future Sons of Atreus

Greek mythology and tragedy appear on the very first page of *Dune* with the use of a single word: Atreides. In mythology, the Atreides were the sons of Atreus, Agamemnon and Menelaus, around whom swirled the most significant events in ancient Greek myth and history.

The brothers married the daughters of Spartan king Tyndareus, Clytemnestra and Helen. When Menelaus' wife Helen was kidnapped (well, kinda) by Paris of Troy, Agamemnon gathered allies and led an army to seize Troy and take Helen back. Having angered the goddess Artemis, Agamemnon's forces couldn't set sail due to contrary winds. Rather than step down as leader, Agamemnon sacrificed his eldest daughter, Iphigenia, and the fleet was underway. After a decade-long siege of Troy in which the Greeks were victorious, Agamemnon went home to Mycenae. There, Clytemnestra greeted him, although she had already plotted his downfall and taken his cousin Aegisthus as her lover. Clytemnestra then either threw a net over him and drowned him in the bath, or trapped him in a new tunic with no sleeves and stabbed him to death, mocking Agamemnon in his last moments by revealing her affair. The cycle of tragedy continued as Agamemnon and Clytemnestra's children, Orestes and Electra, successfuly plotted together to kill Clytemnestra and Aegisthus. Greek traditions differ about the aftermath, though all of them praise and honor Orestes while grudgingly pointing out that killing your mother is probably a bad thing.

These plots and characters were the bedrock upon which Greek Epic poetry and dramatic Tragedy were constructed. The brothers' war to regain Helen found its greatest expression in Homer's *Iliad*, the keystone for all Western literature. Tragedians Aeschylus, Sophocles, and Euripides each wrote their own versions of the Atreides myths, with Aeschylus' *Oresteia* trilogy still celebrated today as a masterwork of drama. Short of Frank Herbert naming the main character of *Dune* "Heracles," there's no more culturally loaded name or family in Greek mythology than the Atreides. In his biography of his father, Brian Herbert confirms and expands upon these connections, noting that place names like "Caladan" and allusions to mythic and tragic plot elements were all drawn from his father's interest in Greek literature and mythology.[3] Many recent authors have also discussed and expanded upon the influence of classical myth and literature on Herbert's work.[4]

From Mythology to History

Much like in the *Dune* series, History emerged in the ancient Greek world by combining mythology, epic narrative, and tragedy. The author of the first true work of History, Herodotus, hailed from the city-state of

Halicarnassus in Ionia (now Turkey).[5] Ionia was a border region between the Greeks to the west and the kingdoms of Asia Minor and Persia to the east, so from an early age Herodotus would've been exposed to many different cultures in addition to the Greeks. The area also produced the first annalists and chroniclers: Cadmus around 540 BCE and Hecataeus around 500 BCE. Hecataeus in particular inspired Herodotus' style and method of research.[6] The young Herodotus took part in a failed popular uprising against the pro-Persian tyrant who controlled his home city; in the wake of this failure, Herodotus fled, ending up in Athens around 447 BCE. After giving a few public readings in Athens, Herodotus received an honorarium of about 60,000 drachmas for his work.[7]

The title of Herodotus' work, *Histories,* would've been more accurately translated as "research" or "inquiries" in his time. Herodotus aimed to be entertaining as well as informative, and his *Histories* borrows structure and ideas from Athenian theater. While he begins his work stating that his purpose was to record "the great works and wonders of the Greeks and barbarians . . . and especially the reason why they warred with one another," Herodotus' work also encompasses ethnography, geography, mythology, and sociology to create an entirely new genre of writing.[8]

Herodotus presents us with the earliest version of "the cycle of empires," an idea that has infatuated historians around the world for centuries, from Polybius to Sima Qian, Niccolò Machiavelli, Edward Gibbon, and Victor Davis Hanson. The cycle is this: empires are founded by a small, impoverished, yet scrappy fighting force that is able to defeat a much larger enemy through sheer grit and determination. Victory makes our scrappy little empire-founders wealthy and famous and they fall prey to vice, license, greed, and *hubris* – the Greek word for excessive pride. Driven to expand by an ever-growing sense of this pride, the great empire is brought low by another small, impoverished, yet scrappy force that embarrasses or even overthrows the old empire, and the cycle begins again. Herodotus even goes so far as to integrate a discussion of geography and the environment as factors in the rise of our scrappy fighting forces. The rocky hills of Greece, the dry plateaus of Persia, and the harsh deserts of Egypt all play a central role in hardening their peoples for expansion and warfare. Herodotus would immediately recognize the idea in *Dune* that the harsh deserts of Arrakis, or forbidding climate of Salusa Secondus, would give rise to elite fighting forces like the Fremen and Sardaukar.

Herodotus begins *Histories* by tracing the conflicts between Asia and Europe back to their sources, but then expands his narrative to encompass Lydia, Egypt, Scythia, Assyria, the Medes and Persians, and several Greek city-states. In his treatment of Croesus, king of Lydia, Herodotus leans heavily on Greek tragedy. Croesus misinterprets an oracle from Delphi and is ultimately undone by his own greed and *hubris*; Herodotus even goes so far as to quote the end of Sophocles' *Oedipus the King,* the lesson that we should count no man happy till his death.[9] The "cycle of empires" starts with the Medes overthrowing the Assyrians, leading to a series of unlikely conquests in which mighty empires were overthrown by small, scrappy forces. The Medes do this to the Assyrians, then the Persians overthrow the Medes, Babylonians, and Lydians.[10] No one is safe or immune to this process, and while Herodotus begins by detailing the exciting backstory of Cyrus and his rise from shepherd boy to king against his evil grandfather, Book 1 ends with Cyrus falling afoul of his own greed when he, now the head of a great empire, challenges the Scythians for seemingly no other reason than his own pride, and ends up with his head in a leather bag full of blood.

In Books 5–9, Herodotus links the "cycle of empires" to the theme of pride, or *hubris*,[11] through which he analyzes the Greco-Persian wars and explains how the Greeks emerged triumphant. Herodotus tells us of a speech to the Persian king Xerxes, where Xerxes is told:

> Look at how Zeus crushes with the thunderbolt the one that stands tall or stands out, never the small; it is always the greatest houses and tallest trees he brings down with his bolts. For Zeus loves to cut down that which stands tall. Thus, the greater army falls to the unworthy when the jealous god strikes with panic or thunderbolt. For Zeus allows pride in none other than himself.[12]

Xerxes' response is that the war must go forward for the sake of his own reputation and pride, stepping right into the divinely set trap.[13] In the aftermath of the overwhelming Greek victory at Plataea, the victory which drives the Persian army entirely from the Greek mainland, the Greek general Pausanius looks over the finery of Xerxes' captured field tent,

> and seeing the preparations in gold and silver, and the brightly colored embroidery, he ordered [the king's] bakers and cooks to prepare a meal for him even as [for the king]. They did as commanded, and Pausanius seeing the couches decked in gold and silver, and the tables in gold and silver, and the magnificence of the prepared meal, he thought it a good laugh to order the servants to prepare beside it a [Spartan] meal. That feast assembled, differing so greatly from the former in its moderation, Pausanius laughing summoned the other Greek commanders, . . . and pointing to the different meal preparations said, "Men of Hellas, I summoned you to me to show you this, for it seems to me the Persian king must have been a fool, having such provisions as these, came to seize from us our poverty."[14]

At the end of his work Herodotus sums up many of his arguments with a quote he attributes to King Cyrus of Persia: "Soft men come from soft lands, for the earth which brings forth wonderous fruits is usually different from that which brings forth men skilled at war."[15]

From Herodotus to Herbert

There is a reflection of this Greek–Persian rivalry on the very first page of *Dune*. We've already seen how the Atreides have the Greekest of Greek family names, and soon we learn of one of their rivals, the Padishah Emperor. It shouldn't be too surprising that the term "Padishah" is Persian in origin. So Herbert is immediately referring to Greek mythology and tragedy – specifically the conflicts between the Greeks and Persians – and therefore to Herodotus, our source for those conflicts. We see Herodotus' ideas about cyclical history at play within the *Dune* universe as well.

In the confrontation between Paul and Gaius Helen Mohiam there is reference to the Butlerian Jihad, a religious war that had wiped out "thinking machines" and most forms of technology.[16] Book One of *Dune* ends with Paul's visions in the desert as he confronts the new jihad that his forces will eventually unleash.[17] Paul spends the rest of *Dune* attempting to avoid, then mollify this second jihad before finally coming to accept it. By *Dune Messiah*, Paul non-judgmentally situates his jihad within the broader history of slaughter and conquest,

> "Stilgar," Paul said, "you urgently need a sense of balance which can come only from an understanding of long term effects. What little information we have about the old times, the pittance of data which the Butlerians left us, Korba has brought in for you. Start with the Ghenghis Khan . . . He killed . . . perhaps four million . . . He killed the way I kill, by sending out his legions. There's another emperor I want you to note in passing – a Hitler. He killed more than six million. Pretty good for those days . . ."
>
> "Statistics: at a conservative estimate, I've killed sixty-one billion, sterilized ninety planets, completely demoralized five-hundred others. I've wiped out the followers of forty religions . . . We'll be a hundred generations recovering from Muad'Dib's Jihad. I find it hard to imagine that anyone will ever surpass this." A barking laugh erupted from his throat.
> "What amuses Muad'Dib?" Stilgar asked.
> "I am not amused. I merely had a sudden vision of the Emperor Hitler saying something similar. No doubt he did."[18]

Dune is presented as the beginning of a new cycle of violence and conquest. The Butlerian Jihad decimated human civilization and technology and led to the Imperial ascension of House Corrino over a feudal society. Paul's dismantling of that society brings about another upheaval, another restructuring, another cycle.

One of the greatest attractions of the *Dune* series is the way in which the series re-packages well-known history and culture. Added to the Greek mythology and tragedy we already looked at, there is the feudal faufreluche system that harkens back to the medieval European nobility, complete with warfare with swords and "shields." There is the relationship of the Emperor and the Landsraad, which has more than a passing resemblance to the Holy Roman Empire and its member states. There are the Fremen akin to Islamic freedom fighters, invoking images from *Lawrence of Arabia*, as well as the echoes in them of Greek Spartans and their laconic turns of phrase. The characters are not ignorant of the power of culture and history: Jessica and the Bene Gesserit make use of the Missionaria Protectiva, which "seeds" worlds with rituals and myths that serve to protect Bene Gesserit sisters in danger.[19] It is through the knowledge and manipulation of these myths that Jessica and Paul find positions of power among the Fremen in the first place.

Brian Herbert's discussion of his father's work gives us another point of comparison with Herodotus:

> Very few readers realized that the story of Paul Atreides was not only a Greek tragedy on an individual and familial scale. There was another layer, larger than Paul, and in that layer Frank Herbert was warning that entire societies could be led to ruination by a hero. In *Dune* and *Dune Messiah* he was cautioning against pride and excessive confidence, the hubris of Greek tragedies that led to the great fall. But it was societal-scale hubris he was warning against . . . the potential demise of an entire society.[20]

When confronted by the jihad in *Dune*, 15-year-old Paul is horrified, determined to take control of the future and do what he can to avoid it. In *Dune Messiah*, an older Paul thinks back to his youth on Caladan, wondering whether he ever actually made the choice to embark on this path; did he ever actually have control?[21] By the time of his blinding, Paul has done away with any pretense of free will: present, past, and future have all simply become part of Paul's vision, but he's lost all direction and destination.[22] Paul's attempt to change the future has brought that very future into existence. As Leto II later remarks in *Children of Dune*, prescience was a trap, prescience was the very way that history repeated itself, and even the prescient became trapped in their own vision.[23]

Another Kind of Sight: Time in the *Dune* Series

Of course, I'm not arguing that Herbert crafted the *Dune* series with a deterministic or fatalistic outlook. In a talk at UCLA, Herbert said, "I like the fact that we cannot predict everything. I like the fact that we live in a universe where anything may happen, because the alternative to me is a constricting dead end."[24] Herbert describes this universe of possibilities in Paul's first experience peering through time:

> He remembered once seeing a gauze kerchief blowing in the wind and now he sensed the future as though it twisted across some surface as undulant and impermanent as that of the windblown kerchief.

He saw people.

He felt the heat and cold of uncounted probabilities.

He knew names and places, experienced emotions without number, reviewed data of innumerable unexplored crannies. There was time to probe and test and taste, but no time to shape.

The thing was a spectrum of possibilities from the most remote past to the most remote future – from the most probable to the most improbable. He saw his own death in countless ways. He saw new planets, new cultures . . .

I have another kind of sight. I see another kind of terrain: the available paths.

The awareness conveyed both reassurance and alarm – so many places on that other kind of terrain dipped or turned out of his sight.[25]

While the Guildsmen could also peer through time, they had never dared to veer off the obvious, easy paths and into the unknown to take control of their destiny.[26] Empires suppressed creativity, stunted progress, killed growth; even guided by Other Memory, all the prescient did was shape the future based on decisions and actions of the past.[27] Within a generation, Paul's dynamic Fremen warriors became the bloated, corrupted Qizarate bureaucracy, whose sole purpose was the propagation of their own power. In truth, Paul's victory and the glorious jihad brought nothing but decay.[28] As Herbert states through Leto II, "The past may show the right way to behave if you live in the past . . . but circumstances change."[29]

Herbert presents Time as open-ended, providing for endless possibilities and processes to play out. The problem is people. People, as Herbert tells us throughout the *Dune* tetralogy, seek not just easy answers, but the same answers over and over again. The cycle of empires exists not because of some natural law of the cosmos, but because human beings keep making the same mistakes. Paul's solution to the corrupt and listless Corrino Imperium is to replace it with his own Imperium, which also rapidly becomes corrupt and listless. With access to Other Memory, Paul and Leto II have full access to all of humanity's failures, the lessons learned again and again. What was needed, though was a way to teach these lessons to the general population, "a lesson their bones would remember."[30]

History, Time, and the Golden Path

In *Children of Dune*, Paul, as the Preacher, introduces Leto II to Gurney as "the ultimate feedback upon which our species depends. He'll reinsert into the system the results of its past performance. No other human could know that past performance as he knows it."[31]

The Golden Path is the death of the constant cycles of imperialism and the freeing of humanity from constantly repeating old mistakes. As the God Emperor, Leto II sees History as a "malleable instrument," a tool used to teach humanity to never seek the easy path, never look for simplicity and solace, and never allow the rise of another tyrant.[32] Tim O'Reilly, in his biography of Herbert, argues *Dune*'s readers play an active role in this process.[33] Herbert presents Paul as an idealized messiah, not just within the text but to the readers as well. Even after Paul fails, Leto II seems to promise the same fulfillment at the end of *Children of Dune*. Both characters are propelled forward by the social and cultural forces around them; humanity in fact *demands* they play these roles even as the results repel us, the readers. Muad'Dib's jihad and the tyranny of the God Emperor are presented as the inevitable result of these messiahs, with humanity celebrating and then appointing to power its own future oppressors again and again. O'Reilly quotes Herbert as saying, "There's a serious question whether humans actually can break out of their self-regulated pattern. It takes audacious methods indeed to explore beyond that pattern."[34]

By founding the *Dune* series on these particular primal themes from Greek culture and history, Herbert draws us as readers into the process of mythologizing Paul's and Leto II's ascents to godhood. *Dune* is constructed in a way that forces us to confront the ways we create not just stories, but history itself. We are just as guilty as the people of the *Dune* universe of looking for an absolutist savior to help us escape from our problems and responsibilities, and so we are just as guilty in an endless cycles of repeated mistakes. But we're also the beneficiaries of the Golden Path, through which we can recognize the pattern in the "cycle of empires" and our ability to break out of that pattern. We can become, as Herbert announces at the end of *God Emperor of Dune*, "the fountain of surprises!"[35]

Notes

1. George Santayana, *The Life of Reason: Introduction and Reason in Common Sense*, in Marianne S. Wokeck and Martin A. Coleman eds., *The Works of George Santayana*, vol. VII, part one (Cambridge: MIT Press, 2011), 172.
2. *Dune* (New York: Ace, 2005), 206.
3. Brian Herbert, *Dreamer of Dune: The Biography of Frank Herbert* (New York: Tor Books, 2003), 179, 191.
4. See Brett Rogers, "'Now Harkonnen Shall Kill Harkonnen': Aeschylus, Dynastic Violence, and Twofold Tragedies in Frank Herbert's *Dune*," in Rebecca Futo Kennedy ed., *Brill's Companion to the Reception of Aeschylus* (Leiden and Boston: Brill, 2018), 553–582; Joel P. Christensen, "Time and Self Referentiality in the *Iliad* and Frank Herbert's *Dune*," in B. Bm. Rogers and B.E. Stevens eds., *Classical Traditions in Science Fiction* (Oxford: Oxford University Press, 2015), 161–175; Lorenzo DiTomasso, "The Articulation of Imperial Decadence and Decline in Epic Science Fiction," *Extrapolation* 48 (2007), 267–291.

5. A.R. Burn, "Herodotus in His Own Words," in *Herodotus: The Histories*, trans. Aubrey de Selincourt (Harmondsworth: Penguin Books, 1972), 7; R.P. Lister, *The Travels of Herodotus* (London and New York: Gordon and Cremonesi Publishers, 1979), 12.

6. Despite these earlier historical authors, Herodotus is still rightly able to claim the title of "Father of History." Cadmus is credited with the invention of the alphabet and a series of annals detailing the founding of Miletus; the *Suda* treats him as actually having been three different individuals, and other authors, such as Dionysius of Halicarnassus, claim that he was purely mythical or actually from Phoenicia. Hecataeus was largely a geographer, and while Herodotus emulates him stylistically, Hecataeus does not present a narrative or analytical history as does Herodotus. Cf. Robert Fowler, "Herodotus and His Prose Predecessors," in C. Dewald and J. Marincola ed., *The Cambridge Companion to Herodotus* (Cambridge: Cambridge University Press, 2006), 29–45.

7. Or about 570 pounds of silver, a little over $200,000 today. This likely included property, a home, perhaps cattle and seed as well.

8. Herodotus, *Histories*, ed. N.G. Wilson (Oxford: Oxford University Press, 2015), 1.1.

9. Herodotus 1.91.1.

10. Herodotus 1.95–96 on the Medes and Assyrians; 1.127–128 on the Persians overthrowing the Medes; 1.86 on the fall of the Lydians to Cyrus; 1.191 on the fall of Babylon.

11. *Hubris*, or overwhelming and destructive pride, is an ancient concept likely familiar to readers from a study of Greek tragedy derived from concepts in Aristotle's *Poetics*. While scholarship on tragedy and discussion of *hubris* has moved well beyond the basic models presented by Aristotle, it is this association between *hubris* and tragedy that Frank and Brian Herbert would likely be most familiar with. For Herodotus, *hubris* certainly had connections to tragedy, though the concept itself also existed in Greek law codes. Acts that were needlessly hateful, destructive, and driven either by the personal pride of the perpetrator or the social debasement of the victim carried additional penalties, including exile and death. For a more thorough discussion, see David Phillips, "Hubris and the Unity of Greek Law," in M. Gagarin and A. Lanni eds., *Symposion 2013: Vortraege zur griechischen und hellenistischen Rechtsgeschichte* (Cambridge, MA, August 26–29, 2013) (Vienna: Austrian Academy of Sciences Press 2014), 75–97.

12. Herodotus 7.10E.

13. Herodotus 7.11.4.

14. Herodotus 9.82.

15. Herodotus 9.122.3.

16. *Dune*, 12.

17. *Dune*, 212.

18. *Dune Messiah* (New York: Ace, 2019), 139.

19. *Dune*, 25, 51, 210.

20. Herbert, *Dreamer of Dune*, 172–173.

21. DM, 215.

22. DM, 235.

23. *Children of Dune* (New York: Ace, 2019), 106–107, 137.

24. "Frank Herbert Speaking at UCLA 4/17/1985," from the archives of the UCLA Campus Events Commission, digitized 2015, at https://www.youtube.com/watch?v=5IfgBX1EW00&t=141s.
25. *Dune*, 206–207.
26. *Dune*, 472–473, 499.
27. *CD*, 176–177.
28. *DM*, 233.
29. *CD*, 171.
30. *God Emperor of Dune* (New York: Ace, 2019), 255.
31. *CD*, 552.
32. *GED*, 176, 389, 529.
33. Timothy O'Reilly, *Frank Herbert* (New York: Frederick Ungar Publishing, 1981), chapter 9.
34. O'Reilly, *Frank Herbert*, chapter 9.
35. *GED*, 587.

THE HUMANITY OF MUAD'DIB: MORALITY AND ETHICS IN *DUNE*

16

Secher Nbiw and the Child's Right to an Open Future

Kenneth R. Pike

> It makes no small difference, then, whether we form habits of one kind or of another from our very youth; it makes a very great difference, or rather all the difference.
>
> Aristotle, *Nicomachean Ethics* 1103b24

The paradox of *Secher Nbiw*, the Golden Path, is that the prescient God Emperor Leto II Atreides – son of Paul – must essentially enslave humankind to bring about its eventual liberation. He knows that a predictable species – one controllable by an enemy with the ability to forecast the future – is an eradicable species. It seems that he cannot know whether his plan will work: if it *can* work, then prescience should mark no difference between a future where humans have been eradicated and a future where humanity has become invisible to prescience. Future humans with the genetics or technology to evade prescience would be invisible not only to their enemies, but to the God Emperor himself. Leto II's paternalism, while cosmic in scope, parallels the decision of Duke Leto Atreides to subject his own son Paul to Mentat training from infancy – training which Paul would not comprehend until adolescence. Each Leto, in his own way, seeks to enhance future autonomy by overriding it in the present.

Parents often wrestle with the same paradox – let's call it the "paternalism paradox" – writ small, when they direct the lives of their children. When I require my daughter to practice piano instead of playing video games, I imagine this will expand her adult possibilities. Today, I limit her authorship and control of her own life, her *autonomy*, predicting she will one day appreciate the eventual result. But this is by no means certain. Perhaps she will grow to resent me – or music! – instead, or otherwise feel that she has been shaped against her interests or preferences. She's not mere property, to be molded according to my every wish and whim. But neither can she be said to pull herself "up into existence by the hair, out of the swamps of nothingness."[1] One of the most important interests humans have is in self-determination – in being the authors of our own lives.

Dune and Philosophy, First Edition. Edited by Kevin S. Decker.
© 2023 John Wiley & Sons, Inc. Published 2023 by John Wiley & Sons, Inc.

By shaping my daughter's values and preferences, am I not shaping her entire life? What, if anything, gives me the right to do that? And how might the answer inform our judgment of the God Emperor's gambit?

Jessica's Choice

The most consequential decision of Paul Atreides' life was made before he was born. The penultimate step of the Bene Gesserit breeding plan called for Leto and Lady Jessica to have a daughter. Jessica's training allowed her to select the sex of her offspring, but love moved her to defy Bene Gesserit orders, instead giving Leto what he wanted – a son and patrilineal heir. Her choice shaped Paul's life from its earliest moments, not only in terms of genetic endowment but also in terms of upbringing. Hoping to raise his successor into a "formidable" duke, Leto submitted the infant to Mentat training.[2] To prepare Paul for the Bene Gesserit's inevitable involvement in his life, Jessica taught him their wisdom and their ways. By the time Paul grasped his "terrible purpose," he wasn't exactly flush with alternatives. Paul's wrestle with destiny was substantially a struggle his parents laid out for him, both deliberately and inadvertently, through their choices.

Like science fiction authors (and prescient God Emperors), philosophers sometimes contemplate different "possible worlds," situations that might exist if only events had gone a little differently. Let's consider one such "possible world," a world where Lady Jessica obeyed her orders and gave birth to a daughter, "Pauline." This daughter would surely have trained in the Bene Gesserit tradition and may even have received Mentat training at her father's behest (though Leto was not exactly a model of gender egalitarianism). But consummation of the Bene Gesserit plan called for an Atreides betrothal to Feyd-Rautha Harkonnen, making Giedi Prime or Lankiveil more likely settings than Arrakis for Pauline's cotillion. We can imagine Pauline eventually accompanying the na-Baron to the Harkonnen fief of Arrakis, possibly giving birth to the Kwisatz Haderach there. Maybe her son would be called Vladimir II – but given access to prescience and the Other Memory of a substantially overlapping set of male and female ancestors, would Vladimir II's hypothetical path have differed meaningfully from the one taken by Leto II? My goal is not to reimagine the saga, but to note that the most consequential role of Leto's scion – Paul *or* Pauline – was to parent the eventual God Emperor. If this is right, then Jessica's choice had minimal impact on the Scattering to come. But even if her choice had muted consequences for the eventual course of history, it had a *significant* impact on the life of her firstborn child. We might well say it made *all* the difference.

For most of human history, selecting the sex of children has primarily been accomplished (if at all) through the crude and costly method of postnatal infanticide. Today, not only do ultrasound and amniocentesis allow a baby's sex to be ascertained far in advance of delivery, some medical interventions allow parents to select the sex of an embryo prior to its implantation in the endometrium. Women wishing to select the sex of their children must still undergo costly and often painful medical procedures to that end, so the dream of bodily autonomy on par with the Bene Gesserit remains distant. But the fact that something approaching Jessica's choice is now medically possible already gives ulcers to ethicists. Is it always, or ever, permissible to select the sex of one's child? Is it always, or ever, permissible to abort a pregnancy based on the child's sex? Details vary across countries and cultures, but our biological sex is often among our most consequential and enduring personal characteristics – and this is something we sometimes have reason to regret. In the past, however, there has been no one to *blame* for one's sex; it was simply a matter of biological chance. But Lady Jessica – in what was, when written, a choice only characters in science fiction novels could make – *decided to bear a son.* If Paul would have preferred to live the life of "Pauline," would this constitute a legitimate moral grievance against his mother?

It is difficult to see how. Paul and "Pauline" are not the same person, in spite of sharing a title – "Jessica's firstborn" – across their respective possible worlds. When contemplating the possible futures of our own children, parents face this puzzle in connection with far more than just sex selection. If I push my daughter to play golf, does the acceptability of my choice hinge on whether my daughter grows to love or excel at the sport? Does the moral legitimacy of James Mill's (1773–1836) method for raising a genius intellect depend on whether the child becomes the next genius like John Stuart Mill (1806–1873)? If I do *not* raise my daughter toward some specific greatness, will she be sorry about that? Will she say, as adults sometimes do, "I wish *my* father had required me to practice the piano, instead of letting me quit?" Since we can't know in advance how our children will respond to the way we choose to shape their lives, on what basis *can* we permissibly make such choices?

Opening the Future

One influential response bears passing similarity to Leto II's own. The philosopher Joel Feinberg (1926–2004) argues that parents hold their children's futures in "trust" – a concept he imports from legal theory.[3] Feinberg writes:

> When sophisticated autonomy rights are attributed to children who are clearly not yet capable of exercising them, their names refer to rights that are to be *saved* for the child until he is an adult, but which can be violated "in advance," so to speak, before the child is even in a position to exercise them. The violating conduct guarantees *now* that when the child is an

autonomous adult, certain key options will already be closed to him. His right while he is still a child is to have these future options kept open until he is a fully formed self-determining adult capable of deciding among them . . . Put very generally, rights-in-trust can be summed up as the single "right to an open future."[4]

The pursuit of an "open future" sounds like *Secher Nbiw* in a nutshell. Just as the God Emperor sought to free humanity from the controlling influence of omniscient foresight, a common approach to parenting is to pursue our dependents' eventual *independence* – that is, to limit their autonomy as children in ways intended to enhance their adult possibilities.

But autonomy seems to require mental and physical abilities that human children spend *years* developing – years during which they may be shaped by mere *proximity* to their parents. While exceptions are far from rare, most children speak the language of their birth, worship the gods of their ancestors, and work and live in the same economic class as their parents. Many settle near their birthplace and even enter the family business. Unlike the characters of Frank Herbert's imagination, we can't transmit our memories along our bloodline, but given all this, an alien anthropologist or thinking machine studying our species might be forgiven for suspecting we can! The extent to which upbringing appears to "close off" certain futures has inspired political philosopher Matthew Clayton to argue that parents must *minimize* the degree to which they direct their children's lives. Some parental influence is apparently unavoidable, because human children need adult caregiving simply to survive. Parents are thus bound to have *some* influence, however inadvertent. Nevertheless, many kinds of influence *can* be avoided, at least in theory. For example, Clayton controversially claims that parents "are forbidden from imparting particular convictions to their child or enrolling her into particular associations or practices . . . [Specifically,] it is morally impermissible for parents to baptize their child or encourage her to believe that religion is mere superstition."[5]

What would Clayton and other "open future" advocates think of Mentat training? Paul Atreides is surprised when he's offered the chance to train as a Mentat because he knows Mentat training begins in infancy. Then he recalls that the subject of Mentat training must also be *unaware* of the fact, implying that early awareness could compromise the training process. To become a full Mentat, Paul must then choose to *continue* the training of which he was previously unaware, but let's consider his position. If, as a teenager, you learned you had received secret, specialized training your whole life, and that if you continued that training, you would develop superhuman powers – is that an opportunity you would feel free to *decline*? In a possible world where Paul had not been trained as a Mentat from infancy, he simply would not have had the choice to become a Mentat. In the world where he *was* trained from birth, it is hard to say with confidence that he was the author of his own life (at least in this regard). The "openness" of a child's future is difficult to maximize because the pursuit of one opportunity often closes off others. To baptize a child, or teach them that religion is mere superstition, or train them as a Mentat, surely shapes their future in some way. But to *not* do those things *also* shapes their future in *other* ways. It seems plausible that parental influence over children's lives ought not be *excessive*, but what qualifies as "excessive?" Many adults who excel in their respective fields do so by virtue of interventions in their upbringing. Even if we assume it is important to open the future for our children (or, if we happen to attain God Emperorhood, for the entire human race), what can that mean in practical terms? Some think it means children should reach adulthood with every possible choice and opportunity available, while others think it is sufficient that children reach adulthood with "enough" choice and opportunity. But David Archard observes that the first interpretation is impossibly demanding, while the second is too vague to be helpful.[6] And either way, the paternalism paradox persists, insofar as it seems contradictory to impose freedom on others.

The interplay between these positions is evident in *Dune*. It is difficult to say what opportunities, if any, Paul lost by becoming a Mentat, but he also presumably spent some portion of his infancy learning how to walk, speak, and read. These mundane abilities were every bit as important to his story as his proficiency with weapons or the Weirding Way. But Frank Herbert did not chronicle Paul's foundational lessons. Why bother? Most of us have personal experience with similar lessons, whether or not we remember them, and so they would make for boring reading. Some foundational skills, like literacy and numeracy, seem to expand future potential without obviously closing off other possibilities, something that can't be said of all childhood pursuits. A child learning to speak and write gains many opportunities, losing few (perhaps none) along the way. But a child who spends 20 hours per week honing their kickboxing abilities has 20 fewer hours to spend excelling at chess, or physics, or philosophy – or enjoying unstructured play. It might be interesting to a philosopher to say that the right to an "open future" identifies a sort of bare minimum upbringing that parents owe to their children to avoid charges of neglect. But that gives no guidance to parents wondering whether it is okay to take their children to church, or enroll them in piano lessons, or send them to secret Mentat school. Some, like Matthew Clayton, seem to think the child's right to an open future requires parents to deliberately minimize the influence they have on children's convictions, associations, and practices, while also *maximizing* their children's future potential. This seems implausibly demanding – like asking the God Emperor to guarantee humanity's eventual freedom without resorting to tyranny along the way.

The Past–Present Alliance

Must parents be tyrants, then? Or, perhaps more perplexingly: *are* parents tyrants, by our very nature? Some think so! "Children's liberationists" resolve the paternalism paradox by rejecting most parental authority; they treat condescension to minors as "childism" – a form of oppression analogous to racism and sexism.[7] At the heart of most liberationist theory is the real concern that children not be *exploited* – that they not be treated as means to ends chosen by adults. But dramatic maltreatment (like selling or abducting children into military service, sexual slavery, or forced labor) is not the only way adults use or abuse children for their own aims. Historically, people have planned to have children to serve as extra hands for the family farm, bargaining tokens in political intrigues, or as a way to carry on the family name. More recently, "savior siblings" have been conceived to harvest genetic material for use in medical therapy. Paul Atreides was conceived based on his father's desire for an heir – and while Leto seems to have given Paul every possible advantage, we might wonder how many advantages were truly for Paul's own sake, and how many served Leto's dynastic ambitions. Conceiving a child in furtherance of one's own aims seems morally suspect. On the other hand, isn't it better to conceive children with good reasons to do so instead of conceiving them only accidentally?

The tension between these positions is wonderfully illustrated by the titular children of *Dune*. In Frank Herbert's universe, a child exposed to spice essence (the Water of Life) *in utero* gains access to the Other Memory – ancestors' recollections. But such vivid access to the lived experiences of others renders the infant susceptible to what the Bene Gesserit call "Abomination." This is the fate of Paul's sister, Alia, who succumbs to possession by Baron Vladimir Harkonnen and carries on the lifestyle, ambition, and vendetta of a man she had, as a child, slain. She becomes a tool of the past, stripped of her autonomy by an ancestor with no regard for her personhood. A similar fate awaited Paul's children, Leto II and Ghanima (though their mother, Chani, did not consume spice essence while pregnant – only large quantities of the spice itself). To avoid their Aunt Alia's fate, the twins mentally ally themselves with the personalities of benign ancestors. They are able to develop their own personalities, either by amalgamating other personalities in a deliberate way, or with defensive assistance from benign predecessors. Paul's children prevailed where Alia failed, not because they were less possessed by spirits of the past, but with the *assistance* of other, benevolent forebears. As David Archard observes:

> [A]n adult can exercise her own autonomy only in relation to the character she already has. An autonomous person must have *some* values, beliefs and dispositions, and it is precisely this that someone acquires in their upbringing. Ironically, parents would fail to produce an autonomous adult if they gave their children *no* outlook on life.[8]

Upbringing is substantially a process of cultural reproduction. Practically speaking, children do not spontaneously develop their own values. If they are not enculturated by their parents, they will be enculturated by someone else. Alia provides the clearest example of the problem – something Jessica seems to recognize later, when she suggests to Ghanima that "perhaps [she] gave up too soon."[9] Had Jessica furnished Alia with an upbringing in spite of the obvious challenges, might certain tragedies have been averted? The lesson for parents is that our children can never be free of us; the bonds of our influence on them cannot be severed. For our children, the past is not optional, so whether it is good, bad, or middling, our children *will* have *some* upbringing, and most of it will not be a matter of *their* choosing. Parental interference can harm children, sometimes irrecoverably. But parental neutrality renders children vulnerable to influence – and exploitation – by others. As Bruce and Jonathan Hafen observe, parents who refrain from guidance in hopes of opening their children's futures risk "abandoning children to their autonomy,"[10] as Jessica abandoned Alia to the ghosts of her ancestors.

Choosing the Future

Whatever family is to us personally, it is most fundamentally the site of biological and cultural reproduction. Not all of us have children, but all of us have parents. These parents, whether biological or custodial, transmit genes and culture into an uncertain future, a future in which they will not (or at least not entirely) take part. Sex and death play important roles in Frank Herbert's epic. The idea that the preservation of humanity is not merely a matter of biological persistence, but also *cultural* persistence, is manifest throughout the saga. Jessica's choices for Paul and Alia were not just informed by her love for Leto, but also, indirectly, by Leto's cultural expectations. Leto's enrollment of Paul in Mentat training was not only a response to Paul's genetic capacities, but also to the demands the empire was likely to place on his son. Whether a child exposed to the Water of Life would become an Abomination hinged not on access to genetic memories, but on *which* of those memories became the basis of their adult behavior. The God Emperor appropriated the Bene Gesserit breeding program, but also enacted broad cultural changes in pursuit of his goals. In fiction as in reality, culture is the secret of our species' success.[11]

So when philosophers suggest that parents have a moral obligation to refrain from enculturating their children, they're stripping away a central feature of parenting. Here, Frank Herbert's epic furnishes a warning: those who do not choose the future will be dominated by those who do. If it's argued that children should be *less* influenced by their parents, then this has the practical effect of arguing that children should be more influenced by someone else. This is sometimes true – for example, when parents are abusive or neglectful. But what we owe to our children is not autonomy *per se*, or at least it is not *only* autonomy. To the extent that children should become authors of their own existence, they must first be handed a stylus, supplied with paper (or sheets of holographic crystal), and taught to write. The paternalism paradox is dissolved when we realize that it was never our role to maximize the autonomy of others – it was only our role to give them the tools they need to eventually maximize their own. We can never know whether we've given our children the best possible or most open future, but we *can* know that we have done what we could with proper intent. The best hope any of us can have, then, is to be formed and guided by benevolent predecessors, and to in turn benevolently select futures when it is in our power to do so. Rarely in literature has there been more clear-eyed and, indeed, prescient contemplation of these matters than in the world of *Dune*.

Notes

1. Friedrich Nietzsche, *Beyond Good and Evil*, trans. Walter Kaufman (New York: Random House, 1966), 21.
2. *Dune,* 40th anniversary ed. (New York: Ace Books, 2005), 46.
3. Kenneth R. Pike, "The Trust Model of Children's Rights," *Moral Philosophy and Politics* 7 (2020), 219–237.
4. Joel Feinberg, "The Child's Right to an Open Future," in William Aiken and Hugh LaFollette eds., *Whose Child? Children's Rights, Parental Authority, and State Power* (Totowa: Littlefield, Adams & Co., 1980), 125–126.
5. Matthew Clayton, "Debate: The Case Against the Comprehensive Enrolment of Children," *The Journal of Political Philosophy* 20 (2012), 353.
6. David Archard, *Children: Rights and Childhood*, 3rd ed. (New York: Routledge, 2015), 76.
7. Elisabeth Young-Bruehl, *Childism: Confronting Prejudice Against Children* (New Haven: Yale University Press, 2012).
8. Archard, *Children*, 199.
9. *Children of Dune*, Ace hardcover ed. (New York: Ace Books, 2008), 283.
10. Bruce C. Hafen and Jonathan O. Hafen, "Abandoning Children to Their Autonomy: The United Nations Convention on the Rights of the Child," *Harvard International Law Journal* 37 (1996), 449.
11. Joseph Henrich, *The Secret of Our Success: How Culture Is Driving Human Evolution, Domesticating Our Species, and Making Us Smarter* (Princeton: Princeton University Press, 2015).

17

The Spice of Life
Hedonism and Nozick in the *Dune* Universe

Luke Hillman

> Without melange, the Sisterhood's Reverend Mothers could not perform their feats of observation and human control. Without melange, the Guild's Steersman could not navigate across space. Without melange, billions upon billions of Imperial citizens would die of addictive withdrawal. Without melange, Paul-Muad'Dib could not prophesy.
>
> *Dune Messiah*

As a *Dune* fan, you've noticed the intricate ways that spice melange is bound up with the motivations of most of the characters. Some forsake everything to gain profit through spice or to ingest it, losing themselves in the drug's intoxicating premonitions. The eyes of Ibad, blue-within-blue, clearly indicate an avid user and identify the indigenous peoples of Arrakis, the Fremen. Spice is as addictive as it is helpful; with each ingestion, users find themselves more entrapped by the addicting, cinnamon-like substance.

After eating a tasty meal, drinking a fine beer, or taking a relaxing nap, have you ever found yourself asking, "What if I went back for seconds, one more beer, or just went back to sleep?" Of course, you have (I admit that I often go back for more than one beer). It's normal for us to want more of what is good in life. But what if you answered "yes" to these questions over and over? In such a heedless pursuit of pleasure, you might make a choice that's bad for your health or compromises something important in your life, like your religious ideals or commitment to your significant other. Now, imagine that you *always* answered "yes." Always answering "yes" to these types of questions is the essence of hedonism.

Jeremy Bentham (1748–1832) understood hedonism as an ethical principle that tells us to minimize pain and maximize pleasure. Hedonism eventually morphed into the ethical theory of *utilitarianism*, which tells us to maximize the pleasure of everyone affected by our actions. The main difference between Bentham's hedonism and utilitarianism is that Bentham

Dune and Philosophy, First Edition. Edited by Kevin S. Decker.
© 2023 John Wiley & Sons, Inc. Published 2023 by John Wiley & Sons, Inc.

is focused on the individual. The pure hedonist does not care who they may hurt with the consequences of their actions. They only seek to maximize their own personal pleasure.

You're probably thinking that hedonism is an outlandish way to live your life (and I'd agree with you!). But there are hedonistic tendencies in each of us, and Frank Herbert, author of the *Dune* series, knew this as well. We're all hard-wired to seek pleasure, much like we're hard-wired to reproduce and survive. This idea, that we have tendencies to seek our own pleasure, is called "psychological hedonism." If ethics is about what we *should* and *should not* do, then "ethical hedonism" says it's always *right* for me to seek my pleasure.

In this chapter we'll explore hedonism in the *Dune* universe. Specifically, we'll consider how the spice melange symbolizes hedonism. By looking at how and why characters in *Dune* seek spice, we'll discover different aspects of the hedonistic lifestyle. Ultimately, Herbert rejected the hedonistic lifestyle: we can find evidence for this in his descriptions of *Dune*'s primary antagonist, Baron Vladimir Harkonnen. Ultimately, we'll see why spice and hedonism should be rejected, using a philosophical thought experiment called "the experience machine."

The Baron: Hedonist Extraordinaire

The Baron Harkonnen, Herbert's pivotal and initial antagonist, fully engages in the lifestyle of seeking his own pleasure above all else. Not only do we see this large, grotesque man – who can barely walk without the help of technology – enjoying the hedonistic lifestyle afforded by his wealth and power, we also see him do all he can to subdue others in his pursuit of maximizing these pleasures. "'A carnivore never stops. Show no mercy. Never stop . . . You must always be hungry and thirsty.' The Baron caressed his bulges beneath the suspensors. 'Like me.'"[1] He plots to destroy his long-time nemesis, the Duke Leto Atreides, in order to recapture Arrakis and gain the exclusive, coveted access to the spice. Harkonnen positions his family in ruling roles on Arrakis so that he can control the natives and maximize spice profits. And he does all of this in search of the most important goal in the universe, the seat of Emperor. In addition to food, drink, spice, and power, the Baron also pursues pleasure from young boys. Indeed, he personifies the extreme position of hedonism: fully indulging in his own pleasures, he will game the system, forfeit relationships and family, harm others, and even disregard his own health.

If Bentham's hedonistic ethics were acceptable, Harkonnen would be a prime example of the ethical theory as practiced by a master. If we did the "pleasure-math," it would show us that the Baron is ahead where many fall behind. However, this can't be right. The Baron is meant to be the immediate tangible evil in the universe of *Dune*.

Herbert, being the subtle author that he is, includes many more interesting ways of thinking about hedonism.

Paul Muad'Dib: Pleasure of Premonition

Spice has a profound effect on Paul Atreides, his family, and the whole universe. Paul sums up his relationship with the drug: "The spice changes anyone who gets this much of it, but thanks to you, I could bring the change to consciousness. I don't get to leave it in the unconscious where its disturbance can be blanked out. I can see it."[2]

Because of the Bene Gesserit training that Paul's mother Jessica implemented throughout his life, Paul now has an ability that many spice users will never possess: premonition through the manipulation of spice ingestion. The side effect of premonition offers an entirely new level of hedonistic addiction.

Imagine that when eating a cheeseburger you were able to glimpse the future. On top of the wonderful burger flavors, you experience premonition. You'd feel compelled to eat burgers all the time (I know I would!). This is the life that Paul finds himself living. Unfortunately for Paul, and perhaps the galactic empire, his introduction to spice is a step into a deep pool. Paul seeks his own pleasure and gain through consistent use of spice and the benefits of the spice's premonition.

Still, should we think that Paul is living a hedonistic lifestyle if the spice is in *everything*? This raises an important question about a person's intention to act hedonistically. While Baron Harkonnen *intentionally* defiles his body, scams his friends and family, and pursues underage boys, it's not clear that Paul *intends* to seek the side effects of the spice melange that ultimately leads to a galaxy-wide jihad. Rather, he finds himself completing a puzzle set in place by the Bene Gesserit.

Nozick's Experience Machine and the Spice Melange

Dune is a universe driven by the desires of humanity, and maybe hedonism is an appropriate way for some to live. One plausible objection to hedonism comes from Robert Nozick (1936–2002) and his speculations about an "experience machine."[3] Suppose there is a machine that could give you the experience of anything you desired (pretty cool, right?). For me, this would be catching a massive, large-mouth bass on a beautiful lake or driving a fast car through the Alps. Think of the experience machine as a VR headset on steroids. To enjoy your wildest desires, all you have to do is "plug in" and stay connected. Nozick's machine would be so effective that it could trick your brain into thinking that you're *actually* experiencing what you desire.

So, the key question Nozick has for his readers is, would you plug in to such a machine? At first glance, it would be hard to pass up such a machine: experiencing all that brings you pleasure with no negative consequences, how awesome! Imagine fishing and always catching fish! But Nozick offers three reasons why we should not use the experience machine.

First, Nozick thinks that a life lived within this kind of virtual environment is not a life that actually *accomplishes* anything. Just because you are experiencing your maximal, pleasure-filled life, does not mean that you are accomplishing anything with your life. For Nozick, there's a major difference between experiencing something and actually living it. In my case, the pleasure of being on a lake and fishing is much more wonderful than playing a fishing videogame. Even if this game is maximally realistic, as Nozick supposes, it's still missing the feature of the actual experience. Think about having an experience contrasted with being told about it. No matter how good a storyteller you are, you probably end up saying, "You had to be there." There's something to be said for experience over observation or simulation.

Imagine that Paul just wasted away in the caves on Arrakis ingesting the Water of Life (plugged into his own version of the machine). Nozick considers a life like that to be not really a life at all. Paul in the caves, or you hooked up to the machine, would be "an indeterminate blob," wasting away, only seeking the experiences that bring the most pleasure. In *Dune Messiah*, we encounter such a character, the Guildsman Edric. Floating completely in a cloud of spice melange and consuming only spice-pellets, Edric is a seer for the Guild, plotting their routes through space by using the spice's gift of prescience. The Princess Irulan – Paul's wife in title only – notes how Edric's disgusting figure is distorted from a life devoted to spice consumption. This parallel makes clear what Nozick had in mind when he pictured the wretched state of a person attached to the experience machine. And while Herbert couldn't include a character that did *nothing*, like a person hooked up to the experience machine, Edric clearly never lives a life as the other characters do. He's just a passive observer. Nozick's second point is strongly against this lifestyle. Doing is so much more than observing. When we are learning new activities, it is much easier to learn by doing than by simply watching a training video. Herbert clearly understood the importance of truly *living* a life as opposed to just existing in a pleasure machine.

Last, and perhaps most importantly, Nozick thinks that we are living a lesser life if we spend our time devoted to the machine because the machine is human-made. In a sense, if you're plugged into the machine, you forfeit your freedom of choice. This is much like the freedom that a drug addict loses: they can fight their addiction, but all too often the addiction wins out by rewiring their brain to desire only the drug. Further, there's a loss of potential, because no matter how clever we are in our creation of machines, we still are limited by our imagination. While the imagination is splendid, we cannot think of everything that would occur in life. Nor could we fully encapsulate lived experience in all its subjectivity. No matter how excellent the fishing simulation, the experience is still not as good as *actually* catching a fish. This is Nozick's final objection to the experience machine.

Of course, the experience machine is human-made, whereas the spice is created by the natural process of the sandworm's life on Arrakis (hence the apt Fremen name "makers"). So, you *could* push back against Nozick's last point by saying that because spice is not artificial, you are living just as good a life as those who do not partake in the spice melange. (Many characters, especially Paul, would probably argue that they are living a *better* life from taking the melange.)

Despite Nozick's three reasons to the contrary, perhaps there could still be good motivations for choosing the experience machine. It might be that real life is far worse than what's possible in the experience machine and you want to experience something better than your current situation.

The Duke Leto: Choosing People Over Pleasure

Perhaps the *Dune* universe is not as bleakly hedonistic as I have painted it. We've focused on the full immersion of Edric the Guild pilot, the disgusting and disturbing habits of the Baron, and the exploitation of spice for prophecy by Muad'Dib, but we have not considered the brief glimpse we get of a caring individual, Duke Leto Atreides.

The Duke often chooses his people over power or financial gain, and he's interested in the locals of Arrakis as people and respects their customs. He's not perfect, of course – he spreads propaganda about his virtues and uses a planet for financial gain, among other things. But one of Duke Leto's shining moments is when he takes Liet-Kynes and some others on a ride over the Arrakeen desert in an attempt to show that he's honorably taking care of his fief. During this trip, the group encounters a mining vehicle with a full crew in imminent danger of a sandworm attack.

With the sandworm closing in, the Duke maneuvers his 'thopter (much to the protest of planetologist Liet-Kynes) to save the mining crew from potential ingestion. In the process, the mining vehicle and the day's haul of spice is returned back to the desert. The Duke knows that this is a substantial loss. If the Duke endorsed hedonism, especially in the cutthroat way that his rival the Baron does, he would have saved his profit and sacrificed the men. Ultimately, though, he meets his untimely end because of his trust and investment in people.

The Fremen: Lost in Spice

The galaxy's most prominent consumers of spice, the Fremen, have their own way to characterize outsiders to Arrakis as hedonists: their plump faces, a stark contrast to Fremen leanness. Several times in *Dune*, the Fremen look down their noses on the water-waste of the off-world visiting elite. Ironically, the Fremen – whose diet consists entirely of food with spice in it – have views on seeking pleasure that differ dramatically from non-natives.

The Fremen value the success of the tribe, religious ideals of a new Arrakis (lush and green with plant life), and water. It would be quite difficult, if not impossible, to develop a lifestyle that is devoted to pleasure when your survival and that of your community weigh so heavily on your mind. Recall that, for Nozick, a life devoted to hedonism (a life plugged into the machine) is a lesser life. If the connection between spice and hedonism holds, then Fremen, unfortunately, are living lesser lives because their diet is rich with spice in every bite. Of course, this is not the case when we first meet the Fremen. They are devoted to one another and to the overall survival of their tribe. Cleverly, Herbert offers this unique combination of a group so engrossed in spice, yet also living by some of the highest moral standards in the *Dune* universe.

To Spice or Not to Spice? That Is the Question!

Hedonism is richly represented throughout the *Dune* universe, and not even Paul is excluded from the spice's tantalizing effects. To evaluate the life of hedonism, you can ask yourself, would you ingest spice? Or, in another scenario, would you plug into the experience machine? Would you forsake all else to enjoy days and days of pleasure with no real consequence? Is it really living a lesser life to seek your own pleasure at every turn? Maybe it is not fair to ask these questions of you. After all, the experience machines that we're used to do not grant longer life, the power to see the past, present, and future, or the blue-within-blue eyes of Ibad. Yet the cinnamon-like substance beckons all within Herbert's works and none are left the same after they embrace the tantalizing effects of spice melange.

Notes

1. *Dune* (New York: Ace, 2005), 386.
2. *Dune*, 318.
3. Robert Nozick, *Anarchy, State, and Utopia* (New York: Basic Books, 1974), 42–45.

18

"Less Than a God, More Than a Man"

Is It Morally Wrong to Make a Kwisatz Haderach?

Alexandru Dragomir

> He was warrior and mystic, ogre and saint, the fox and the innocent, chivalrous, ruthless, less than a god, more than a man. There is no measuring Muad'Dib's motives by ordinary standards.
> From "Arrakis Awakening" by the Princess Irulan[1]

Take a look to your left, now to your right – you'll be sure to find at least one piece of "smart" machinery for the comfort and necessities of your life. In the *Dune* universe, humans relied on computers for thousands of years. Their immense capacity for mathematical calculations made space travel possible, until the Butlerian Jihad ended that era. But what comes after humanity puts an end to the use of intelligent computing machines? Humans found the means to cognitively and physically enhance themselves to replace and outmatch intelligent machines by using nootropic drugs, revolutionary training methods, artificial selection, and genetic engineering. *Dune* is about the coming into being of the Kwisatz Haderach, the pinnacle of 90 generations of Bene Gesserit selective breeding to create the Superbeing. As the Kwisatz Haderach, Paul Muad'Dib is endowed with prescience, the Other Memory of his ancestors, and extraordinary perceptiveness and intelligence. But what are the consequences of creating such a radically enhanced human being? Is it morally wrong to seek to create a Kwisatz Haderach?

Human Enhancement in the Duniverse

Imagine a universe in which scientists, engineers, and educators concentrated on improving human cognition and physical traits instead of building better computers. Frank Herbert lays out a smorgasbord of

Dune and Philosophy, First Edition. Edited by Kevin S. Decker.

enhancement drugs for denizens of his universe: the spice melange grants prescience, extends lifespan, and improves overall health; the Truthsayer drug allows the Bene Gesserit to go into a trance that distinguishes truth from lie; the juice of sapho enhances the Mentats' mental powers to out-match computing machines; rachag, a stimulant, is consumed during debriefings and strategy meetings; both Duke Leto Atreides and Thufir Hawat take anti-fatigue and energy pills; and gladiators are given the Elacca drug to go berserk in the fighting pits.

The Bene Tleilaxu are master genetic engineers, renowned for being able to create gholas, or clones fully equipped with the memory of the original individuals. They also create Face Dancers, who can mimic the appearance of any human, and "twist" Mentats into human computers unconstrained by moral laws and principles. As farmers breed animals with desired traits to get offspring with improved versions of those traits, the Bene Gesserit selectively breed with men who have characteristics deemed suitable for the Kwisatz Haderach. Their interest in identifying such traits is evident when Lady Margot and her husband, like two athletic talent scouts, remark on Feyd-Rautha's agility and cunningness in the fighting arena.

Besides these forms of intervention, the Bene Gesserit and the Guild of Navigators created education programs to identify and cultivate the talents of children from an early age: "The Great Revolt took away a crutch . . . It forced *human* minds to develop. Schools were started to train *human* talents."[2] While the Guild focuses on mathematical training, the Bene Gesserit aims at gaining perfect self-control through the improvement of both mental and physical capacities: prana-bindu training enhances perception of environmental and social factors, and gives the trainee the capacity to memorize, recollect, and analyze vast amounts of information. To illustrate, Paul, in an extraordinary feat of perceptiveness, figures out the existence of a secret exit from a Fremen hideout simply by inspecting the air currents in the room. If Jessica, with her highly trained senses, hadn't been able to figure that Paul was still alive after taking the Water of Life, the story of Muad'Dib would've been cut short – to the Fremen's and the reader's disappointment. Extreme psychological and muscular self-control developed through prana-bindu training makes the Bene Gesserit into fearsome fighters. Although the Fremen are presented as highly proficient warriors, Jessica quickly manages to immobilize Stilgar at the Tuono Basin, and Paul easily defeats the much more experienced Jamis.

Though these kinds of improvements might be attractive and spectacular, there are also moral and social problems that come along with human enhancement technologies. They are *enhancement* technologies, so their purpose is to extend a human's abilities beyond the statistically normal.[3] As a result, such technologies might disadvantage people who cannot afford them. In a society where enhancement is popular, the poor would have fewer chances to succeed in social and economic competitions: "the rich get smarter, and the smart rich get richer."[4] In *Dune*, only the most privileged can afford spice and benefit from its mind-enhancing, lifespan-extending effects. This small, elite group includes the Emperor, the leaders of the Great Houses, and the Guild Navigators. Duke Leto teaches Paul: "all fades before melange. A handful of spice will buy a home on Tupile. It cannot be manufactured, it must be mined on Arrakis. It is unique and it has true geriatric properties."[5] Access to large amounts of the drug allowed the Guild a monopoly on space travel, causing its emergence as one of three major powers in the Universe. Human enhancement would deepen social inequalities, and it would also influence our understanding of *personhood*, the very thing that guarantees our freedoms and basic rights.

Personhood and Post-personhood

Many moral philosophers argue that our freedoms and basic rights are guaranteed by a special moral status, *personhood*. Because we are persons, we can't be harmed in certain ways without government intervening on our behalf, and our interests and well-being weigh more than the interests and well-being of things with lower moral status, like rocks and non-sentient animals. Early in *Dune*, Duke Leto's decision to save the spice-workers' lives instead of the spice in their harvester is an example of the respect for human lives that the status of personhood guarantees. It also explains Liet-Kynes's admiration for the Duke and his family, who contrast starkly with the Harkonnens and their abusive ways.

But why do we deserve such a privileged status? It's not because we belong to the species *homo sapiens*. After all, wouldn't we welcome as an equal the lovable alien from Spielberg's (1982) *E.T. the Extra-Terrestrial*? Or any Earth animal advanced enough to understand our social structure, communicate, and philosophize with us about the meaning of life? On the other hand, if personhood is more like a badge that allows entrance to an exclusive social club – if it's "a free-floating honorific that we are all happy to apply to ourselves, and to others as the spirit moves us, guided by our emotions, aesthetic sensibilities, considerations of policy, and the like"[6] – then we might lose it if policies and emotions change over time. Since these two roads are blocked, let's see if there's another.

Let's ask what really matters to having the moral status of a person. According to John Locke (1632–1704), persons are "rational, self-conscious beings who are aware that they have interests that persist over time."[7] So what matters to Locke are the mental powers that allow you to conceive of what's good and bad for you over time, but that also make you able to anticipate paths and obstacles to your future well-being. More specifically, according to Immanuel Kant (1724–1804), personhood is based on mental capacities that allow us to accept and act on "universal" principles – that is, moral principles that could and should be followed by all rational beings.[8] Either way, what makes a being (and not necessarily a human being!) a person does not depend upon membership in a species or the changeable rules of human sympathy or society.

But if mental abilities are so important, what happens if your abilities highly surpass the norm for deserving personhood? Would you deserve a higher moral status – *post-personhood* – and so *more* protection of your interests and rights?

Post-persons in the Duniverse

Nicholas Agar has proposed that post-personhood could be seen as the end of a continuum of intelligence and reasoning abilities.[9] Along the continuum there would be three categories of moral status: inanimate things, like rocks and chairs, that have zero-moral status; things that have "sub-personal" moral status, like non-sentient animals; and, finally, personhood, which includes not only human beings but, perhaps, some animals like dolphins and apes. Now, if we think of these three categories of moral status as a continuum of lowest-to-higher mental capacities (*à la* Locke or Kant), then a huge increase in those capacities would imply an even higher category of moral status, post-personhood. Clearly, the enhancement technologies that Frank Herbert imagined would give a being the higher moral status of post-personhood.

Looking at them from Agar's perspective, the inhabitants of the *Dune* universe already fall into a greater variety of moral statuses. So under the faufreluches system, the Padishah Emperor, his family, and everyone in the Great Houses of the Landsraad are top of the hierarchy. Their interests are assumed to have precedence over the interests of other denizens of the Duniverse. The weight of the nobility's rights helps explain the institution of slavery in Herbert's universe, Rabban's abuse of the indigenous Arrakeens, and the ease with which the Padishah Emperor threatens the entire Fremen population with annihilation.

On the other hand, at the lower extreme of *Dune*'s categories of moral status, we find those kept in slavery. Clearly, the slaves in the Harkonnen fighting pits or love chambers don't have the basic moral protections of personhood; they may be harmed or killed at the whim of their masters. To take two gruesome examples, Feyd-Rautha practices his fencing skills fighting and killing slaves, and for the purpose of punishing Feyd's plot against his life, Baron Vladimir Harkonnen commands him to kill every woman in the pleasure chambers of the slave quarter.

Situated between these two extremes, the fanatic Sardaukar warriors are taught to see themselves as superior human beings. Mentat Thufir Hawat finds that the Sardaukar mindset is part of their tradition and argues that creating a similar fighting force requires just the same belief in superiority: "I'd fill them with the mystique that their planet had really been a secret training ground to produce just such superior beings as themselves. And all the while, I'd show them what such superior beings could earn: rich living, beautiful women, fine mansions . . . whatever they desired."[10]

Straight from the Philosopher's Toolkit

Science fiction like *Dune* shares with philosophy the use of *thought experiments* to think about the possible existence and nature of things that don't appear to exist – like gholas and sandworms. David Hume (1711–1776) justified such thought experiments when he said, "*whatever the mind clearly conceives includes the idea of possible existence*, or in other words, *that nothing we imagine is absolutely impossible*."[11] In other words, if we are able to *imagine* beings of higher moral status, then they are at least *possible*. Two such thought experiments can help us see that the Kwisatz Haderach is a likely candidate for the status of post-person. The first comes from Thomas Douglas, and the second comes from Jeff McMahan.

Thomas Douglas invites us to imagine a time and place in which the mental abilities that moral status depends on, such as intelligence, altruism, and self-control, are enhanced to the point where humans can engage in forms of social cooperation that do not lead to collective action problems.[12] Douglas uses the possibility of "enhanced cooperators" like these to argue that such creatures deserve a superior moral status.[13] Collective action problems arise when people facing the same or similar problems find themselves in a situation where their cooperation would benefit the group most, but by acting separately and selfishly, many individuals in the group would gain more. To illustrate, let's look at one of the most useful and famous thought experiments, what contemporary political scientist Robert Axelrod called "the *E. coli* of social psychology" the *Prisoner's Dilemma*.[14]

In our imagined *Dune* scenario, a Harkonnen spice harvester has been destroyed by the Fremen, and the Baron asks Rabban to find the culprits. The Sardaukar have been increasingly vigilant and caught two young Fremen who, wanting to prove their valor to the sietch, attempted to steal an Ornithopter. Unsurprisingly, they do not confess to attacking the harvester, so Rabban tells each of them, in private:

> If you testify, saying that you both attacked the harvester, but your partner refuses to confess, then I'll let you go, and he'll get ten years in my dungeon of Carthag! However, if he testifies you both did it and you do not, then I'll let *him* go and *you'll* be spending ten years in the dungeon. If both of you testify you did it, I'll grant you two my mercy (*cough*) and reduce the maximum punishment to only six years for each of you. If you both keep quiet, remember that you're still guilty of trying to steal a 'thopter, so you'll both get one year detention for that.

Importantly, the two young Fremen cannot communicate with each other during or after their interrogation. That means they're on their own in making a decision.

If they want to minimize their losses, each will choose to betray the other: no matter what the other Fremen does, testifying grants either fewer years in Rabban's dungeon than keeping silent (remember, no jail if the other does not confess, six years otherwise; compare with choosing not to confess: six years if the other keeps silent, ten years otherwise). But – and here's the catch! – the penalty for the less risky strategy of confessing, six years, is worse than what they'd gain if both chose to protect each other, one year in detention. This is a collective action *problem* because lack of communication or of trust makes them unlikely to choose this last option. But the "enhanced cooperators" of Douglas's thought experiment would choose to act in this altruistic (yet individually risky) way, looking for the best outcome for them both.

The Bene Gesserit education and selective breeding program claims to be all about producing human beings who maximize the well-being of all humankind. The gom jabbar test, as Reverend Mother Helen Gaius Mohiam explains it to Paul Atreides, is used to determine someone's potential for inhibiting the instinctive reaction to pain, but also for selfless behavior: "You've heard of animals chewing off a leg to escape a trap? There's an animal kind of trick. A human would remain in the trap, endure the pain, feigning death that he might kill the trapper and remove a threat to his kind."[15] Bene Gesserit education's effects on both Jessica and Paul emerge when they exhibit spontaneously selfless behavior after being ambushed by the Fremen at the Tuono Basin. Jessica puts herself at great risk by attacking Stilgar, while Paul retreats to a safer place to try and gain a threatening position to ensure her escape. So, a capacity similar to what Douglas considers necessary for the moral status of post-personhood is nurtured by the Bene Gesserit, and is a desired trait of the Kwisatz Haderach.

Expanded Consciousness and Empathy

Jeff McMahan speculates that since the capacity for empathy is necessary for personhood, the enhancement of empathy would give a being a higher moral status than just personhood.[16] He thus invites us to imagine beings that can experience the thoughts and feelings of others as if they were their own, while also being able to reflect on these experiences.[17] This "expanded consciousness" is not an outlandish thought experiment: we can already imagine feeling the pain or anxiety of others, even though we don't actually feel them. The enhancement of our ability for empathy would have consequences for our moral behavior and policymaking: for example, directly feeling the suffering of an immigrant child might change our immigration policies. Likewise, feeling the anxiety and pain of animals might alter our attitudes toward harming them.

McMahan's idea of "expanded consciousness" also finds a home in the *Dune* universe. Something quite similar is attainable by Reverend Mothers, the Fremen, and the Kwisatz Haderach. Upon taking the Water of Life, Jessica senses the terror that her unborn daughter is experiencing, and gains access to all the memories of the dying Reverend Mother Ramallo: "the old woman was dying and, in dying, pouring her experiences into Jessica's awareness as water is poured into a cup."[18] During the spice orgy after Jessica converts the Water of Life, Chani reveals that ingesting the substance allows the Fremen people to telepathically share thoughts and feelings: "We're together – all of us. We . . . share. I can . . . sense the others with me, but I'm afraid to share with you."[19] Yet the Kwisatz Haderach can do all these things, and much more! For instance, he is able to access the experiences of all his ancestors, both maternal and paternal, a feat impossible to Reverend Mothers. These parallels to McMahan's sense of "expanded consciousness" again point to the Kwisatz Haderach as a likely candidate for post-personhood.

"That Which Makes a Man Superhuman Is Terrifying"[20]

Paul Muad'Dib is the perfect example of an enhanced human: he's cognitively and physically enhanced through the Bene Gesserit genetic selection program, taught by the best teachers and warmasters spice can buy (Mentat Thufir Hawat, Suk doctor Wellington Yueh, Duncan Idaho, Gurney Halleck), trained in the Weirding Ways by his mother, and, after settling among the Fremen, has access to as much spice as a human being can tolerate. All these enhancements are responsible for his becoming the Kwisatz Haderach, the Superbeing.

So is making a Kwisatz Haderach morally wrong? If we incline toward answering "yes," maybe the worry is that the Kwisatz Haderach – an enhanced being of higher moral status than us – might be entitled to more rights and freedoms, his interests and well-being having more importance than ours. In effect, the Superbeing might be able to legitimately sacrifice the freedoms, rights, and interests of non-enhanced beings if it is to his benefit. To use an analogy, he might treat mere people the way humans treat cats, dogs, and Sligs. As Nicholas Agar reminds us, we've sacrificed the health and lives of countless animals to develop vaccines and cures.[21] Beyond this concern, if the Duniverse's Superbeing were created, it would make the lives of those in the lower ranks of the hierarchy even worse. Just imagine three circus acrobats, each weighing 140 pounds, doing a human ladder. The one on top has it easy until a fourth acrobat climbs up – but it's even worse for the one at the bottom: now it's 420 pounds on their shoulders!

It seems that seeking to create a Kwisatz Haderach is morally wrong. But we shouldn't rush to this conclusion. Allen Buchanan, for example, argues that an extension of the ladder of moral status doesn't necessarily mean that those below would no longer benefit from the rights they already have.[22] In other words, "once a person, always a person!" So Superbeings and mere persons could cohabitate peacefully. What's more, if enhancing mental capacities entails the enhancement of moral sentiments – as our "enhanced cooperator" and "expanded consciousness" thought experiments suggest – then the Kwisatz Haderach might not only be smarter, but also kinder and more thoughtful toward lower moral status beings.[23] Consider that Paul Muad'Dib fears for the billions of lives that would be lost in the jihad he presciently saw; much of his inner turmoil stems from trying to prevent it.

So, the question of whether it is morally wrong to bring about the Kwisatz Haderach is not an easy one to answer. If we pressed the wisest of the Mentats to respond, they'd probably take a sip of sapho juice and reflect on all the interrelated issues: the mental capacities that ground personhood, the technologies that aim at improving them, our notions of rights, freedoms, and moral status, and their intricate relationship with each other. As discussed, the inhabitants of Herbert's universe, with their already multi-tiered moral status system backed by the feudal-like faufreluches system, are in for double trouble. First, drawing on Nicholas Agar's lessons, the more statuses a society accepts, the easier it is to accept a new one. And if moral status is tied to mental capacity, the Superbeing's status would top all others – as we've seen, with bad prospects for everyone else of lower status. Second, since they live under the faufreluches system, if a Superbeing infringed on their rights and freedoms, they couldn't rely on any of our democratic institutions. A safe bet, though, is that the Mentat would advise keeping human enhancement technologies in check. Not as in prohibiting them, since, remember, they'd still need substitutes for computers and other technologies banned after the Butlerian Jihad, but merely making sure that the technologies nurture moral virtues like wisdom, kindness, fairness, and tolerance, alongside quick logical reasoning, memory, and physical power. This way, either Superbeings would not claim a higher status, or they would refrain from infringing the freedoms and rights of lesser beings.

On a different note, what's in it for us, the *readers* of *Dune*? Philosopher Richard Rorty (1931–2007) argued that reading literature is necessary for our moral education, making us more empathic, imaginative, and open-minded.[24] As children we take our lessons in moral virtue from fairy tales and fables, and as adults we learn from more mature fiction. Science fiction is particularly instructive because it ponders the effects of technology on our lives and societies. Think about George Orwell's *Nineteen Eighty-Four* world, in which surveillance technology is used as a tool for dominance and control. Read Philip K. Dick's *Do Androids*

Dream of Electric Sheep?, and you'll get to explore the problems of creating artificial humanoid slaves. Look at A.C. Clarke's *2001: A Space Odyssey* as a forewarning about our reliance on artificial intelligence. Dive into Ursula K. Le Guin's *The Word for World Is Forest* for a cautionary tale on the effects of colonizing other planets and alien cultures. Read *Dune* and you'll be like a Mentat (but without the sapho juice), reflecting on the consequences of the widespread use of enhancement technologies. In the end, it's still not easy to decide whether it's right to make a Kwisatz Haderach, is it?[25]

Notes

1. *Dune* (New York: Ace Books, 2010), 757.
2. *Dune*, 18.
3. So eyeglasses that correct poor vision wouldn't count as an enhancement technology, but bionic eyes that help you see farther or at night would.
4. Anders Sandberg and Julian Savulescu, "The Social and Economic Impacts of Cognitive Enhancement," in Julian Savulescu, Ruud ter Meulen, and Guy Kahane eds., *Enhancing Human Capacities* (Chichester: Wiley Blackwell, 2011), 104.
5. *Dune*, 68.
6. Daniel Dennett, "Conditions of Personhood," in Amelie Oksenberg Rorty ed., *The Identities of Persons* (Berkeley: University of California Press, 1976), 176.
7. Nicholas Agar, *Truly Human Enhancement: A Philosophical Defense of Limits* (Cambridge, MA: The MIT Press: 2013), 159.
8. Immanuel Kant, *Groundwork for the Metaphysic of Morals*, trans. Jonathan Bennett, at https://www.earlymoderntexts.com/assets/pdfs/kant1785.pdf.
9. Agar, *Truly Human Enhancement*, 176–180.
10. *Dune*, 610.
11. David Hume, *A Treatise of Human Nature*, Book I, Part II, Section 2 (Oxford: Clarendon Press, 1896), at https://oll.libertyfund.org/title/bigge-a-treatise-of-human-nature.
12. Thomas Douglas, "Human Enhancement and Supra-personal Moral Status," *Philosophical Studies* 162 (2013), 473–497.
13. I borrowed the term from Agar, *Truly Human Enhancement*, 173.
14. Robert Axelrod, *The Evolution of Cooperation* (New York: Basic Books, 1980), 28. To explain the metaphor, *E. coli* is one of the most analyzed organisms on Earth.
15. *Dune*, 13.
16. Jeff McMahan, "Cognitive Disability and Cognitive Enhancement," *Metaphilosophy* 40 (2009), 582–605.
17. Something similar can be found in Kathryn Bigelow's 1995 movie *Strange Days*.
18. *Dune*, 578.
19. *Dune*, 585.
20. Feyd-Rautha, thinking about a superhuman feat of the gladiator he just killed. *Dune*, 544.

21. Agar, *Truly Human Enhancement*, 194.
22. Allen Buchanan, "Moral Status and Human Enhancement," *Philosophy and Public Affairs* 37 (2009), 346–381.
23. See Emilian Mihailov and Alexandru Dragomir, "Will Cognitive Enhancement Create Post-persons? The Use(lessness) of Induction in Determining the Likelihood of Moral Status Enhancement," *Bioethics* 32 (2018), 308–313.
24. Richard Rorty, "Is Philosophy Relevant to Applied Ethics? Invited Address to the Society of Business Ethics Annual Meeting, August 2005," *Business Ethics Quarterly*, 16 (2006), 369–380.
25. I'm grateful to Kevin Decker and William Irwin for their feedback on earlier versions of the chapter, and to Louise Spencely for copyediting. For their suggestions and comments, I would also like to thank Corina Stavilă, Emilian Mihailov, Constantin Vică, Radu Uszkai, and my father, Ion, who introduced me to the wonderful world of *Dune*.

19

That Which Does Not Kill Me Makes Me Shai-Hulud
Self-overcoming in Nietzsche, Hinduism, and *Dune*

Steve Bein

Life is a mask through which the universe expresses itself. We assume that all of humankind and its supportive life forms represent a natural community and that the fate of all life is at stake in the fate of the individual. Thus, when it comes to that ultimate self-examination, the *amor fati*, we stop playing god and revert to teaching. In the crunch, we select individuals and we set them as free as we're able.

Lady Jessica Atreides, *Children of Dune*

One of the major themes in the *Dune* novels is what Friedrich Nietzsche (1844–1900) calls *self-overcoming*. This is an internal struggle against one's own physical, mental, and moral limits, in pursuit of a more powerful form of self-expression. The Fremen and the Sardaukar capture the concept perfectly: by situating them on a hellish planet, Frank Herbert commits entire cultures to Nietzsche's famous maxim, "That which does not kill me makes me stronger."[1]

We see self-overcoming in Duncan Idaho, who overcomes his Tleilaxu conditioning after being reborn as a ghola. We see it in Lady Jessica, who thwarts the centuries-long genetic program of her Sisterhood by giving her duke a son instead of a daughter. We see it most clearly in Paul Muad'Dib, whose self-overcoming began with the gom jabbar (a Nietzschean device if ever there was one: if the test doesn't kill you, it will make you stronger). Paul later overcomes his Bene Gesserit training, bending it to his will. As a Fremen, he overcomes the name Atreides, freeing Muad'Dib from the fetters of aristocracy. He even overcomes the limits of time, space, and mortality as the prescient Kwisatz Haderach.

But when it comes to self-overcoming, there's one little boy who puts all of them to shame: Leto II, son of Chani and Paul Muad'Dib. The Fremen spend 10,000 years forging themselves into the deadliest fighters in the

Dune and Philosophy, First Edition. Edited by Kevin S. Decker.
© 2023 John Wiley & Sons, Inc. Published 2023 by John Wiley & Sons, Inc.

cosmos, and Leto says, "Hold my beer."[2] In becoming Shai-Hulud, he makes himself a god. In fact he *must*, for he faces a moral conundrum too great for mere mortals: should he follow his Golden Path? If he does, he ends the eternal jihad, but he also shatters the galactic economy irreparably, condemning humanity to theocratic dictatorship for millennia. On the other hand, stepping aside from the Golden Path spells the end of the spice, the end of interstellar travel, and the condemnation of all humankind to the provincial consciousness of life on a single planet.

Luckily, you and I don't have to decide the fate of humanity, as Leto does. But there's still a big philosophical question for us to answer: does Leto's decision represent an unprecedented exercise of willpower, or is it actually no decision at all? Is it the only thing he could have done in a present already written by the future? This is a question in the age-old debate of *free will versus determinism*. Nietzsche toys around with this question, and Hinduism does a lot more than toy with it. In this chapter we'll see what they have to say about Duncan, Jessica, Paul, and the God Emperor himself.

Are We Fremen or Unfremen?

We all know our decisions are influenced by forces beyond our control. Here's an easy example: would you like to walk as you normally do, or do the Fremen shuffle-step? It depends on where you're standing, right? In the deep desert, your normal pace gets you eaten by a sandworm. But once you're home in the sietch, the shuffle-step makes you look like a jackass. We're all immersed in an ocean of prior causes and conditions, and these nudge our decision-making in one direction or another. In the desert, basic survival instinct taps you on the shoulder and says, "Hey, let's not get swallowed today." Then, in the sietch, social conditioning chimes in: "Okay, but let's not become the laughingstock of the tribe either."

The big question is, are we capable of defying these external influences, or do they always predetermine our choices? If you believe we have free will, then you believe that we can sometimes overrule the countless factors that shape our decision-making. (This general school of belief is called *libertarianism*.[3]) Consider Dr. Yueh, who betrays House Atreides to avenge his wife, whom he already suspects Baron Harkonnen has murdered. If he tells Duke Leto, "I'm sorry, I had no choice," the libertarian will say, "Sure you did. You could have failed your wife instead of failing your House. You just chose not to."

On the other hand, if you're a *determinist*, you believe the factors that exist before any given decision – including genetics, upbringing, environment, past experiences, current circumstances, and so on – influence every single one of our choices, such that none of us ever acts freely. For example, suppose you cut yourself with a crysknife (or a kitchen knife, if that's all you have handy). Can you accurately predict the first word to come out of your mouth? I can. Mine starts with *f*, and it isn't "faufreluche."

Can you predict your next steps after that? Would you grab the first aid kit? How about squeezing a lemon directly into the wound? It often *feels* like we could choose to go either way, but the determinist will say even this feeling is predetermined. If we hit replay on your life a thousand times, so a thousand times you cut yourself just the same way, and a thousand times in a row you dress your wound with the first aid kit instead of freshly squeezed lemon juice, then the lemon isn't really a choice. It only seems like one.

Nietzsche never heard of a replay button, but he offers us a similar thought experiment with the *eternal return* (sometimes called the *eternal recurrence*).[4] He asks,

> What if a demon crept after you one day or night in your loneliest solitude and said to you: "This life, as you live it now and have lived it, you will have to live again and again, times without number; and there will be nothing new in it . . .?"[5]

Nietzsche suggests you might have one of two responses. The first is to gnash your teeth and curse, and the second is to thank the demon for bearing such wonderful news. It all depends on what you think of your life and your decisions so far. Prior to Arrakis, Duke Leto and Lady Jessica might have thanked the demon. They had a comfy life on a comfy planet, with a brilliant baliset player strumming away like their own personal Spotify. But after? Thanks, but no thanks. Returning eternally to betrayal and murder doesn't sound so nice.

Nietzsche didn't say the eternal return is true. To him it's just a question. But there's one school of thought that says all of us really *are* living in a version of the eternal return, and it's got some interesting things to say about free will and determinism.

If the Stillsuit Fits, Wear It

Hinduism says we're all born into *saṃsāra*, the unending cycle of birth, death, and rebirth. As individuals, we don't replay the exact same life over and over again (as in Nietzsche's thought experiment), but collectively we're all bound up in the same universal collaboration of actions and reactions, lives and deaths, good karma and bad karma. We go round and round the wheel of *saṃsāra*, reincarnating into one body after the next, sort of like exchanging a worn-out stillsuit for a new one.

In effect we're all players in the repertory theater of the cosmos, and our director is the *dharma*, the cosmic law behind both nature and morality. As it turns out, Bene Gesserit philosophy agrees with Hindu philosophy on the idea that the moral order mirrors the natural order. We see this in Lady Jessica's epigraph at the beginning of this chapter, where she comes pretty close to the *dharma*: "All of humankind and its supportive life forms represent a natural community."[6] The actors change with every reincarnation, but the roles are familiar: the deep thinker, the fiery protector, the shrewd calculator, the diligent worker, and so on. Through karma and reincarnation, we have infinite roles to audition for, and infinite opportunities for self-betterment, always tested by the *dharma*.

In the end, Hinduism says, we all reap what we sow. (And hey, you don't have to be a Mentat to understand that what goes around comes around.) With each rebirth, karmic momentum sends us along a certain trajectory, and if you want to alter that trajectory, you've got to do some moral self-overcoming.

What is moral self-overcoming? In each cosmic (re)play, your job is to gain a deeper understanding of your character. That's *character* in both senses of the word: the role you're to play, and also your innermost nature. When you're reborn, the stillsuit is new, but the *you* slipping into it isn't. You have a history, and your past actions (called *karma*) continue to bear fruit (called *karmabandha*, the bonds of karma). No one knows this better than Duncan Idaho. In his first rebirth, as the ghola Hayt, he's sent to Paul Muad'Dib knowing his Tleilaxu creators plan for him to assassinate Paul. His psychological conditioning is a kind of karmic bond, but so is his ghola body. Ultimately the body wins out: some part of him still loves Paul like a son, and it overrules the programming of the murderous Bene Tleilax.

According to Hinduism (and determinism too), you and I are no different. We are bound not only by our present circumstances but also by our past actions, and by the character we formed through those actions. For Beast Rabban torturing the defenseless is as natural as eating and sleeping. If he were to suddenly start believing in reincarnation and wanted to purge himself of cruelty (which is certain to earn him a miserable rebirth), then he would have to achieve a self-overcoming of Herculean proportions. Sadism disturbs the natural order *and* the moral order. How do we know? Because humans are the only animals to engage in it, and almost all of them find it appalling. To align himself with the *dharma*, Rabban would have to overcome his own character, formed by long habit and karmic momentum.

No matter what he does, his choices have ripple effects. Yours do too, and remember, they don't just affect you. They radiate to all the rest of us, just as ours radiate back to you. That's the grand cosmic play: *karma* and *karmabandha*, creating patterns, cycles, feedback loops so far-reaching that even Thufir Hawat couldn't track them all.

Can Unfremen Act Freely?

A case like Rabban's tests whether or not there are good reasons to believe in determinism. If determinism is true, then Rabban doesn't have free will, in which case why should he worry about becoming a better person? A being who lacks free will hasn't got much need to hem and haw over ethics. The choice to be a better man is *hard* for him to make, doesn't it follow that it is in fact a *free* choice?

Well, no. The determinist will say there's an important difference between what the decision *feels like* and what *actually happens*. For example, in *Children of Dune*, Lady Jessica plays Prince Farad'n Corrino like a baliset, leading him inexorably to conclude – of his own free will (or so he thinks) – that his own mother has been manipulating him. In the end he becomes Ghanima's concubine and Leto II's official scribe, effectively bringing House Corrino and its fearsome Sardaukar to heel – which, of course, was Lady Jessica's goal all along. Farad'n *thinks* he chose freely, but we readers know better.

Nietzsche says we know better even when it comes to our own lack of freedom. "The total unfreedom of the will," he insists, is "our strongest knowledge."[7] He calls free will "a piece of nonsense," something we believe in because of our "excessive pride," and likens libertarians to Baron Münchhausen, a fairy tale character with delusions of his own powers.[8] And yes, this does sound odd coming from the guy who advocates self-overcoming and the will to power. What could be more libertarian than exercising your willpower to overthrow your physical limitations and social conditioning?

The short answer is, Nietzsche is tricky to pin down when it comes to the free will debate. He writes not of freedom but "the idea of freedom," which he calls "the will to be responsible for yourself."[9] So there's some wiggle room there: what you *can* do isn't the same thing as what you can *will* yourself to do. And this raises a deeper question: even if all our so-called "decisions" are as inevitable as Farad'n's, could there still be room for freedom of choice?

It turns out there's more than one determinist answer. If you're a *hard determinist*, you believe 100 percent of our choices are zero percent free. We're like sandworms, drawn mindlessly to the sound of footfalls on the slip face of a dune. But if you're a *soft determinist*, you believe we're capable of steering some of our decisions, even if only a little. For example, consider Duncan Idaho's fateful standoff with Stilgar in *Children of Dune*. Duncan knows only one of them will leave the sietch alive, but he gets to choose which one. By forcing Stil's attack, he sacrifices himself to save his friend and keep an important Atreides ally on the field.

The Hindu philosopher Sarvepalli Radhakrishnan (1888–1975) makes an argument for *compatibilism*, a version of soft determinism that says free will is compatible with a determined universe. "Human freedom is a matter of degree," Radhakrishnan says, and he compares our lives to a game of bridge.[10] Here, Duncan and Stilgar can't play any old cards they want. They can only play the ones they're dealt. Like any card game, the rules of bridge make some plays better than others, and that by itself imposes certain limits on the players' choices.

At the beginning of their "game," Duncan and Stilgar are as free as they're ever going to get. But as soon as Duncan plays his first card, that has a determining effect on how the game will unfold. (Not just his plays, but Stil's too.) Each time he plays a card, he limits his freedom even further, until at last he's left with two dreadful options: he dies or Stilgar dies.

Poor Duncan! He doesn't want to play either card. He tried playing his hand so he wouldn't end up here. But if you know your way around card games, you know that sometimes you just get a bad hand. And sometimes the other players outplay you no matter what you're dealt. So Duncan never had the kind of freedom libertarians believe in – that pure, 100 percent unbounded choice – but in the end, he *can* choose which of his two no good, lousy, fatal cards to play.

Of course, the hard determinist will say it only *feels* like a free choice. What seals Duncan's fate is his loyalty to House Atreides, a loyalty so deeply ingrained in his psyche that, when you get right down to it, he was never going to choose otherwise. But Radhakrishnan says Duncan's freedom of choice isn't a matter of defying his mental habits; it's all about whether he chooses wholeheartedly or halfheartedly. As he puts it,

> Freedom of the will really means freedom of the self. It is determination by the self . . . Self-determination means not determination by any fragment of the self's nature but by the whole of it. Unless the individual employs his whole nature, searches the different possibilities and selects one which commends itself to his whole self, the act is not really free.[11]

In other words, if Duncan is torn between devotion to the Atreides and saving his own skin, then his decision isn't really free. But since he's selfless in his loyalty, and *also* a selfless friend to Stilgar, and *also* a Zensunni Mentat whose calculations tell him this choice is best for House Atreides, then he isn't choosing as a fragment of himself. It's the whole Duncan who chooses how this game of bridge will end, and that makes him as free as human beings (and probably gholas) can get.

Speaking of Bridges . . .

Radhakrishnan's bridge analogy applies to another bridge: the one spanning the Idaho River, the final, fateful, fatal terminus of Leto II's last peregrination along his Golden Path. The big question is, could his reign have ended any other way?

He certainly doesn't think so, but you and I may still have doubts. Yes, humanity needs to be freed of its God Emperor if it is ever to venture out in the Scattering. But why doesn't he just abdicate the throne? And yes, the future of humankind depends on all those sandtrout becoming the next generation of sandworms, but why get peeled apart in the rapids when he could just sit in a hot tub? That sounds like a much nicer place to hang out with his beloved Hwi Noree – especially when the alternative has her plummeting to her death alongside him.

Leto doesn't take the easy way out, presumably because there's no other way to set humanity on the Golden Path. So Leto does exactly what Nietzsche would have him do: he embraces his fate. Oh, and by the way, let's not rule out the possibility that he's actually a distant relation of Nietzsche himself. Leto shares the memories of his ancestors, and several times he uses a Latin term that otherwise comes to us only through Nietzsche: *amor fati*, the love of fate.[12] In *Children of Dune*, Leto speaks several times of "the *amor fati* which I bring to humankind, the act of ultimate self-examination."[13] Could that term be a memory bubbling up from the depths of Leto's pre-born consciousness? Does Friedrich Nietzsche have a seat beside the pharaohs as one of Leto's illustrious ancestors? I like to think so.

To love your fate is to "thank the demon" in Nietzsche's thought experiment of the eternal return. It is to engage in "the ultimate self-examination," as both Leto and Lady Jessica describe it, and to emerge from that examination capable of rejoicing in the inevitable. But the libertarian must ask, couldn't that itself be a free choice? He's a God Emperor, after all; no one can tell him what to do. Just because following the Path is his best option doesn't *force* him to choose it.

The hard determinist will say force doesn't enter into it. If all of your options are terrible except for one, then they're not genuine options. Even if it *seems* like I could, I'm never going to reach for the lemon juice when I can reach for the first aid kit. But the soft determinist takes a middle path. Leto is playing the final hand of a 3500-year-long game of bridge. He's played masterfully, but the best players in the universe still winnow their options down to just one card. There's no freedom in choosing to cross the bridge, but it doesn't follow that he never had it.

The End of the Path

Leto's reference to "fate" in *amor fati* implies he's a determinist. But what kind? His *magnum opus*, the Golden Path, is his great gift to humankind: a "new kind of time" where prescience no longer weaves divergent futures back together. Schemers like the Bene Gesserit can no longer manipulate variables to converge in a single "concurrence" under their control. That cuts the strings from all the would-be puppeteers with the gift of prescience, but all the ordinary influences on our decisions still hold sway: genes, beliefs, experiences, roving Laza tigers, and so on. God Emperor or not, Leto is still subject to the laws of cause and effect, just like the rest of us. So we're back to our original question: does Leto's decision represent an unprecedented exercise of willpower, or is it the only thing he could have done in a present already written by the future?

Framed in Nietzschean terms, Leto's will to power is unequalled in human history (though he has an unfair advantage: the rest of us only get a few decades to try it). Likewise, his self-overcoming is beyond compare;

he transcends every limit imaginable, attaining a level of self-expression that is truly godlike. But he's too wise to believe in the "piece of nonsense" that is "the idea of free will."[14] He accomplishes his superhuman feats by *embracing* his fate, not by pretending it doesn't exist.

Framed in Hindu terms, Leto was born to protect. In ancient India, House Atreides would have been *kshatriyas*, members of the warrior and protector caste. (Who but the *kshatriyas* would have a specialized Chakobsa battle language?) In following his Path, he sought to protect humanity by aligning it more closely with the *dharma*.[15] Whatever the cosmic order may be, surely it isn't endless jihad, or enslavement to machines with minds, or 13,000 worlds wholly dependent on the one planet with the spice melange. But it isn't thralldom under the thumb (or flipper?) of a God Emperor either. As a protector from a House of warriors, Leto's final recourse can only be to sacrifice himself for his people.

Framed in Radhakrishnan's terms, "we are most free when our whole self is active and not merely a fragment of it."[16] That's a tall order for a boy with a thousand extra minds floating around in his head. Even so, it's clear that following the Golden Path is a selfless choice for him. He surrenders so many things he would otherwise have wanted: his own humanity, a long life with Hwi Noree, normal friendships, a legacy as something other than a tyrant. If he chooses with his whole self – which it seems he does – then he is as free as any human–sandworm hybrid can be.

In the end, Leto's Herculean labor is a Nietzschean labor: self-examination and self-sacrifice in the name of self-overcoming. But it's not selfish, as Nietzsche's philosophy is so often thought to be. He upholds his warrior's duty to protect, not selfishly, nor with a fragmented self, but through the wholehearted self-overcoming of the karmic bonds of selfishness.

Notes

1. Friedrich Nietzsche, Maxim 8 of "Maxims and Arrows" in *Twilight of the Idols*, trans. Judith Norman (Cambridge: Cambridge University Press, 2005).
2. Or is it spice beer? Truth to tell, he probably shouldn't be drinking beer of any kind. Despite the generations of pre-born wisdom he inherited at birth, his body is still only eight years old.
3. In philosophy, *libertarianism* is the name given to two unrelated schools of thought, one in political philosophy, the other in metaphysics. In metaphysics – which is what we're talking about here – libertarianism is the belief that human beings (and maybe human–sandworm hybrid beings too) have free will. That is, they are capable of acting contrary to what pre-existing conditions would otherwise direct them to do.
4. If you want a deeper dive into the eternal return in the *Dune* universe, see Brook Pearson's "Friedrich Nietzsche Goes to Space," in Jeffery Nicholas ed., *Dune and Philosophy: Weirding Way of the Mentat* (Chicago: Open Court, 2011), 189–205.

5. Nietzsche, *The Gay Science* 341, in R.J. Hollingdale ed., *A Nietzsche Reader* (London: Penguin, 1977), 249.

6. *Chapterhouse: Dune* (New York: Berkeley, 1977), 305.

7. Nietzsche, *Human, All Too Human*, trans. R.J. Hollingdale (Cambridge: Cambridge University Press, 1996), 50.

8. Nietzsche, *Beyond Good and Evil*, trans. Judith Norman (Cambridge: Cambridge University Press, 2002), 21. To extricate himself from a swamp, Münchhausen pulls himself up by his own hair. Nietzsche implies that those who believe in free will must replicate this impossible feat, escaping from their "strongest knowledge" – namely, that determinism is true – by pulling themselves up by their own pride.

9. Nietzsche, *Twilight of the Idols*, 38.

10. Sarvepalli Radhakrishnan, *An Idealist View of Life* (London: George Allen and Unwin, 1932), 278. "Bridge" was an ancient card game played on Old Terra in the centuries preceding the Butlerian Jihad. What's important for present purposes is that four players are dealt 13 cards each, and then must take turns playing one card at a time.

11. Radhakrishnan, *An Idealist View of Life*, 277–278.

12. We might split a philosophical hair here and observe that Nietzsche is the first to express this idea *in Latin*. The Stoics of ancient Greece advised us to embrace our fate a good 2000 years before Nietzsche got around to it. But the phrase *amor fati* originates with Nietzsche, because, well, it ain't Greek.

13. CD, 270.

14. Nietzsche, *Human, All Too Human*, 50, and Nietzsche, *Beyond Good and Evil*, 21.

15. It's worth noting that Leto himself seems to deny the existence of the *dharma*. In the Stolen Journals he says, "In all of my universe I have seen no *law of nature*, unchanging and inexorable. This universe presents only changing relationships which are sometimes seen as laws by short-lived awareness," *God Emperor of Dune* (New York: Ace, 1987), 456.

16. Radhakrishnan, *An Idealist View of Life*, 278.

LESSONS OF THE GREAT REVOLT: POLITICS AND WAR IN *DUNE*

20

The God Emperor and the Tyrant

The Political Theology of Frank Herbert's *Dune* Saga

James R.M. Wakefield

> When religion and politics ride the same cart, [and] that cart is driven by a living holy man . . . nothing can stand in their path.
>
> Bene Gesserit teaching, *Dune*

Politics and religion certainly ride together throughout the *Dune* saga. Paul "Muad'Dib" Atreides and his son, Leto II, become the most powerful rulers in the known universe, revered respectively as a prophet and a living god. That political leaders are somehow godlike is an old idea in philosophy. Equally old is the idea that leaders might exploit myths to make people support them. Plato (ca. 428–348 BCE) argued that the best form of government would operate without any input from ordinary people, who should be appeased with fictions to explain the social order.

Similar rationales were given to support twentieth-century dictatorships, whose citizens were encouraged to see their leaders as infallible. In this way, politics in a totalitarian state resembled a religion, with a community of faithful followers and its own special theology to justify the dictator's authority. In this chapter, we'll draw parallels between the religious dimensions of politics in Frank Herbert's *Dune* novels and some philosophers' views on tyranny and justice here on Earth.

Vice-regents of Heaven: Political Leaders and Political Religions

How do Paul and Leto come to be such powerful political and religious leaders?

Let's start with Paul. Before the events of the first novel, the religious culture of the Fremen has been primed for the arrival of a messiah, and

Dune and Philosophy, First Edition. Edited by Kevin S. Decker.
© 2023 John Wiley & Sons, Inc. Published 2023 by John Wiley & Sons, Inc.

Paul is – not coincidentally – ideal for that role. The Bene Gesserit's Missionaria Protectiva has already cultivated "infectious superstition[s]" on planets across the Imperium.[1] When they did this, the Sisters anticipated that they'd have control of the Kwisatz Haderach, and through him they'd be able to muster a galaxy's worth of true believers in support of their agenda. This isn't quite how things turn out, however. Even so, the Fremen are "beautifully prepared to believe" that an outsider, the son of a Bene Gesserit, will come to "lead [them] to paradise."[2]

Paul fits neatly into the Fremen's existing belief system, so they have no trouble accepting him as an infallible leader. And yet, as he soon discovers, he can do little to control them. Soon after the 12-year jihad has been carried out in his name, Princess Irulan describes him as

> the Mahdi whose merest whim is absolute command to his Qizarate missionaries. He's the mentat whose computational mind surpasses the greatest ancient computers. He is Muad'Dib whose order to the Fremen legions depopulates planets. He possesses oracular vision which sees into the future.[3]

This is true, but it gives a misleading impression of Paul's power. He's powerless to *stop* his followers believing that he's more special, more godlike, than he really is. He's more a catalyst than a component in the chemical reaction that awakens the "sleeping giant" of the Fremen, who are like an "unconscious single organism."[4]

Here on Earth, by contrast, prophecies and talk about leaders as actual gods don't feature much in political philosophy, but plenty has been said about leaders or institutions being in some sense god*like* or otherwise connected to the divine. In the Catholic Church, for example, there's a long tradition of regarding the pope as infallible, at least with respect to moral and spiritual matters. The great medieval philosopher St. Thomas Aquinas (1225–1274) argued that the pope is infallible because he is "the vicar of the apostolic throne" – the earthly representative of God, occupying the position originally held by St. Peter, who, according to the New Testament, was personally appointed to the role by Christ.[5] In similar vein, other leaders have sometimes claimed that while they're not *themselves* gods, they are appointed by God, so they effectively rule on His behalf, with His authority, and are answerable to no one but Him.[6]

Paul is accepted as a messiah or prophet, and we're told that he tries to be "a supreme moral symbol while [renouncing] all moral pretensions" and is "a saint without a god."[7] The Fremen come to think of him as a god, though he doesn't want this. He sees that, for all his special powers of prescience and wisdom, he is still a fallible person. He aims to do the right thing (as "a supreme moral symbol"), but he doesn't have the right answers to every question (hence the lack of "moral pretensions"). When his followers make the mistake of thinking him infallible, they treat everything he says with more significance and certainty than he intends.

Leto II, on the other hand, leans into the role the Fremen give him. By the time he's born, Paul's political religion is well established. The jihad has spread it across the inhabited universe. Yet when Paul renounces his role and disappears into the desert, Leto sees that this religion needs "a living god" to keep it from breaking down without its messiah.[8] Leto becomes the human–sandworm hybrid "God Emperor," whose powers are even greater than his father's. As well as prescience, enhanced computational powers, and ancestral memory, he is nearly (but not quite) invulnerable to harm, and can live much longer than an ordinary human. For the first 300 years of his reign, the Fremen take him to be a "delegate" of a nameless "supreme deity" – equivalent, perhaps, to Aquinas's pope in his relation to God. He then performs what they see as a "miracle" to convince them that *he* is their god.[9] In this way he tightens his control over them: they literally believe him to be a deity, and so are all the more willing to do as he commands without question.

We might think that this is pure science fiction, without any direct bearing on real-world politics and political philosophy. For better or worse, our leaders are made of the same stuff as the rest of us, and they'd be hard-pressed to convince us otherwise. They can't reliably predict the future, draw directly on a collective consciousness, or perform anything like miracles. Yet according to Carl Schmitt (1888–1985), the modern sovereign state now bears many of the special characteristics traditionally assigned to God. Though shorn of explicit ties to religion, the positions of leaders in the apparatus of government makes them effectively – if only metaphorically – godlike.

The modern view, says Schmitt, is not that political leaders have second-hand divinity – a kind of political authority borrowed or passed down from some higher power. Instead, godlike characteristics such as infallibility, lack of accountability to any higher authority, and the power to define right and wrong are *built into the idea* of the sovereign state. As the "omnipotent lawgiver," the state acts "in many disguises but always as the same invisible person."[10] This "invisible person" exists mainly as a metaphor. Political leaders are not *personally* infallible, and they do not *really* have a hotline to any kind of all-knowing deity, but as leaders it must be assumed that they have the last word.

This conclusion might seem like a rationalization by Schmitt, who favored dictatorship in his own country. But we can understand his claim in more mundane, psychologically plausible terms. Think of the old business expression, "The boss is always right." People who work for the boss might not agree, but the buck must stop somewhere, and it's the leader's job to make final decisions one way or another. Even in democratic countries, leaders still tend to think of themselves as in service to some higher, impersonal standard, like a set of principles, a tradition, a flag, or a constitution. They have few qualms about treating these with near-religious reverence, even when it's really *their* collective decisions that make the difference. Citizens might disagree with those decisions, but in the end, they're not the boss.

Playing God: Knowledge and Justice

According to Paul, "the problem of leadership is inevitably: Who will play God?"[11] With this in mind, let's ask: is it good news for the people of Arrakis (and the wider Imperium) when the Atreides start playing God? Is there any special reason they should become objects of religious devotion? Should their leadership have a distinctly religious aspect, when past leaders, like the Padishah Emperor Corrino, did not? Paul and (especially) Leto have some qualities that set them apart from other rulers. While their rule is uncompromising, they are undoubtedly wise, smart, and well-informed. But how are wisdom, intelligence, and knowledge related to good leadership?

Plato thought these traits were all part of the same package. He was a *moral realist*, believing general concepts, or universals – justice, for example, or goodness – *actually exist*, and are out there for us to discover, albeit in some perfect, non-sensible realm accessible only to philosophers. Plato's readers have sometimes described the relation between the higher plane of reality of universals and the world of everyday experience in terms of the relation between heaven and earth in the Abrahamic religions (Judaism, Christianity, and Islam). In each case the mundane world is an imperfect reflection of the divine one.

The more a person knows, Plato reasoned, the more closely their ideas about the world correspond to the way the world really is. This is true not only of the imperfect, observable world around us, but also the perfect world of universals, where justice can be found. The wisest, smartest, and most knowledgeable people have the clearest insight into what justice *really* requires, so they are best qualified to rule well.[12] Other people might have their own opinions about justice, but these can safely be ignored, thinks Plato, since they aren't grounded in knowledge of these higher truths. He argues that in the ideal state, government would be left to philosophers, who would live apart from the rest of society. To keep everybody else from trying to change things according to their mistaken views of justice, the philosophers could spin a "magnificent myth," saying that the ruling class had souls made of gold and non-philosophers had souls made of baser metals. While untrue, this would be simpler to explain than the theory about justice and the world of universals. It would stop people from rebelling and keep them doing the jobs for which they were best suited.[13]

We might wonder whether justice, as Plato pictures it, is really the most important issue for Paul and Leto. They don't seem to believe, as he does, that there's an independent, objective world of universals out there for us to find and use as the basis for moral judgments. Their view of justice is more cynical. They see people's ideas about justice as being similar to their ideas about religion: they can be useful for political purposes, but they can also be changed by careful political manipulators. Their distant descendant, the Mentat Miles Teg, expresses a view like this when he characterizes justice as a "fickle mistress, subject to the whims and prejudices of whoever

THE POLITICAL THEOLOGY OF FRANK HERBERT'S *DUNE* SAGA

administer[s] the laws."[14] But Paul and Leto do have principles of a kind: they're motivated by their foreknowledge of the ultimate fate of humanity. They justify their oppressive politics by reference to the terrible thing that will happen without their intervention.

This is an example of moral reasoning that treats consequences as most important. Paul and Leto (especially Leto!) think that we ought to do whatever leads to the best outcome. By this standard, any action that makes it less likely humanity will die out is better than one that makes it more likely, even if it involves treating people poorly here and now. They might be better consequentialists than any of us can be, since they have (and again, this is especially true of Leto) a more comprehensive view of the future, whereas we have to make predictions with more limited knowledge. Since their special insight into the future isn't shared by everyone else, the people they govern just have to accept that they're being oppressed for a good cause.

The Full Glare of Awareness: Justice and the Big Picture

Philosophers have long talked about the tension between immediate needs and deeper longer-term interests, whether of a person or of a society. We might think of the question of what a leader should do as one about the point of view needed to think about justice. Since societies contain people with different, sometimes mutually opposed needs, interests, and preferences, it's not always possible to satisfy everybody equally well. Some kind of rationale is needed to decide who is given priority. Should leaders treat societies as collective units or as groups of separate individuals? Should they focus on the longer-term needs of society or on people's more immediate interests? Should they aim to get the best outcomes overall, even if this requires that some people be treated poorly, or to respect rights, even if this results in worse outcomes overall?

Perhaps Paul and Leto's higher consciousness forces them to look on the world from the wrong point of view for good political leadership. They see every individual as a tiny part of a big picture, a grand historical narrative including countless past and future people. In this respect their special powers might make them unfailingly impartial and to that extent fair, if only in the sense that any given person is worth about as much as any other, and the same standards are applied to everybody. But it's hard to see how or why a leader looking at the world in this way could *value* anybody, except to the extent that that they know that person will play an important role in changing the big picture.

Why does this matter? The everyday problems people face might not count for much in the grand scheme of things, but they are still important to the people who face them. This makes big-picture conceptions of justice intuitively unappealing. Leto suggests this when he explains why people oppose him, even when he's doing humanity a favor in the long run. He says his detractors consider him a "sham," who governs "under false pretences, never consulting the needs of his people." He adds that "all gods have this problem. In the perception of deeper needs, I must often ignore immediate ones. Not addressing immediate needs is an offense to the young" – and everyone's young compared to the God Emperor.[15]

Religious language is sometimes used to explain the differences between the perspectives we can take when thinking about what we ought to do. R.M. Hare (1919–2002) pictured moral thinking as an attempt to view the world from the perspective of an "archangel," imagined as "a being with superhuman powers of thought, superhuman knowledge and no weaknesses."[16] Hare's concern was not whether angels actually exist. Instead, he used the archangel as a model for moral reasoning, as opposed to other kinds of reasoning – in a self-interestedly rational way, for example, or according to our personal preferences. The archangel cares about us and, not having any stake in our decisions, is also scrupulously fair. Of course, we who are trying to figure out what's the right thing to do aren't actually superhuman like an archangel, but we can try to think methodically to compensate for our weaknesses and limitations.

In some ways, Paul and Leto are closer to the ideal of Hare's archangel than the rest of us are, but it isn't self-evident that the archangel would favor their kind of big-picture consequentialism. As Hare said, the archangel's view will sometimes clash with our intuitive, unprincipled sense of what ought to be done – hence the dissatisfaction of Leto's detractors, despite his rationale. A god's perspective may not be the best one, and certainly isn't the only one, from which to look on our particular problems.

Creating the Church-state: Some Earthly Precedents

"Do not assume I merely created a Church-State," says Leto, looking back over his long reign. "I was leader and outsider. That was my function as leader and I copied historical models." In doing so, he adds, he denied people "the right to choose a place in history."[17]

What real-world precedents might Leto – or rather, Frank Herbert – have had in mind? Plato could be one, but his ideal city-state never existed in reality. In medieval Europe, there was a long dispute over the relations between the Catholic Church and rulers of different countries. If the pope was God's highest earthly representative, did he have the authority to overrule political leaders, like kings and queens? Philosophers like Marsiglio of Padua (ca. 1275–1342) argued that political leaders had authority in the "secular" domain of worldly affairs and religious leaders in the "spiritual" domain of conscience, so neither should try to control the other.[18] The legacy of this idea can be seen in the legal separation of church and state in many countries today.

Twentieth-century dictatorships tried more systematic means of social control, with governments reshaping culture and thought to match their political agendas. As Hannah Arendt (1906–1975) put it, each of these governments enforced its own "theology," giving citizens an emotional connection to their leaders as well as a corresponding ideology and world-view. It made them dependent on the government for their sense of who they were and what they stood for. As a result, they couldn't be brought around, argued with, or persuaded to rethink their convictions, at least while that government was still in power.[19]

Schmitt, who supported the Nazi regime in Germany in the 1930s and 1940s, thought it was a mistake to think of the world of politics as distinct from the domains of religion, culture, and society at large. Instead, he argued, if there's to be any decisive, firm, and final answer to any question about what ought to be done, those domains must be folded into politics, and placed under the control of the dictator – the embodiment of the "omnipotent lawgiver" we saw earlier.[20] Arendt described the distinctive form of totalitarian tyranny using a metaphor apt for a "sandy" subject like *Dune*. If we compare the totalitarian regime with older forms of tyr-anny, she wrote, we see that it tries "to set the desert itself in motion, to let loose a sand storm that [can] cover all parts of the inhabited earth." The whole point of totalitarianism, she argued, was to stifle thinking under this heap of "sand" – an ideology that permeates every part of life.[21]

Is there any philosophical case to be made *in favor of* denying people "the right to choose a place in history"? One consideration is strictly pragmatic. The Imperium is very large, insurrections will inevitably crop up from time to time, and Leto's supporters can't be everywhere at once. Neither can they bring the growth of "human experience and knowledge" to a complete stop: people will always be able to find ways to resist if they feel so inclined. However, Leto can try to keep people from *wanting* to resist.[22] This calls for a kind of social engineering, examples of which he can find in both the his-tories of the Bene Gesserit and the totalitarian efforts of dictators here on Earth. As Paul discovered soon after he came to power, religion is a conve-nient means of achieving this, since people internalize its commandments and effectively police each other, ensuring that thoughts of rebellion have "a smell of blasphemy" and that lawbreaking is identified with sin.[23]

In fascist Italy, the philosopher Giovanni Gentile (1875–1944) argued that if the state were to make everybody see its leader as the ultimate source of authority, there wouldn't be any deep or irreconcilable con-flicts of interest. Instead, people would share a common purpose, explic-itly articulated by the leader – for Gentile, the dictator. What's more, if the leader is seen as the exclusive source of authority, a god (or God Emperor) rather than just the delegate of some higher power, the peo-ple's "common purpose" can be updated as circumstances require. The leader isn't bound by any preconceived idea of what should or should not be done.

An obvious objection to this rosy view of totalitarianism is that its rationale works backward from an imaginary end-point – that is, a situation where everyone is on board with the demands their leaders make of them. Gentile assumed that unity and order are preferable to disunity and disorder (and, more controversially, that there can't be order without unity), so it's in the interests of any government to bring citizens' beliefs, interests, and preferences in line with its own.

Reforming people's values would not be easy. From the perspective of someone already wholeheartedly committed to an identity or set of values, it will never make sense to adopt a completely different one. Any attempt to force them will strike them as oppressive. But eventually, argued Gentile, the combined powers of education, propaganda, and brute force will make people internalize the values imposed on them. If citizens *actually want* what the state wants them to want, they won't feel its authority to be a burden.[24] In this way, submitting to the state's authority is like undergoing a complete religious conversion.

Still, it's hard to imagine putting this case to the people with their own particular beliefs, interests, and preferences in place. It's like saying, next time someone disagrees with you, "If only you'd take *my* side, we'd get along just fine!" They might answer that that's not a reason for *them* to give in. Why don't you take their side instead?

Gods Die Hard: Does It Ever Make Sense to Give Up Power?

Leto uses religion as a tool to help him rule. The Imperium under his reign is close to a pure form of totalitarianism. Real-life regimes built on those lines rarely last longer than the lives of the dictators that lead them, ending up isolated and worn down by external pressure much sooner than their propaganda promises. Yet with a vastly increased lifespan and actual (rather than only figurative) superhuman power, Leto is able to maintain peace for thousands of years. He and his supporters try, as far as possible, to suppress the development and spread of new ideas, ensuring that history unfolds in line with the "Golden Path." He keeps the society of each planet closed, depriving people of interplanetary travel, competition, and conflict. He carefully controls religion and culture to keep people "in awe" of him, as Thomas Hobbes (1588–1679) says of the "Mortal God," the sovereign state.[25]

And yet he finally gives it all up. "Government," says Lady Jessica, "is a cultural organism particularly attractive to doubts."[26] Leto works to bring about his own downfall, to cultivate those doubts, and to have people remember him as "an ordinary tyrant" rather than a true god or legitimate ruler.[27] This seems to contradict the Bene Gesserit view that, over time, governments work increasingly in the interests of the ruling class, as well as the tendency of real-world religions and totalitarian governments to perpetuate themselves as long as they can.[28]

We might think that, from the leader's point of view, it can never make sense to stop being a leader, and that it can't make sense for a religion to have no followers. For the same reason, a winning strategy in chess never involves overturning the board and vowing never to play again. Of course, it's easy enough to imagine someone having reasons to stop playing chess that aren't *about* chess – maybe pursuing excellence in chess makes them anxious and unhappy, and they'd make better use of their time if they spent it on some other pursuit. But this would never make sense to them *as a chess player*. Their reasons for stopping don't arise within the logic of the game, where the aim is always to win. Maybe politics works the same way, only there the minimum condition necessary to "win," whatever else leaders might want to do, is to keep hold of power.

How, then, do we explain Leto's decision? Consider that the disadvantages of all-encompassing social and ideological control might outweigh the advantages. A Bene Gesserit credo tells us:

> Religion (emulation of adults by the child) encysts past mythologies; guesses, hidden assumptions of trust in the universe, pronouncements made in search of personal power, all mingled with shreds of enlightenment. And always an unspoken commandment: Thou shalt not question! We break that commandment daily in the harnessing of human imagination to our deepest creativity.[29]

Paul and Leto's political religions serve to unify people across the Imperium through a common state of dependency. But those religions can't be insulated from the kinds of doubts Jessica mentioned unless people are prevented from thinking or harnessing their imaginations and creative capacities, which makes them unable to learn the lesson Leto is trying to teach. He needs them to see that dependency on any one great leader is ultimately a bad thing, despite the security it might bring. While they rely on him for answers, there can be no progress, and they'll be no better off in the long run. His departure – his decision to give up his godlike position in exchange for future notoriety, ensuring that he'll be remembered, for the most part, as a tyrant – keeps humanity on the Golden Path that he and Paul foresaw.

Notes

1. *Heretics of Dune* (Sevenoaks: New English Library, 1984), 196.
2. *Dune* (Sevenoaks: New English Library, 1965), 328–329.
3. *Dune Messiah* (Sevenoaks: New English Library, 1969), 16.
4. *Dune*, 416.
5. Thomas Aquinas, *Contra Errores Graecorum*, trans. Peter Damian Fehlner and Joseph Kenny, chapters 32–37, at https://isidore.co/aquinas/english/ContraErrGraecorum.htm; and Matthew 16:17–18.
6. This way of thinking about political authority had supporters well into the seventeenth century. See, for example, Robert Filmer, *Patriarcha and Other*

Writings, ed. Johann P. Sommerville (Cambridge: Cambridge University Press, 1991; originally 1680).

7. *Children of Dune* (Sevenoaks: New English Library, 1976), 390.
8. *CD,* 417.
9. *God Emperor of Dune* (Sevenoaks: New English Library, 1981), 232–233.
10. Carl Schmitt, *Political Theology: Four Chapters on the Concept of Sovereignty,* trans. George Schwab (Chicago: University of Chicago Press, 2005; originally 1922), 37.
11. *GED,* 226.
12. Plato, *The Republic,* trans. Desmond Lee, 2nd ed. (London: Penguin, 2003); and *Meno,* in *Five Dialogues,* trans. G.M.A. Grube and John M. Cooper (Indianapolis: Hackett, 2002), 73d–e.
13. Plato, *The Republic,* 414b–415d.
14. *HD,* 42.
15. *GED,* 277.
16. R.M. Hare, *Moral Thinking: Its Levels, Method and Point* (Oxford: Clarendon Press, 1981), 44.
17. *Chapterhouse: Dune* (Sevenoaks: New English Library, 1985), 32.
18. Marsiglio of Padua, *Defensor minor and De translatione imperii,* ed. and trans. Cary J. Nederman (Cambridge: Cambridge University Press, 1993), 44.
19. Hannah Arendt, *The Origins of Totalitarianism* (San Diego: Harcourt, 1968; originally 1951), 233, 308.
20. Schmitt, *Political Theology,* 7.
21. Arendt, *Origins of Totalitarianism,* 478.
22. *GED,* 270–271.
23. *CD,* 6.
24. Giovanni Gentile, *Origins and Doctrine of Fascism,* trans. A. James Gregor (New Brunswick, NJ: Transaction, 2002; originally 1927), 28–29.
25. Thomas Hobbes, *Leviathan,* ed. J.C.A. Gaskin (Oxford: Oxford University Press, 1996), 84, 114. For more on the Hobbesian undercurrents in *Dune,* see Rebeccah Leiby's chapter in this book (Chapter 22).
26. *DM,* 171.
27. *GED,* 253.
28. *CD,* 200.
29. *CHD,* 120.

21

Lessons from Islamic Philosophy on the Politics of Paul Atreides

Galipcan Altinkaya and Mehmet Kuyurtar

> The problem of leadership is inevitably: Who will play God?
>
> Muad'Dib, from the Oral History

Frank Herbert's novel *Dune* not only warns us about charismatic leadership, it looks to answer a very crucial question: What happens when ethics, religion, and politics intertwine?

When his dynasty falls into ruins and Paul acquiesces to being a prophetic leader to the Fremen, he finds need for an answer to this question. Neither he nor Jessica, being the nobles they are, are strangers to the realities of political life and the political purposes of religion. In the Imperium, politics is a balance between CHOAM, the houses of the Landsraad, the Spacing Guild, and the Bene Gesserit. But as an adept seer, Paul can see beyond the short-term interests and machinations of everyday politics. The destiny of humankind is available to his vision, including the possible paths to take humanity to that point. But while Paul is in the guise of a religious leader, he hesitates to take this Golden Path, fearing totalitarian rule and the stagnation it brings.

Paul's hesitation endangers the moral authority of his religious rule and turns faith into religious fanaticism. Deprived of its original Fremen morality and an ultimate direction, his political rule turns into mere power plays. Intrigues and conspiracies bedevil him as he finds himself fighting for his family's lives. Indeed, Paul is unable to control the jihad declared in his name. Ultimately, we see Paul as a frayed man, a plaything in the hands of lesser people. What he leaves behind is an abomination masquerading as the ruler of a powerful and sovereign state.

But where did it all go wrong? Which choice or action caused Paul's demise? To find an answer, we should turn to the prophetic and religious side of his leadership. Because even at the peak of Paul's power, religion is the most disquieting aspect of his government. As he says himself, to effectively

Dune and Philosophy, First Edition. Edited by Kevin S. Decker.
© 2023 John Wiley & Sons, Inc. Published 2023 by John Wiley & Sons, Inc.

control something, you should be able to destroy it. And this Muad'Dib could not manage to do because of the myth created around his name. But what is the proper way of controlling a religion?

Religions of Truth

According to Muslim philosophers, or *Falasifah* as they were known by the Muslim public, this was a very important philosophical question. The combination of divine and secular leadership, which we see both in Paul Atreides and Leto II, was also a trait of Prophet Mohammed (570–632 CE). His roles as the bearer of revelation and founder of the Islamic government made him a natural, charismatic leader in his lifetime. But after his passing, political organization of the Muslim community (*ummah*) rapidly degenerated and then disintegrated. Since then, how to determine the fundamental principles of legitimate rule has been a central debate for the Muslim community.[1]

Muslim philosophers argue that one has to know the essence of religion in order to address this issue. Alfârâbî (ca. 872–ca. 951 CE) says, "religion is opinions and actions, determined and restricted with stipulations and prescribed for a community by their first ruler, who seeks to obtain through their practicing it a specific purpose with respect to them or by means of them."[2] Alfârâbî means that religion is a specific design, customized to a community by a leader for the sake of endowing his people with a purpose. He calls this leader the "first ruler," a person who acts as the original religious lawgiver for a community.

And this is basically how the elites of the Duniverse see religion. For Jessica, it's an elementary Bene Gesserit teaching: all priestesses know about Missionaria Protectiva and its purpose. Apart from this, Duke Leto advises Paul to capitalize on superstitions of the Fremen if he has to go renegade. Therefore, Paul learns from his parents how to make religion his *mystique*.[3] As the *Lisan al-Ghaib* (which means both "Voice from the Outer World" and "Giver of Water"), Paul turns religion into political and military power.

A philosopher of the Platonic tradition, Alfârâbî did not think religion was only a pragmatic tool. Alfârâbî's first ruler is an extension of Plato's idea of the "philosopher-king." In his *Republic*, Plato argued that, to achieve true happiness, a political institution must be organized according to principles of justice.[4] For this, we need true knowledge of what justice is, and why it is a virtue.

Plato believed that to really know justice, one needs the eternal "idea of justice." Such knowledge is only accessible through reason. Contemplation, as the methodic use of rational abilities, is the only way a philosopher can obtain the knowledge of the "the Ideal Realm" (*al-alam al-musul*, as Muslim philosophers translated the term). This, in turn, provides the true essence of "the idea of the Good," and from this the philosopher can proceed to the true essence of the just order of things. This pure, absolute knowledge is possible only for a true philosopher. Hence, Plato says, "unless . . . the philosophers rule as kings or those now called kings and chiefs genuinely and adequately philosophize, and political power and philosophy coincide in the same place . . . there is no rest from the ills for the cities."[5]

Plato provided fertile ground for Muslim philosophers: they agreed that the one who knows must rule, and this person gets his authority from reason alone. But Muslim philosophers went further in trying to fit religious phenomena like revelation and prophecy into this picture. Islamic jurisprudence experts (*faqīh*) were inclined to label philosophers as dangerous heretics and infidels. Facing the possibility of religious prosecution, philosophers tried to show that even Muslim jurisprudence (*fiqh*) gets its principles (*uṣūl*) from reason and philosophy.

Their conclusion was that a philosopher or prophet-legislator should be above the law, for only he knows the eternal normative principles that give authority to particular laws. This person should be free to alter any law in changing circumstances. The important thing was to establish a harmonious society that rests on a hierarchy allowing it to move toward the objectives set by the ruler.

Think of how Muad'Dib, or "Usul," as he was known among the Fremen of Sietch Tabr, rejects the idea of a constitution, even a religious one. According to him, a constitution is an unstable balance point with no limitations; it eventually eradicates individuality and causes a tyranny of its own making. Without a constitution for Paul's religious rule to rest on, we must answer two questions: Can his rule be defined as virtuous according to this idealistic scheme? And what happens to the relationship between religion and politics if the law-giver is corrupted?

Truth of Religion and Truth of Science

According to Alfârâbî, religion can be virtuous or vile – it can even become degenerate in time. When a philosopher or prophet has demonstrable metaphysical knowledge and pure intentions, his religious teachings and laws will also be virtuous. But if it is the opposite and the community is subjected to laws or teachings of false philosophers or prophets, society will be corrupted.[6] To see if Paul's sense of religion is virtuous or corrupt, we have to examine the quality of the knowledge that legitimizes his rule as a prophet or philosopher-king.

A philosopher takes his authority from his knowledge of the natural order of the universe. This order is strictly dependent on God, an eternal, omnipotent entity that exists necessarily. Just like Aristotle (384–322 BCE) with his idea of a "prime mover," *Falasifah* believed in a God who does not intervene in the natural order of things. God might be the first cause of the world as a whole, but due to His grace the natural order He creates is also stable and unchanging. Because of the stability of this order and because God knows Himself as the ultimate cause of all things, God knows what was, what is, and what will be. This means that God is omniscient, His knowledge unchanging.

This natural order affords the world rational harmony and stability. Knowledge of this order is what grants the philosopher-prophet the information needed to order his society. Similarly, the vision of the Golden Path revealed to Paul and Leto II represents the destiny of all humankind. Leto II sacrificed his humanity to attain this goal. If it were not for promise of the knowledge he obtained, he would not have considered, even for a moment, turning into a millennia-old, disfigured – and very bored – tyrant.

Falasifah theorized that supernal (cosmic) intellects – beyond philosophers and prophets – were key to acquiring this knowledge. Divine revelations (*wahy*) occurred to help recipients penetrate the realm of the unknown (*al-alam al-ghaib*) and establish laws for a people. This "practical philosophy" yields a "Virtuous City" (*al-madīna al-fādila*) or, in Plato's terms, the ideal state. Any religion in compliance with this scheme can be defined as a virtuous religion.

Now, all this may sound like mysticism, but this was not the intention of Greek or Muslim philosophers. The same goes for Frank Herbert's narrative, which was intended to be more "philosophical fiction" than science fiction.[7] As an example, the Bene Gesserit and Mentat training that created Muad'Dib must come from a far advanced civilization that excels not only in physics and technology, but also in "soft" sciences like psychology, biology, sociology, and politics – including religion *as a science.*

With his training as a noble, Paul was well-versed in scientific knowledge. Moreover, he was the unexpected product of a genetic program aimed at creating a male Bene Gesserit (a Kwisatz Haderach) who was supposed to be able to see what Reverend Mothers could not during Water-of-Life experiences. Paul can control both his body and emotions to a high degree and, as a Mentat, he can make computer-like calculations. Finally, and most crucially, he can tap into the symbolic language of a community in order to mobilize them politically. This ability is the most important one Muad'Dib had in common with the philosopher-prophet of the *Falasifah.*

According to the *Falasifah*, a philosopher-prophet can use his abilities to report truths from an unknown (*ghaib*) past, present, or future, or unknown realms of space. If the philosopher-prophet is prudent, he uses this knowledge to create myths and parables that transmit moral values. Excellence in this art requires rhetorical skills, since the philosopher must be able to convey the truth to the everyday believer who lacks the ability to grasp the truth philosophically. Therefore, it is not far-fetched to call the philosopher-prophet "the voice of the unknown" (*al-lisan al-ghaib*), just like the Fremen called Paul.

Let's return to the previous questions regarding Paul's virtue and corruption as a law-giver. If we define the Golden Path as the politically idealistic choice, then Muad'Dib can't attain the high moral standards of the Muslim and Greek philosophers. Yes, the Golden Path implies tyranny, but oppression is not its main aim. The main objective is the breeding program that Leto carries out. The stagnation and dormancy Paul fears more than the jihad is a side effect of this design. But Herbert gives different accounts of how much Paul knew about the results of this path, and nobody, himself included, knew whether he was *the* Kwisatz Haderach. Therefore, from the Muslim philosopher's perspective, Muad'Dib is either a false or an ignorant prophet. But does that make Paul the *villain* of the story?

Let's consider another perspective before making a hasty conclusion about Paul's leadership. For that perspective we will turn to another philosopher who tried to scientifically analyze society and politics in the context of their religious and moral aspects: Ibn Khaldun (1332–1406), the North African philosopher, sociologist, and historian of the "Islamic Golden Age."

Political Ideals versus Human Realities

In a climactic scene from the first novel, Paul berates his Fremen followers for demanding he challenge Stilgar to mortal combat. According to Fremen traditions, this is the only way for Muad'Dib to rise to leadership. Paul gets aggravated by the suggestion that he should kill Stilgar, or as he says, "cut his right arm off," just to provide them with a "circus," on the eve of a great war.[8]

It's likely that Paul as "Usul" was the only human being who could characterize Fremen traditions as a "circus" and walk out alive. But how? Because he was the most skilled warrior in that room? He was skilled indeed, but he also faced an army. Yet at that moment Paul *knew* the Fremen were ready for change as a society. They had outgrown their tribal way of life because of the military and social power introduced by Paul's and Jessica's leadership. He knew that the brotherhood of all Arrakeen sietches, the Ichwan Bedwine, was ready to act as a superior civilization in the face of upcoming galactic challenges.

The choice of the word Bedwine is not a coincidence. The Arabic "Bedouine" was sometimes used to address all Arab peoples. But Ibn Khaldun used this term in a technical sense in his work on social science (the *ilm al-umrān*), which he developed in his *Mukaddimah* ("introduction") to *Kitab al-Ibar* ("Book of Lessons"). It would be naive to think that Herbert simply stumbled on the same title for the Fremen catechism manual.

In his science of *Umrān*, Ibn Khaldun distinguishes between morality in general and morality in politics. Moral issues could be a part of scientific research only insofar as they affected the social life of *Umrān* (in this sense, *Umrān* can be translated as "the necessary sociability of human beings").[9]

This research investigates the economic, geographic, and psychological conditions for social structures (like the state and the family) and their consequences. In addition to this, the word "sietch," which originally means "place of assembly in time of danger," can be translated into Arabic as *Umrān*.

In his criticism of the Platonic *Falasifah* approach to politics, Ibn Khaldun argues that a solid social science must depend on concrete data. For social life, such data is provided by historical experience. Ibn Khaldun says:

> History makes us acquainted with the conditions of past nations as they are reflected in their national character. It makes us acquainted with the biographies of the prophets and with the dynasties and policies of rulers. Whoever so desires may thus achieve the useful result of being able to imitate historical examples in religious and worldly matters.[10]

So experience shows us that societies can rise and prosper without ever needing the transcendent guidance of celestial beings or prophets. All a people need is a leader powerful enough to cultivate respect and to legislate and enforce the laws. Societies do not need prophetic leaders and otherworldly, transcendent knowledge or utopian aims to function.

But this does not mean social behavior and political action are any less rational, at least in some cases. Social order occurs not because political actors are supreme rational beings capable of determining ultimate aims and leading people to happiness. On the contrary, human beings are mostly amoral, cruel, and aggressive. Their natural sociability arises from a need for defense and nutrition – these are needs that leaders can meet more or less rationally. Ibn Khaldun calls this ability to garner loyalty and create solidarity *asabiyyah*. And relations of *asabiyyah* in societies can also be investigated rationally.

For Ibn Khaldun, the first phase of human society is tribal solidarity, or *Badouin Umrān*. In this phase, laws don't really provide social structure. Governors are not yet powerful enough to enforce laws, but they are the most esteemed members of a tribe, and thereby tribal *asabiyyah* is founded on *reverence*, similar to the way Stilgar rules. This creates solidarity among tribal people, leading them to a traditional kind of pre-law morality. The Fremen seem to share this sort of *asabiyyah*.

When this kind of young society can easily provide for its members and the means of its food and technological production change, some members start to specialize in the military, the bureaucracy, and even finance. Once social complexity increases, tribal rule or Bedouin *asabiyyah* is not enough anymore. This is because the tribal *asabiyyah* turns outward to seek affirmation from other societies.

This demands a different kind of leadership that can make other social groups who don't share tribal solidarity bend the knee, pay taxes, and obey laws. This is the leadership of Paul as Duke and as Emperor. Now we have a *sovereignty* relationship that may overstep the consent of the governed. Paul is claiming this kind of sovereignty when he describes his leadership:

> Production growth and income growth must not get out of step in my Empire. That is the substance of my command. There are to be no balance-of-payment difficulties between the different spheres of influence. And the reason for this is simply because I command it. I want to emphasize my authority in this area. I am the supreme energy-eater of this domain, and will remain so, alive or dead. My Government is the economy.[11]

Paul sees that to control this energy, the tribal way of life must change. In the words of Ibn Khaldun, Bedouin *asabiyyah* must give way to *Hadari* (civilized) *asabiyyah*. In this phase, tribal solidarity becomes state sovereignty, which he calls *Mulk*.[12] The practical act of directing political power is called Rational Politics (*al-siyasah al-aqliyyah*). But in the civilized state, a sovereign must still promote the older Bedouin morality. Otherwise, subjects will succumb to luxury due to abundant wealth, prosperity, and power. According to Ibn Khaldun, and as Stilgar complains time and again, comforts lead to the loss of warrior qualities and turn honest men into insatiable political predators. Or maybe the writers of the Missionaria Protectiva are more on the point when they say, "All governments suffer a recurring problem: Power attracts pathological personalities. It is not that power corrupts but that it is magnetic to the corruptible."[13]

But it was the original Bedouin morality that made the Fremen so appealing to Jessica in the first place. Their military discipline and their sense of honor suited the familial *asabiyyah* of the Atreides.[14] Further, she sees the future-oriented mindset of the Fremen as something Paul can exploit.[15] Maybe this is why Leto II stressed that Paul was never truly a Fremen. As a political realist in the same vein as Khaldun, Paul knew how to manage Fremen morality to strengthen his political dynasty.

So far, religion seems to have no role in Ibn Khaldun's thinking. For him, prophecy is not a necessity of reason or of nature, although it may be necessary by imposition of religious law (*sharia*). Religious politics is a possible but very rare occurrence in an *Umrān*.

Ibn Khaldun knew that some kind of religion had been a part of every society. But when he compared religions with political power, he saw that religions were not the main force in the political structure. The same goes for the Imperium before Paul's rule: the teachings of the Orange Catholic Bible were applied by rote and quasi-religious Bene Gesserit were natural consultants to governors, but Shaddam's rule was mostly based on balancing power groups like the Landsraad, CHOAM, and the Guild. Ibn Khaldun would've pointed out that political sovereignty depends on strong *asabiyyah* and that Shaddam's secular government was only relatively successful at this.

But things quickly changed when Paul Muad'Dib showed up as a messianic figure. According to Ibn Khaldun, religion can create *asabiyyah*, and in the course of time, this *asabiyyah* can create religious-political power. For example, Ibn Khaldun claims Bedouin Arabs were able to transform into civilized *asabiyyah* only because they embraced Islam. Prior to that time, it's not that they were dim-witted or barbaric, but they were too free-spirited, individualistic, and anarchistic to belong in any state. Islam showed Bedouin Arabs the way to civilization, preserving these qualities and also elevating them.[16] Under Mohammed's rule, Arabs did not bend the knee before any secular leader, only before God. But after Mohammed's passing and the rule of Rashidun Caliphs, the Umayyad and Abbasid dynasties led the Muslim community back to Rational Politics (*al-siyasah al-aqliyyah*) and state sovereignty.

Paul's spiritual and political influence created a similar miraculous elevation for the Fremen people and, in turn, a similar degeneration and demoralization. The core of Ibn Khaldun's political realism is acceptance of the idea that even political sovereignty founded on religion must pass through all the phases marked by a secular society. Charismatic leaders like prophets say they have the key to the salvation of their people. But when they seize power, they become power players at Rational Politics. However, this is nothing surprising since, as Ibn Khaldun shows, when it comes to the evolution of social life, there are some realities that an insightful leader – even a prophet – should not ignore.

Paul's Decision

We began with the questions, "Where did it all go wrong for Paul?" and "Which choice or action caused his ultimate demise?" Even though Paul was not an Abomination like Alia, was he a better ruler? After only 12 years of rule, a single conspiracy brought him down and claimed the life of his beloved. But how could this happen to a prescient and capable military leader? The answer is that Paul was torn between his inherited powers as Kwisatz Haderach and his birthright as the Duke's son.

From the very beginning, our hero was disturbed by the visions he had: they filled him with a terrible purpose, a race consciousness that would devour everything in its path. We do not know exactly when Paul acquired the fuller picture of the Golden Path. As we see throughout the novels, there were two main directions in front of him: one of them lead to jihad, and the other clearer and safer path to dormancy and stagnation. He might have been prescient enough to anticipate the consequences of his choices, but this did not allow him to finally choose. Instead, he kept swaying between possibilities.

The choice of jihad was due to his political realism: he took the path of religious warfare even though he was disturbed by it, thinking that he could dictate the undetermined strands of his future through political prowess. But he did not purely follow a politically realist path either. He kept increasing his influence as a religious figure, all the while ignoring the safer choices his visions presented. He saw no threat in unlimited power, even though he refused the "ideal" direction in which to steer the Imperium. Eventually, he created yet another kind of oppression, a tyranny of religious bureaucracy under his Qizarates.

If we consider the human stagnation Paul feared as being similar to the ideal regime that philosophers like Plato and Alfârâbî desired, we see where Paul (in his "Preacher" guise) stands on political idealism versus political realism: "Muad'Dib showed you two things: a certain future and an uncertain future. With full awareness, he confronted the ultimate uncertainty of the larger universe. He stepped off *blindly* from his position on this world. He showed us that men must do this always, choosing the uncertain instead of the certain."[17]

Paul always seemed to think that truth had an unstable nature. So, such blindness is a fitting metaphor for a character who faces the truth and resolutely ignores it – the truth itself becomes the very curtain that keeps him from seeing what is right in front of him. That is why Paul walked so blindly into the area of power politics, where defeat is always a possibility. In this sense, Paul was unable to see for a very long time.

Of course, the Golden Path did not bring the perpetual happiness sought by idealists like Alfârâbî, but at least Leto listened to good advice. As the voice of the "father-presence" in his head told Leto, "It is not the present which influences the future, thou fool, but the future which forms the present. You have it all backward. Since the future is set, an unfolding of events which will assure that future is fixed and inevitable."[18] The stagnation he created was meant to end all stagnation. But we're not taking sides and arguing that the God Emperor is the true hero of this saga. Honestly, when we reflect on Herbert's novel, we feel grateful that all this is mere fiction. But as we witness the current global rise in authoritarian and populistic tendencies and the heartbreaking search for charismatic leadership, *Dune* is even more relevant today.

Notes

1. Zerrin Kurtoğlu Şahin, "The Foundations of Islamic Political Theology," *Felsefi Düşün Dergisi* 4 (April 2015), 137–158.
2. Alfârâbî, *The Political Writings: Selected Aphorisms and Other Texts*, trans. Charles E. Butterworth (Ithaca: Cornell University Press, 2001), 93.
3. *Dune* (New York: Ace, 2005), 483.
4. Plato, *The Republic*, trans. Allan Bloom, 2nd ed. (New York: Basic Books, 1991), 433a.
5. Plato, *The Republic*, 473 e.

6. Alfârâbî, *Political Writings*, 93.
7. Frank Herbert, Rare DUNE Interview with Frank Herbert, Video, September 28, 1987, at https://www.youtube.com/watch?v=CFWIKR1b_N8.
8. *Dune*, 540–541.
9. Ahmet Arslan, *İbni Haldun* (Istanbul: İstanbul Bilgi Üniversitesi Yayınları, 2017).
10. Ibn Khaldun, *Ibn Khaldun: The Muqaddimah, An Introduction to History*, trans. Franz Rosenthal, vol. 1 (New York: Pantheon Books, 1958), 18.
11. *Dune Messiah* (New York: Ace, 2020), 188.
12. Ibn Khaldun, *Ibn Khaldun*, 381–382.
13. *Chapterhouse: Dune* (New York: Ace, 2020), 59.
14. *Dune*, 366.
15. *Dune*, 404.
16. Ibn Khaldun, *Ibn Khaldun*, 260.
17. *Children of Dune* (New York: Ace, 2020), 263.
18. CD, 325.

22

Why Settle for Hobbes's Sovereign When You Could Have a God Emperor?

R.S. Leiby

If you're a political figure in the Corrino Empire or the later Atreides Empire, chances are that you're feeling some anxiety. Palms a little sweaty? Chest a little tight? Don't worry, that's normal. After all, depending upon your rank and relationships, you'll probably find yourself conspired against, soon if not already. There's always a danger that once-close allies might betray you. Potential assassins lurk around every corner and poison snoopers hover over every meal. *Maybe* you're lucky enough to have a really top-notch Master of Assassins watching your back, but maybe you're not. Either way, even the absolute best security officers have been known to miss things (looking at you, Thufir Hawat).

But don't worry, it's not just you! The anxiety you're feeling is an anxiety that most – and maybe *all* – political figures in the world of *Dune* feel from time to time. It's the kind of anxiety, as Thomas Hobbes (1588–1679) would say, that comes from living in a world in which our enemies are many and frequently hidden; a world in which there isn't a sufficiently powerful, central ruler to keep everyone on their best, or possibly least treacherous, behavior.

Why does this kind of anxiety seem so built into the politics of the *Dune* universe? Hobbes would say that this level of apprehension is inevitable in any society that isn't governed by a sufficiently powerful central ruler. And that ruler can't just have an impressive title (like "Padishah Emperor") or a great army (like one made of Sardaukar). That ruler needs to be absolute, his power untempered and undivided, according to Hobbes. We need someone, in other words, as close to a God Emperor as we can get. We need a Leto Atreides II. Without a single, all-powerful figure who can make the laws and hold everyone to them, Hobbes might say, we're always going to be looking over our shoulders . . . Or at least down into our spice beer.

Dune and Philosophy, First Edition. Edited by Kevin S. Decker.
© 2023 John Wiley & Sons, Inc. Published 2023 by John Wiley & Sons, Inc.

Is It Just Me, or Is It Feeling Kind of State-of-Nature-y in Here?

This kind of scenario, in which there is no absolutely powerful single ruler, no "common power to keep [men] all in awe," is what Hobbes calls man's natural state: a State of Nature, if you will.[1] Now let's imagine that the Duniverse is such a place. What would that look like?

Just as in our world, some people or groups would have more power than others, and some of these might have more power than most. But no one individual or group would be in a position to enjoy *unlimited* power. The Emperor would still be subject to the demands of the Spacing Guild, for example, while the Spacing Guild would still need to be on good terms with the governor of Arrakis because of the Guild's absolute dependence upon spice, and so on. And in the background, everyone would eye each other with appropriate suspicion as Houses, Greater and Lesser, jockey for positions of prominence, power, wealth, and security. This is starting to feel awfully familiar.

Now imagine that two political entities in this landscape find themselves in a messy disagreement. Let's say, just hypothetically, that House Harkonnen wants control over a resource that has been entrusted to House Atreides. How can they resolve this dispute?

> *Option #1*: They can shake hands, agree to disagree, and move on peacefully.
> *Option #2*: They can fight.
> *Option #3*: They can appeal to some higher authority to resolve the dispute.

Given the ancient feud between these two Houses, option #1 doesn't look especially likely. Kanly – a formal vendetta – isn't the kind of thing you just shrug off and walk away from. And you could do that only if you were absolutely positive that your opponent wouldn't stab you in the back. Hobbes thinks that rationality demands we do things to protect ourselves from harm, to keep ourselves alive, and to avoid doing things that will lead to our deaths. Not only *should* we do those things, says Hobbes, we're *morally permitted* to do those things in any circumstances. The right to be safe and defend ourselves from harm is what Hobbes calls our "right of nature."[2] When we're in the State of Nature, that right is unlimited: we can do *anything* to preserve ourselves, including betraying, hurting, and even killing others. By "right," Hobbes just means something that we're morally allowed to do. And if we're free to do whatever it takes to keep ourselves safe (as are our opponents), it might be hard to see how walking away from a vendetta would be a viable option.

What about option #2? There are lots of ways to fight, after all, not all of which violate the Great Convention. The Houses could seek to injure each other in ways big and small, from compelling a traitor to deactivate the opponent's house shields, to hiding a poison capsule in a fake tooth, to everything in between. Okay, now this is starting to sound *really* familiar.

What's more, this isn't a special matter unique to the relationship between House Harkonnen and House Atreides. All of the political players on the galactic stage seem to bear this relationship to one another: everyone is scheming (or *could* be scheming) against everyone else, and everyone confronts disagreements that often are met with violence (or with diplomacy backed by polite threats of violence). So what should we do?

Well, there's always option #3: appeal to some higher authority. Oh, great: we have one of those! Let's go ask the Padishah Emperor. Well, we could do that . . . But probably not if the Emperor is one of the disputing parties. Or if the Emperor is too weak to compel adherence to his mandates. Or if we can't be absolutely sure that the parties to the dispute will abide by whatever the Emperor decrees, no matter what. Or if a sizable enough portion of the Landsraad takes one side or the other. Suddenly, it's starting to look like the Emperor might not be enough of an authority to settle all of this. And at the end of the day, we still have that disagreement to worry about.

Hobbes's mission in his 1651 masterwork, *Leviathan*, is to show that this kind of state – a State of Nature without an absolute, undivided, central authority – can't help but devolve into a State of War. By State of War, Hobbes doesn't mean that battles are constantly occurring. The effects can be much more subtle (and much more anxiety-inducing).

Think about war as though it were like the weather. When we say there's a stretch of bad weather near Sietch Tabr, it doesn't have to be true that there's a violent sandstorm happening every moment of every day. Instead, it feels like there *could* be a sandstorm at any moment. Maybe the wind is a little higher than usual and the visibility is a little lower than usual, so we need to go about our daily tasks *as if* a sandstorm could happen at any moment. We need, in other words, to be constantly prepared for a potential sandstorm. The so-called State of War is similar: it's simply that we continue to be aware that "the will to contend by battle is sufficiently known."[3] And if fighting could break out at any moment, then we always need to be prepared to respond to violence. And if that's the world we're living in, then it seems like we have good reason to feel anxious.

Diffidence Is the Mind-killer

This picture of Imperial life that Hobbes would paint doesn't seem attractive. But we might think that he's blowing out of proportion the dangers of a state lacking a sufficiently powerful single ruler. Sure, the other Houses *could* attack us, but they might not. In fact, they probably won't, as long as we play our cards right – right? So why does Hobbes think that this constant tension is going to be insurmountable, our anxiety unavoidable?

It's because of what he terms "diffidence" and by which he means anxiety or distrust.[4] Hobbes's argument about diffidence goes something like this:

First, *we're all pretty much equal*. We might be better at some things than others, but at the end of the day we're all vulnerable in the ways that human beings are. No one individual is absolutely impossible to kill. Anyone can be poisoned; a bunch of enemies working together can gang up on the strongest or the most intelligent; even a prescient person could, however unlikely, have a blind spot that leaves them open to attack (so even if some of us turn out to be slightly-more-than-human, we're still not completely invincible).

Second, *since we're all pretty much equal, we have good reason to distrust each other*. Because of our relative equality, we're all (somewhat) vulnerable to being attacked and (somewhat) confident in our ability to successfully attack others. So everyone else is a potential aggressor or a potential victim, and that means we have to always keep our guard up.

So, *since we have good reason to distrust each other, we find ourselves in a State of War*. If it really is the case that we can't reasonably feel secure with regard to each other's intentions, then we're going to have to be prepared for battle all the time (like we might brace for what seems like an imminent sandstorm). For Hobbes, this is what must occur without a higher authority keeping all in check: "persons of sovereign authority, because of their independency, are in continual jealousy and in the state and posture of gladiators, having their weapons pointing and their eyes fixed on each other, that is, their forts, garrisons, and guns upon the frontiers of their kingdoms, and continual spies upon their neighbors, which is a posture of war."[5]

In a world like this, it would be difficult not to see potential threats around every corner, and with good reason. And in this state of wariness, political and social stability will be tough to attain. It's going to be difficult to know who you can trust and with whom you can form a reliable alliance – not because everyone is evil and self-serving – but because you just can't know the intentions of others. For example, when we leave our house, most of us lock the doors not because we think that everyone is out to rob us, but *just in case*. And when we are invited to dinner at the Arrakeen Great House, we're glad there's a poison snooper concealed in the rafters *just in case*. When he hosts a dinner shortly after arriving on Arrakis, Duke Leto Atreides understands what the omnipresence of poison snoopers signifies in the society of *Dune*. Subterfuge and intentions to harm are so woven into the fabric of the Duniverse that there exist "*precise and delicate delineations for ways to administer treacherous death. Will someone try chaumurky tonight – poison in the drink? Or will it be chaumas – poison in the food?*"[6] So central is the experience (and fear) of political treachery in this society that virtually no aspect of life is free of it.

Again, we might worry that Hobbes is being a bit too dramatic. Sure, there are a lot of other contenders to worry about, and sure, meeting a violent death at the hands of one's enemies isn't vanishingly rare in this society . . . But isn't *some* sustainable trust possible? In this sort of world, we might trust our loved ones (as Duke Leto Atreides trusts Lady Jessica, despite the way things look). We might give our confidences to comrades, friends, and most trusted advisors. But Hobbes might say that we are never really far from doubting those close to us. When Paul and Gurney spar together during their final day on Caladan, Paul feels a flicker of anxiety about even Gurney the Warmaster's loyalty:

> Paul fell back, parrying. He felt the field cracking as shield edges touched and repelled each other, sensed the electric tingling of the contact along his skin. *What's gotten into Gurney?* He asked himself. *He's not faking this!* Paul moved his left hand, dropped his bodkin into his palm from its wrist sheath. "You see a need for an extra blade, eh?" Halleck grunted. *Is this betrayal?* Paul wondered. *Surely not Gurney!*[7]

Because collaboration relies on trust, and trust is necessarily fragile in the political world of *Dune*, the kinds of beneficial projects that depend on collaboration are going to be difficult to undertake. Working for the good of all humanity starts to look a lot less doable when you're always looking over your shoulder and side-eyeing your partners. So you'll probably find yourself unable to accomplish much good for humanity, and you probably won't be able to enjoy your own life very much. After all, no one looks forward to the possibility of meeting a violent death, no matter how good their prospects are for finding their way into (and back out of) a Tleilaxu tank. In such a state, life as a political figure is going to be stressful, dangerous, and probably pretty brief if you're not exceedingly careful (and maybe even if you are). So what can we do about it?

According to Hobbes, the *only* thing we can do to get rid of this instability is to undermine the diffidence (or distrust) with which we regard each other. And the only way to do that is to erect a higher authority to keep everyone in line: an all-powerful monarch, or, to use Hobbes's term, a Sovereign.

Seeking Sovereign, BYOM (Bring Your Own Makers)

Let's go back for a moment to our dispute between Houses Harkonnen and Atreides. Their simply agreeing to disagree probably wouldn't be a useful path forward, since material gain and power are at stake for both parties. Fighting *could* be an option, but not a great option: in addition to the very real human costs of warfare, the fight will just make everyone's anxieties worse and might even cascade into an empire-shattering galactic war. All that's left is appeal to a higher authority to resolve the dispute. But, as we saw, it's not clear that Shaddam IV, or any of his predecessors, is actually a high enough authority to accomplish this satisfactorily. They're *certainly* not capable of remaining above the fray. After all, Shaddam IV conspires against House Atreides because he feels threatened by Duke Leto's popularity among the Great Houses, so it seems clear that Shaddam is just as much a part of the culture of anxiety and diffidence as anyone else. At the end of the day, the quasi-feudal political arrangement between the Bene Gesserit, the Spacing Guild, and the Landsraad means that House Corrino only has as much power as it can muster, wheedle, and compel. It is not invincible, and it certainly doesn't hold all the cards.

If Shaddam IV isn't up to the task, then we need an absolute Sovereign. And we don't just need them, Hobbes thinks we should *want* them. For Hobbes, nothing (not even 3500 years of jihad) could be as terrible as the uncertainty, dread, and fear that comes with political instability. It tears communities and families apart, it makes collaboration difficult or even impossible, it makes us suspicious, miserable, and liable to meet a violent end. It's in our best interest, always, to avoid political instability – and the way we do that, according to Hobbes, is to transfer some of our natural rights to the Sovereign. We give up our right to do whatever we want to others, as long as they give up their right to do whatever they want to us. We'll no longer hurt people preemptively to stay safe, the logic goes, because we'll have given our *Sovereign* the moral permission to hurt people to keep us safe. The downside: we no longer have the right to kill each other and take each other's wealth and holdings. The upside: other people no longer have the right to kill us and take our wealth and holdings! And if they do, the Sovereign will be there to punish them. This is not because the Sovereign needs to be benevolent, or even because they feel a strong moral obligation to defend us from our would-be enemies. The ruler just needs to be interested in maintaining stability – which Hobbes thinks we all should be if we're thinking carefully about the issue at hand.

So while it certainly couldn't hurt the Sovereign to be a good and virtuous ruler, beloved by all, it's not necessary. All the Sovereign *must* do is be powerful enough to remain the single, universally recognized source of authority in the society (or planet, or galaxy, or Known Universe). That way, when we're in the midst of a dispute, we can avoid both the unrealistic alternative #1 (agreeing to disagree) and the undesirable alternative #2 (fighting) and go with safe old option #3: appeal to a higher authority to resolve things.

Of course, one of the disputing parties might not abide by the Sovereign's arbitration, though Hobbes thinks it would be in their best interest to do so. Or they could betray their opponent without regard for the Sovereign's opinion at all. No ruler, Hobbes grants, will be able to prevent any and all bad actions. Someone could still betray us, after we transfer our rights to the Sovereign. It's just that no one could betray us with *impunity*, because the Sovereign will be there to punish them accordingly and, as a bonus, disincentivize other parties who might be getting ideas about betrayal. And since there will be a pretty good chance that our acting against the wishes of the Sovereign and the stable order will result in our punishment and death, it's no longer going to seem rational for us, in most cases, to take the risk. Because doing harm to others in ways that violate the Sovereign's dictates invites severe punishment, we'll ultimately have fewer reasons to distrust one another. Without the diffidence that locks us into an endless cycle of anxiety and violence, we'll be better able to achieve the goals of humanity without getting sidetracked into tangential power struggles.

Is Leto II a Hobbesian Sovereign?

At first glance, the God Emperor Leto II seems to cut a Hobbesian figure. After all, his power is absolute and undivided. He retains a monopoly on the distribution of melange, and the peace he imposes upon the known universe with this leverage "is an enforced tranquility which humankind knew only for the briefest periods before [his] ascendancy."[8] Maybe folks aren't living with as much wealth, convenience, and spice-enhancement as they once were, but at least there's stability. At least the diffidence or distrust that characterized political relationships under the Corrino Empire, and even during the reign of Paul Muad'Dib, has been somewhat diminished.

So Hobbes might be a fan of Leto's approach. After all, Hobbes had lived through the English civil wars of 1642–1651, a violent struggle between competing branches of government. Hobbes had seen firsthand the terrible destruction that civil war could unleash, the horrific loss of life and destruction of security. For Hobbes, this sort of instability is the worst fate that could befall a people. Virtually any government, he suggests, is better than anarchy, civil conflict, and a State of War in which every man is pitted against every man (even potentially, as we've seen).

Perhaps if the circumstances of Leto II's reign were different, this would be the end of things. But Leto II isn't Hobbes, and his concern is with more than just social and political stability. For the God Emperor, the worst thing that can befall a people is not a State of War; it's a state of stagnation, decline, and ultimately annihilation. While Hobbes thinks that the greatest disaster befalls us when we're fractured and apart, Leto II thinks the greatest disaster occurs when we're together and complacent, since "[when] you are together, you can share a common catastrophe. You can be exterminated together."[9] Ultimately, both Hobbes and Leto II are looking for a path toward survival. But while Hobbes's notion of survival is focused on this day or the next, Leto II's notion of survival is focused on the trajectory of the human race as a whole. At some point along the path, Hobbes's thinking and Leto II's are going to pull apart, and when that happens, we find ourselves in a position to ask: what's more important? A cure for our anxiety, a Sovereign? Or a cure for our species' destruction, a God Emperor who engineers his own destruction?

Notes

1. Thomas Hobbes, *Leviathan*, ed. Edwin Curley (Indianapolis: Hackett Publishing, 1994), 76.
2. Hobbes, *Leviathan*, 79.
3. Hobbes, *Leviathan*, 76.
4. Hobbes, *Leviathan*, 75.
5. Hobbes, *Leviathan*, 78.
6. *Dune* (New York: Ace Books, 2005), 162.
7. *Dune*, 44.
8. *God Emperor of Dune* (New York: Ace Books, 2019), 19.
9. *GED*, 558.

23

The Mind at War
Conflict and Cognition in Frank Herbert's *Dune*

Sam Forsythe

Practically speaking, Frank Herbert's *Dune* is a story mostly about war. It is a strange sort of war – an aristocratic vendetta waged by the spymasters, strategists, and knifemen of two feuding Great Houses – but it forms the weave within which the whole tapestry of narrative and concept is knotted together.

The heroes and villains of the *Dune* universe live in a world where violent conflict is an inevitable and necessary part of life. In their harsh and adversarial society, political self-interest guides every action, while personal meaning is found only in contest and struggle. Almost all of the problems that *Dune*'s characters face arise from the challenges of warfare and politics, and much of the enjoyment we readers experience comes from watching cunning minds grapple with problems of strategy and statecraft. Through trials of physical danger and political peril, *Dune*'s warrior-reasoners continually search for advantages that will allow them to succeed despite doubt and uncertainty.

Dune, like real-world philosophy that deals with war and power, such as Niccolò Machiavelli's *The Prince*, Thomas Hobbes's *Leviathan*, or Carl von Clauseiwtz's *On War*, confronts us not only with ethical problems, but with questions about how reason and cognition can be turned toward the goals of conflict.

In this context, *Dune* has a *pragmatist* character, in the sense intended by Charles Sanders Peirce (1839–1914). For Peirce, philosophy is the study of how logic, belief, and reasoning can best guide practices of inquiry – the search for new knowledge despite doubt and contingency.[1] However, the pragmatic perspective adopted by *Dune*'s combatants and commanders is not the cooperative inquiry of scientific discovery, but a darker, bloodier vision, deformed by violence and domination.

In the brutal worlds of the galactic Imperium and the Arrakeen desert wilderness, inquiry, perception, and logic are no longer tools of scientific

Dune and Philosophy, First Edition. Edited by Kevin S. Decker.
© 2023 John Wiley & Sons, Inc. Published 2023 by John Wiley & Sons, Inc.

truth-seeking, but have become weapons in a war between minds as sharp as the cutting edge of a crysknife.

The Political Logic of Kanly

A common view of truth is that true accounts of the world conform to some reality independent of our thinking. Peirce added that truth can only be approached through a community of inquirers with a shared interest in pursuing truth. As a first lesson in the dark rationality of covert warfare, *Dune* illustrates how such ideals are deformed and replaced with principles of power and conflict. The inquiries of *Dune's* characters don't follow the logic of scientific discovery but instead the wartime logic of advantage.

The conflict between House Atreides and House Harkonnen stretches back to the earliest days of the empire. But their feud is not the outright violence of open warfare; it's the covert struggle of kanly, an organized form of vendetta where treachery and deception are not only permitted but expected.

The Baron Vladimir Harkonnen, aided by his Mentat assassin Piter de Vries, has woven an elaborate trap for his nemesis, the honorable Duke Leto Atreides, and has even manipulated Leto into unknowingly giving the Baron the political cover he needs to move against Leto. The Padishah Emperor, Shaddam Corrino IV, jealous of the renown of the Duke and fearful of the superb Atreides fighting forces, has secretly intervened on the side of House Harkonnen, committing both his own elite Sardaukar warriors and the might of imperial influence. Compelled to take charge of the desert planet Arrakis, source of the mind-enhancing spice-drug that binds the networks of empire, Leto faces espionage, assassination, and military deception. The questions of what is true and who can be trusted loom over every action and judgment.

The political circumstances of *Dune* present the Duke and his trusted strategists – Thufir Hawat, the Lady Jessica, and Paul Atreides – with three kinds of problems that shape their approach to adversarial reasoning and decision.

Niccolò Machiavelli (1469–1527) thought that these three types of problems were:

- *necessity*, an incentive to action arising from the perceived threat of danger to oneself, which Machiavelli thought justified expedient or unethical acts;
- *fortune* – which we might think of as *chance* – the uncertainty of changing circumstances and the resulting risks or opportunities; and
- *prowess*, or what the characters of *Dune* call *bravura*: the combination of mental brilliance, technical skill and practical boldness needed to face necessity and navigate uncertainty.[2]

While necessity and chance are factors in dangerous circumstances and the unpredictability of events whose outcomes also depend on others' actions, *bravura* represents a kind of "cunning intelligence," a mental attitude that Machiavelli thought was required to succeed despite the opposition of fickle fortune and devious adversaries.

Necessity and the Knowledge Advantage

In the conflict between Atreides and Harkonnen, the necessity both Houses perceive depends on the fact that the rules of kanly permit the use of tactics and techniques otherwise forbidden or taboo: poison, treachery, the murder of family members, or even House-wide slaughter. Constant, hidden danger guarantees a cycle of threat and escalation, which can only be ultimately resolved through the total destruction of one or both Houses.

In response to this necessity, the "terrible purpose" of war and political self-interest, the superhuman minds of Mentat assassins, strategist Aristocrats, and cunning Bene Gesserit are all brought to bear on the problem of discovering and developing the advantages of strategic knowledge, perceptive insight, and the use of logical inference to anticipate opponents' moves in advance.

Leto is confronted with the pressing issue of limited and unreliable information, which is all that he has available to make his most important and high-stakes decisions. Occupying what was until recently the source of Harkonnen wealth and power, Leto is unsure who can be trusted, and he struggles to cultivate reliable allies and informants. While his staff officers and spy networks give him some idea about where to position his limited armed forces, or how best to pursue secret diplomacy with the Fremen, his intelligence channels also give him worrying and uncertain reports on traitors, sabotage, and enemy infiltration. While most of this information would ordinarily not be worth acting on until it was thoroughly double-checked and factually verified, the terrible necessities of his situation force Leto to depend entirely upon his small community of trustworthy inquirers and upon their extremely limited and fallible forms of inquiry.

The problems facing the Duke as he tries to consolidate power on Arrakis compel him to adopt what ethicist Jean Maria Arrigo calls an *adversarial epistemology*, a rational framework of conflict that arises in high-stakes circumstances "where competition for knowledge is crucial to the attainment of a limited good, such as military and political power."[3] This approach to knowledge highlights the difference between the *validity* of knowledge and its *utility* – what matters is not whether information is true but whether it is advantageous.[4]

In most cases, accurate information would still be preferred, but in this case rapidly formed beliefs that enable a timely decision are ultimately more useful than carefully verified knowledge. While uncertain or hypothetical beliefs might support speedy action, they also pose the risk of being factually incomplete or simply wrong. The pressures of necessity on the conduct of inquiry force Leto to accept a trade-off between the speed and accuracy of his beliefs, an acceptance which is ultimately his undoing.

In the paranoid and suspicious interactions of kanly, the force of necessity degrades Leto's standards for forming beliefs, but it also influences his willingness to communicate truthfully. An advantage in strategic knowledge is not only dependent upon seeking out secret sources of information, but also may require denying similar advantages to the adversary. If the adversary makes their decisions based on information which they also can't verify, this opens up options for deception and disinformation.

Even the honorable Duke Leto wasn't above using the instruments of deception to his advantage, not only against the Harkonnens, but also against his own people. Through his networks of intelligence and diplomatic communication Leto learns of a Harkonnen plot to sow doubt in his ranks by implicating the Lady Jessica as a traitor. Despite knowing the accusations were false, Leto nonetheless decides to play along, allowing Thufir Hawat to believe that he suspects the mother of his child of plotting his downfall. Through this subtle trick, Leto hoped to be able to control the knowledge and expectations of the Harkonnens, thereby to stay one step ahead of them as he established his foothold on Arrakis.

Considering the imbalance of power between House Atreides and the Harkonnen–Imperial alliance, Machiavelli might say that the Duke Leto would be prudent to use both force and deceit. But to deceive the enemy while covertly making his own moves would require that Leto receive a constant stream of advantageous secret intelligence. Yet in wartime conditions, time is short and deception goes both ways. Leto's ruses and countertrickery eventually leave him full of doubt and entangled in a web of his own making. By deceiving Hawat and Jessica, his closest and most trusted advisors, Leto undermines their ability to participate fully in the project of wartime inquiry, thereby depriving him of their valuable contributions.

Deceived by Harkonnen disinformation and surveilled by Imperial spies, Leto is outmaneuvered and manipulated by adversaries who, thanks to their skillful and relentless use of intelligence and information warfare, are able to stay several steps ahead of him. Trapped by danger and stressed by necessity Leto is compelled to lower his standards for the truth of his beliefs and his communication with others, and ends up paying for this compromise with his life.

Uncertainty and Mentat Mentality

The grim necessities of kanly force *Dune's* characters to value the utility of knowledge over its truthfulness; it also gives rise to the problem of reasoning under uncertain conditions.

The Prussian military general and philosopher of war Carl von Clausewitz (1780–1831) thought that war was infinitely adaptable to circumstances, but that its nature was to be found in the strange three-way interaction between the blind force of hatred and violence, the play of chance and uncertainty, and the role of war as an instrument of politics. And while war is always characterized by violence and finds its purpose as a tool for achieving political objectives, Clausewitz thought (like Machiavelli) that the most distinctive facet of war was the influence of chance and uncertainty. Clausewitz notes, "No other human activity gives it [chance] greater scope: no other has such incessant and varied dealings with this intruder. Chance makes everything more uncertain and interferes with the whole course of events."[5] In *Dune*, much of the responsibility for navigating this aspect of war is given to two Mentat Masters of Assassins, Thufir Hawat for the Atreides and Piter de Vries of House Harkonnen, both renowned for their dangerously cunning and devious intelligence. As rigorously trained "human computers" in a world that banished artificial intelligence in the Butlerian Jihad, Mentats are employed by the wealthy and powerful to process, analyze, and calculate probabilities far beyond the reach of normal human minds. While the Duke and the Baron steer their political interests and ultimate ambitions, it is their Mentats who are responsible for the formulation of strategy and its realization in operations.

From a cognitive (knowledge) perspective, Mentat abilities involve rapid assimilation and evaluation of an abundance of quantitative and qualitative data, precise calculation of probabilities, and, most importantly, the creation of *inferences* – conclusions reached by reasoning about the analyzed information. Despite great differences in their personal character, both Hawat and de Vries share the Mentat cognitive training allowing them to devise strategic and logistical schemes out of a bewildering array of variables and contingencies.

In a meeting between the Baron Harkonnen and his nephew Feyd-Rautha, de Vries is asked to demonstrate one of his strategical functions. Calling on data and calculations, de Vries describes the "plans within plans within plans" of the Harkonnen plot to destroy House Atreides. Piter details the precise choreography through which the Duke Leto will be made to dance, right up until his doom, revealing his incredible ability to plan for contingencies, estimate capabilities, and calculate probable outcomes from complex data. However, as the plot of *Dune* reveals, despite their superhuman gifts, Mentat minds suffer from many of the same limitations of mechanical and digital computers: they risk being overwhelmed by rapidly changing circumstances and remain blind to unaccounted variables. In other words, if you give a Mentat bad information, they will give you worse results.

On the Atreides side, the tempo and contingency of unfolding events prevent Thufir Hawat from verifying vital information, allowing him to be anticipated and manipulated. Controlling what, when, and how much Hawat learns, de Vries employs a slightly different strategy than the one used on Duke Leto. Instead of being blindsided through secrecy and deception, Hawat is fed a constant stream of half-true, contradictory, and outright false information designed not to induce total ignorance but instead to provoke profound uncertainty. Outwitted and overwhelmed, Hawat becomes lost in an impenetrable fog of war that doesn't lift until it is far, far too late. As philosopher Don Fallis notes, "to acquire knowledge despite the fact that there may be epistemic adversaries out there, we need to find things that are *robust* indicators of insincerity."[6]

And yet, despite his formidable foresight and venomous cunning, even Piter de Vries is brought down by his own failure to appreciate contingencies in the unfolding of his plans. Overconfident and blinded by the promise of wealth and power, the Mentat assassin fails to anticipate Dr. Yueh's suicidal counter-scheme, and is killed by the treacherous stratagem of the Duke's poisoned tooth.

The Mentat mind, trained only in rigid, mechanistic reasoning and dependent on high-quality sources of information, proves to be unsuited to the pragmatic task of perceiving hidden risks and opportunities in the war's uncertainty and the contingency of human affairs.

The Secret Intelligence of Perception

For the young Duke Paul Atreides, warrior-Mentat, Muad'dib of the Fremen, and Kwisatz Haderach of the Bene Gesserit legend, the demands of conflict and survival compel success where his father and mentors failed. He must perceive opportunity where others see only uncertainty and discern traces of the future in the chaos of the present.

The first time we meet Paul he's lying in bed, secretly surveilling the Bene Gesserit Truthsayer who is visiting his mother, his mind filled with vague hints of catastrophes and triumphs to come. Already demonstrating the slyness and cunning that will prove so important for his future, Paul exhibits an uncanny degree of control over his perception and his psychophysical processes. He also reveals his ability to arrive at hypotheses about what *may* be the case in the future through the imaginative constructs of dreams. In his experience, these always correspond in great detail to actual future events. The unique quality of these anticipatory dreams marks them out as special, because after he has dreamt them, Paul knows that what they suggest is true in the same way that the things he usually perceives with his senses are true.

And as we learn from his meeting with the Bene Gesserit Reverend Mother Mohiam and his trial with the gom jabbar – a brutal test of his ability to exert conscious and rational control over instinctual processes – Paul possesses an innate superhuman ability to *perceive truth*. And this ability stems from the way Paul's mind has been shaped by his life-long training as an Atreides, as the son of a Bene Gesserit, and as an aspiring Mentat.

Since Paul was a child, the Lady Jessica – an adept of the Bene Gesserit Sisterhood – has been training her son in the deep mysteries of *the Way,* a secret system that teaches the ability to exert conscious control over normally unconscious and automatic perceptual and cognitive processes. The Sisterhood, an organization deeply complicit in the political dealings of the Empire, have their own secret program to eugenically engineer a superhuman mind. It trains its initiates to detect, interpret, and exploit signs of vulnerability that are hidden in human speech patterns and unconscious behavior. In effect, every Bene Gesserit is trained to become a perceptual spy, operating by way of secrecy, espionage, elicitation, and manipulation, controlling others through hidden points of leverage. From the perspective of the mysterious Sisters, the world is a skein of exploitable significance, a web of interconnected indices, icons, and symbols which can be induced to reveal their secrets.

Combined with his Mentat abilities and his natural capacity for truth sensing, the Bene Gesserit training provides Paul with the key elements for success that were missing from his father and Hawat. Over and again we witness Paul's ability to reason almost instantly and correctly about his environment and its potential opportunities for action. He shrewdly discerns hidden motives from the smallest conversational clues, infers unknown truths from habitual gestures, detects secret sietch exits from air currents and flight paths from storm turbulence, always seeing hints of opportunity in the shifting of desert sands. Paul extracts significance from observations that, for most of us, would be mute and meaningless.

The value of this ability to read the potential in any situation is revealed at key moments of overwhelming danger and contingency – piloting the Ornithopter through the Coriolis storm, the duel with the Fremen Jamis, the trial of the sandriders, and the turmoil of the final assault on the Emperor. In these moments, his Mentat logic is blinded by uncertain data and uncountable probabilities, yet Paul can depend on his heightened perceptions and its practical insights.

Armed with Ducal prudence, Mentat calculation, and Bene Gesserit perception, Paul is finally equipped to face the final tests of terrible necessity and cruel fortune.

The Power of *Bravura*

When Clausewitz considered the question of how reason might best guide war and strategy, he arrived at something very much like the *bravura* with which the heroes of *Dune* are so well endowed:

> If the mind is to emerge unscathed from this relentless struggle with the unforeseen, two qualities are indispensable: first, an intellect that, even in the darkest hour, retains some glimmerings of the inner light which leads to truth; and second, the courage to follow this faint light wherever it may lead. The first of these qualities is described by the French term, *coup d'oeil*; the second is *determination*.[7]

Clausewitz's *coup-d'oeil* describes the ability to make a penetrating appraisal of a situation from an instantaneous "sweep of the eye," to perceive the world at a glance without doubt in a way that enables immediate and decisive action. It is a "power of judgment raised to a marvelous pitch of vision, which easily grasps and dismisses a thousand remote possibilities which an ordinary mind would labor to identify and wear itself out in so doing."[8] In this description, it's easy to see Paul's powers of predictive imagination in moments of crisis and danger and his ability to rapidly perceive, orient, decide, and act.

This resonates with the view of Charles Sanders Peirce that perceptual judgments – the *meanings* of our innate, pre-conscious perceptions – contained two incredible characteristics.

First, Peirce argued that sense perceptions already include *generalities*: we can infer from them general principles or law-like regularities that structure the world. Second, he thought that perceptual judgments already included *hypotheses* about the world. These were the often fallible but ultimately effective inferential insights that lead us to *new* knowledge.[9]

When we use it consciously, Peirce called this latter kind of reasoning *abductive* inference. He contrasted abduction with *deductive* inference, which proves that something *must* be so, and with *inductive* inference, which shows that something is merely probable. *Abductive* inference suggests that something *may* be true, and provides us with a hypothesis which could explain a set of facts. Abduction can be used to reconstruct unseen causes and meanings lying in the past, as well as to reason about future consequences. It has both an explanatory (past-facing) and a predictive (future-facing) capacity.

In Peirce's pragmatism, abduction finds its hypotheses through the perception and interpretation of *signs* – anything that stands for or represents something else, for some observer. Signs range from tracks and traces to images and symbols. Through the interpretation of signs, abductive hypotheses can become premises in creating theories, and then inductively tested through experimentation. Abduction, for Peirce, was the engine of any and all scientific discovery.[10]

In *Dune*, Peirce's abductive inference is the key to adapting to the extreme adversity, necessity, and contingency of war and conflict. From the moment Paul wakes from the coma induced by ingesting the Water of Life – both the spice-exhalation of a dying sandworm and the strongest truth-perception catalyst known to the universe – his ability to interpret past, present, and future is no longer a mere instinct upon which he can only semi-reliably depend. It's now a mental faculty under his conscious and rational control. While Bene Gesserit techniques aim to slightly roll back the moment when instinctual perception passes into conscious control, Paul's Kwisatz Haderach cognition gives him control of the perceptual-abductive process, the inner-eye that sees the significance of every tiny event. Combining this insight with his accelerated Mentat computation, Paul is able to mentally model circumstances in order to instantly explore the consequences of countless hypotheses and then respond decisively.

What this spice-awakened super-abduction brings to Paul's strategic thinking is not some mystical power of omniscience, as his continued experience of temporal blindness demonstrates. Rather, the truth-drug opens up in Paul an ability to draw out the active general principles of both nature and history at work in particular circumstances. In the gyre of desert war and imperial politics, these abductive visions are key to Paul's final victory. Paralyzing the Harkonnen defense with his slow escalation of guerrilla war, anticipating and manipulating the Imperial invasion of Arrakis, Paul is able to plan and enact a surprise strategy that entraps and dominates the most powerful political players in the Universe: the Emperor and the Spacing Guild. From necessity through uncertainty, and into the domain of skillful control that realizes an inner vision, Paul pursues an adversarial form of pragmatism at once more capable and more comprehensive than his predecessors and his enemies.

The Tragedy of Strategy

Equipped with such profound strategic intelligence, it's hardly surprising that Paul Atreides finally, after many trials and tribulations, overcomes his adversaries. Paul's pragmatism is a synthesis of Machiavelli's ruthless and prudent Prince, Clausewitz's genius tactician and strategist, and Peirce's ideal inquirer.

The great tragedy of Frank Herbert's *Dune* lies in the fact that despite their successes in the most difficult circumstances imaginable, the superhuman minds of *Dune*'s strategists, spies, and soldiers simply cannot conceive of a life beyond the brutal one in which they find themselves complicit. Despite their incredible powers of reasoning, calculation, perception, and invention, we never find them considering courses of action other than traveling the path that their dark worldview tells them is inevitable. As a guide for action, this adversarial kind of pragmatism utterly lacks the true virtue of Peirce's vision: that we should delight not only in discovering things for ourselves, but in sharing them with others, for the benefit of all.

Notes

1. Charles Sanders Peirce, *Pragmatism as a Principle and Method of Right Thinking: The 1903 Harvard Lectures on Pragmatism* (Albany: SUNY Press, 1997).
2. Niccolò Machiavelli, *The Prince*, ed. and trans. Peter Bondanella (New York: Oxford University Press, 2005).

3. Jean Maria Arrigo, "The Ethics of Weapons Research – A Framework for Moral Discourse Between Insiders and Outsiders," *Journal of Power and Ethics: An Interdisciplinary Review* 1 (2000), 317.
4. Arrigo, "The Ethics of Weapons Research," 307.
5. Carl von Clausewitz, *On War*, trans. Michael Howard and Peter Paret (Princeton, NJ: Princeton University Press, 1976), 101.
6. Don Fallis, "Adversarial Epistemology on the Internet," in David Coady and James Chase eds., *The Routledge Handbook of Applied Epistemology* (New York: Routledge, 2018), 58.
7. Clausewitz, *On War*, 102.
8. Clausewitz, *On War*, 112.
9. Peirce, *Pragmatism as a Principle and Method*, 221–227.
10. Peirce, *Pragmatism as a Principle and Method*, 230.

Index

Page locators in *italics* indicate figures. This index uses letter-by-letter alphabetization.

Dune and Philosophy, First Edition. Edited by Kevin S. Decker.
© 2023 John Wiley & Sons, Inc. Published 2023 by John Wiley & Sons, Inc.